AMBASSADORS OF Cl

"In the discussions now going forward about restructuring ministerial education, a book like the present volume has a huge contribution to make, not just to the intellectual and institutional history of the Church of England but to that Church's self-understanding. As we read this excellent memoir of a history both brave and complex, we can be grateful that the Church of England has been so wonderfully served; and we can strengthen our resolve to make sure that such a service is still available to the Church of the future"

The Most Revd Rowan Williams, Archbishop of Canterbury

Ambassadors of Christ commemorates 150 years of theological education in Cuddesdon College, Oxford. Presenting a detailed history of England's most famous theological college, *Ambassadors of Christ* also contributes to the wider discussion of theological education in the nineteenth and twentieth centuries and discusses prospects for the future.

Following a forward by the present Archbishop of Canterbury, Mark Chapman discusses the revival of theology and education in the early years of the nineteenth century. An essay on Samuel Wilberforce as a pastoral theologian follows from Alastair Redfern, and a revision by Andrew Atherstone of Owen Chadwick's Centenary History explores several of the leading figures of the time, including Henry Liddon and Edward King, and brings the focus up to the 1880s. For the first time Ripon Hall, which merged with Cuddesdon in 1975, receives a thorough historical treatment by Michael Brierley. Mark Chapman then discusses the 1960s under Robert Runcie, and Robert Jeffrey examines the theological and churchmanship issues which emerged from the merger and the issues in debate today. Recent developments in theological education throughout the Church of England are explored further, before the appendices presenting Michael Ramsey's 1958 sermon and Owen Chadwick's 1966 sermon.

This special commemorative volume will appeal to past and present students as well as specialists in nineteenth and twentieth church history and all those interested in ministerial education and spiritual formation.

"A theological college endeavours, so far as human agency can do this, to give the tongue of the learned, the power of spiritual instruction to the future ambassadors of Christ. … It would fain teach them to listen, morning by morning, for the Divine Voice, explaining, deepening, fertilising within them the truth which is thus committed to their guardianship" (Henry P. Liddon *Clerical Life and Work*, pp. 49-50).

Ambassadors of Christ

Commemorating 150 Years of Theological Education
in Cuddesdon 1854-2004

MARK D. CHAPMAN
Ripon College Cuddesdon, Oxford, UK

ASHGATE

Published by
Ashgate Publishing Limited
Gower House
Croft Road
Aldershot
Hampshire GU11 3HR
England

Ashgate Publishing Company
Suite 420
101 Cherry Street
Burlington, VT 05401-4405
USA

Ashgate website: http://www.ashgate.com

British Library Cataloguing in Publication Data
Ambassadors of Christ : commemorating 150 years of theological education in Cuddeson 1854-2004
   1. Ripon College Cuddesdon – History 2. Theology – Study and teaching (Higher) – England – Oxfordshire
   I. Chapman, Mark D. (Mark David), 1960 –
   230'.071142574

Library of Congress Cataloging-in-Publication Data
Ambassadors of Christ : commemorating 150 years of theological education in Cuddesdon, 1854-2004 / edited by Mark D. Chapman.
     p. cm.
   Includes bibliographical references and index.
   ISBN 0-7546-3754-9 – ISBN 0-7546-3755-7 (pbk.)
    1. Cuddesdon College – History. I. Chapman, Mark D. (Mark David), 1960-

   BV4160.C86A69 2005
   230'.07'3342574—dc22

2003025122

ISBN 0 7546 3754 9 (Hbk)
ISBN 0 7456 3755 7 (Pbk)

Printed and bound in Great Britain by MPG Books Ltd, Bodmin, Cornwall

Contents

List of Figures

Notes on Contributors

Andrew Atherstone studied at Cambridge and took his doctorate in Oxford on the work of C. P. Golightly. He is curate at Christ Church, Abingdon.

Michael W. Brierley is Chaplain and Research Assistant to the Bishop of Oxford.

Owen Chadwick was Master of Selwyn College and Regius Professor of History, University of Cambridge.

Mark D. Chapman is Vice-Principal of Ripon College Cuddesdon.

Robert Jeffery was until recently Sub-dean of Christ Church, Oxford, and was previously Dean of Worcester.

The late **Michael Ramsey** was Archbishop of Canterbury.

Alastair Redfern is a former Vice-Principal of Ripon College Cuddesdon and is currently Bishop of Grantham in the Diocese of Lincoln.

Preface

For good or ill the village of Cuddesdon has probably made more of an impact on the Church of England than any other in the country. Its life has been dominated by a theological college since 1854 when Samuel Wilberforce decided to build his diocesan seminary across the road from his Palace. The story of its founding was brilliantly told fifty years ago by Owen Chadwick for the centenary of Cuddesdon College.[1] This book commemorates another important milestone, that of the 150th anniversary of theological education in Cuddesdon. It does not aim to be comprehensive – that would make it too much like the ponderous and prosaic *Cuddesdon College 1854-1929: A Record and Memorial* of 1930.[2] Instead the different essays present snapshots of the history of Cuddesdon College, Ripon Hall and Ripon College Cuddesdon. Each offers some fresh insights into some of the great personalities who have helped shape the ethos of all three insitutions over a century and a half.

Most importantly, this collection pays proper attention not just to Cuddesdon College, which many liked to think of as the Sandhurst of the Church of England, but also to Ripon Hall, its perhaps unlikely partner in the merger of 1975 which formed Ripon College Cuddesdon. While location is obviously a crucial part of any theological education and buildings can do much to shape a spiritual outlook, it is absolutely vital that the contribution of Ripon Hall on Boar's Hill, with its academic excellence and its emphasis on unfettered theological exploration, is not lost to the wider church in what often seems like an era of managerialism and shallowness.

The book begins with an introduction which locates Cuddesdon in the history of theological education more generally. This is followed by a re-evaluation of the early years of Cuddesdon College. Since Owen Chadwick wrote his book, much new light has been shed on the ritualist controversies which marked the time of Pott and Liddon, and later Furse and Willis. These controversies, which were dominated by the arch-controversialist, Charles Portales Golightly, are brilliantly discussed by Andrew Atherstone in chapters two and four. In chapter three Alastair Redfern has drawn out the implications of Samuel Wilberforce's preaching and

---

[1] *The Founding of Cuddesdon*, Oxford: Oxford University Press, 1954.
[2] *Cuddesdon College 1854-1929: A Record and Memorial*, Oxford: Oxford University Press, 1930.

teaching for contemporary pastoral theology. This is followed by Michael Brierley's *tour de force* in chapter five which presents the first thoroughgoing history of Ripon Hall, as well as a portrait of Henry Major, its great principal and the leading figure in English liberal theology for many decades of the twentieth century. In chapter six I have tried to re-assess Cuddesdon College of the 1960s in the context of rapid social and theological change, but also to paint a portrait of Robert Runcie, whose personality shaped the college through that decade of change. Finally Robert Jeffrey brings the story up to date by charting the many ups and downs of the past twenty-five years or so since the merger.

All the contributors have tried to tell the story warts and all, making an effort to avoid the triumphalism that inevitably comes with institutional histories. And all of us are conscious that we are writing at a time when the finances of the Church of England are becoming increasingly limited and when a residential education is seen by many as something of a luxury. Ripon College Cuddesdon is meeting this challenge by reshaping itself for the new century and opening up its resources to the wider church and to other forms of theological training. However things might develop in the next few years it is our earnest hope that something of the ethos of Cuddesdon College, Ripon Hall and Ripon College Cuddesdon will survive – alongside a solid and rigorous academic education a good priest needs the space to learn how to pray and to be able to live together with all sorts and conditions of people. Something of those qualities were displayed in Michael Ramsey, whose 1958 College Festival Sermon is reproduced in Appendix One.

I would like to acknowledge a special debt of gratitude to John Davies, the College Assistant Archivist, who has helped all the contributors by keeping the archives in such good order and by sharing his infectious enthusiasm for the past. The College has benefited much during his time as librarian and archivist. Thanks are also due to Owen Chadwick, a great friend of the College during his distinguished academic career. He has graciously allowed us to use his earlier research and to cite from his letters. I hope that the re-publication of his memorable sermon preached at the Cuddesdon Festival in 1966 (Appendix Two) will serve as a fitting tribute. Finally, it seems fitting to dedicate this book to all the students and staff of Cuddesdon College, Ripon Hall and Ripon College Cuddesdon and to give thanks for the enormous contribution they have made to God's church.

Mark D. Chapman
Cuddesdon
Michaelmas, 2003

Abbreviations

ABM	Advisory Board of Ministry
ACCM	Advisory Council for the Church's Ministry
Bodl.	Bodleian Library, Oxford
CACTM	Central Advisory Council on Training for the Ministry
CCA	Cuddesdon College Archives, Ripon College Cuddesdon
ECU	English Church Union
KCL	Keble College Library, Oxford
LHP	Liddon House Papers
LP	Liddon Papers
LPL	Lambeth Palace Library
MCU	Modern Churchmen's Union (now Modern Churchpeople's Union)
PHL	Pusey House Library
RCC	Ripon College Cuddesdon Archives
RHA	Ripon Hall Archives, Ripon College Cuddesdon
SSC	Society of the Holy Cross

Foreword

At least once a decade, the pattern of ministerial education in the Church of England becomes a matter of fierce debate and widespread anxiety. Both financial constraints and shifts in the understanding and expectation of ordained ministry have repeatedly unsettled the process of preparing people for ordination and other recognised ministries – with a good deal of cost in terms of personal unsettlement for teachers and students as well.

Such a period of unsettlement is upon us once again. And perhaps the greatest dangers in this context are short-term visions of both the past and the future. We don't remember quite why ministerial education has developed as it has, we ignore the often very elusive element in the process that is provided by the ethos and history of institutions. And we are in a hurry to sort out clearly defined new patterns that will accord with current thinking (fashion, if you want to be a bit sceptical).

In the discussions now going forward about restructuring ministerial education, a book like the present volume has a huge contribution to make, not just to the intellectual and institutional history of the Church of England but to that Church's self-understanding. What we have here is the record of two dramatically different enterprises in theological education which finally came together to find some sort of common vision. The story tells us that it is not a new thing to reshape ministerial training by provoking deeper conversation and negotiation between diverse traditions; but it also serves as a salutary reminder of the dangers of supposing too quickly that we know exactly what authentic Anglicanism looks like. Some of this record is painful reading because it tells of people under pressure to rethink some very profound convictions about Anglicanism – pressure as great for 'liberals' as for Tractarians.

But pervading the whole is one common assumption, boldly held and argued. Ministerial education is the training of theologians, not technicians; of men and women who are committed to being immersed daily in the common life of praying, thinking and imagining that is the reality of the Body of Christ and who are therefore daily ready to confront clichés and conventions in the name of God's revelation, God's self-gift. For this, both an intensive common life within the institution and a strong discipline of intellectual maturation are essential.

These things are not irrelevant luxuries. Whatever emerges from our current review of possibilities, the twin disciplines of common prayer and intellectual labour at the highest possible level are matters we cannot afford to sideline. As we read this excellent memoir of a history both brave and complex, we can be grateful that the Church of England has been so wonderfully served; and we can strengthen our resolve to make sure that such service is still available to the Church of the future.

The Most Revd Rowan Williams, Archbishop of Canterbury

Chapter 1

Living the Truth:
Cuddesdon in the History of Theological Education

Mark D. Chapman

The Rise of Theological Education in the Nineteenth Century

There was always something inherently vague about theological education as it developed in the Church of England in the nineteenth century, at least when it is compared with models on offer elsewhere. Where German and American theological curricula were highly structured and often resembled other forms of "professional" education, the character of Anglican theological education was more usually described in terms of the assimilation of an ethos, the ownership of a tradition and the development of a way of life or a pattern of being, rather than being primarily focused on the education of the "clerical practitioner".[1] Furthermore, Anglican theological education has traditionally been rooted in the praying life of a religious community rather than in the purely intellectual atmosphere of the university. Indeed, as this opening section shows, it was the perceived failure of the university as a religious community that led to the development of theological colleges in the Church of England in the first place. What will be shown is that Anglican theological education provides a good

---

[1] On the history of theological education in the nineteenth century, see F. W. B. Bullock, *A History of Training for the Ministry of the Church of England, 1800-1874*, London: Home Words, 1955; *A History of Training for the Ministry of the Church of England, 1875-1974*, London: Home Words, 1976; Alan Haig, *The Victorian Clergy*, London: Croom Helm, 1984, pp. 116-76; D. A. Dowland, *Nineteenth-Century Anglican Theological Education: The Redbrick Challenge*, Oxford: Clarendon Press, 1997; K. Sterling, "The Education of the Anglican Clergy, 1830-1914", Ph.D. diss. Leicester University, 1982.

example of what Edward Farley called "theologia",[2] that is, a conception of theology rooted in the practice of the church. This chapter discusses this model of education as it has developed in the Church of England, particularly at Cuddesdon, its counterparts in the early church and in the present day, as well as addressing some of its inherent problems. It concludes with a vision of a possible direction for the future.

Things developed very differently elsewhere. In Prussia, for instance, the rise of the modern university and the reform of the theological curriculum under the influence of Friedrich Schleiermacher (1768-1834), the first professor of theology at the newly-founded University of Berlin, was to focus on the historical and philosophical knowledge and skills base required for the practice of ministry. In his short classic, *Brief Outline on the Study of Theology* of 1811,[3] he justified theology in terms of the practical tasks of ministry. "Theology," he claimed, "is a positive science [which itself is] a compass of scientific elements which do not cohere as though they formed a necessary part of scientific organisation as a result of the idea of science, but rather to the degree that they are required for the solution of a practical task."[4] Similarly, theology was "the compass of academic knowledge and skills, which unless possessed and used, there could be no leadership of the church or a church government".[5] Theology was no longer the science of God, on the medieval model, but instead was the theory behind a practical task. Indeed, without the practical ministerial orientation of theology "the same items of knowledge cease to be theological and each become part of a different science".[6]

For Schleiermacher, then, the study of theology in the university was primarily the acquisition of historical knowledge and a set of practical methods, analogous to the learning of medical or legal theory, for the clerical practitioner, and is justified in terms of the functional requirements of an indispensable activity of the modern state – the need for the "cure of souls".[7] The minister, like the lawyer or the doctor, learns a particular tradition, works out its "historical" essence (using ordinary historical tools), and then passes this on, using the techniques of practical theology. Unlike the alternative model of theological education, which was developed in most Anglican theological colleges in the later nineteenth century as will be shown

[2] Edward Farley, *Theologia. The Fragmentation and Unity of Theological Education*, Philadelphia: Fortress, 1983.

[3] *Brief Outline on the Study of Theology*, tr. Terence Tice, Richmond: John Knox, 1966.

[4] Ibid., §1.

[5] Ibid., §5.

[6] Ibid., §6.

[7] On this see Wolfhart Pannenberg, *Theology and the Philosophy of Science*, London: Darton, Longman and Todd, 1976, esp. p. 249.

below, Schleiermacher's is an extreme example of what might be called the clericalisation of theology whereby a specially trained leadership is equipped with a distinctive professional knowledge and a set of skills to perform a particular function in the church and state at large: theology is defined in terms of ministerial practice and thereby becomes a "technical rationality" rather than a spiritual discipline. This becomes clearest in Schleiermacher's famous description of the ideal clergyman:

> Imagine the concern for religion and the scientific spirit united, for the sake of theory and practice, in the highest degree and in the most perfect balance, and you have the idea of a "prince of the church".[8]

In many ways things could not have been more different in England. There was no undergraduate study of theology as a distinct and separate discipline: as one writer comments, compared with Germany, "the Church of England was uniquely uninterested in theological training for its ministers".[9] Whereas in the protestant churches in Germany from the Reformation onwards a degree in theology had been a general requirement for ordination, in England all that was needed was a simple arts degree. At the same time, however, at least in Oxford, a modicum of theological study, together with subscription to the Thirty-Nine Articles, was a requirement for all degrees, making the university a confessional establishment. At the turn of the nineteenth century, for instance, knowledge had to be shown in the Gospels in Greek, the Thirty-Nine Articles, as well as Bishop Butler's *Analogy of Religion*. On this model of theological study, the system of thought on which it was based was fixed and final, and did not allow for even a limited degree of critical study. Critics like Sydney Smith might have questioned such a limited understanding of theology, but other influential figures were prepared to defend it. Thus Edward Copleston, Provost of Oriel College, Oxford, and afterwards Dean of St Paul's and Bishop of Llandaff, could write:

> There is one province of education indeed in which we are slow in believing that any discoveries can be made. The scheme of revelation we think is closed, and we expect no new light on earth to break in upon us ... We hold it our especial duty ... to keep strict watch around the sacred citadel, to deliver out in due measure

---

[8] *Brief Outline*, §9.

[9] L. W. B. Brockliss, "The European University, 1789-1850" in M. G. Brock and M. C. Curthoys, *The History of the University of Oxford*, Oxford: Clarendon Press, 1997, vol. vi: *The Nineteenth Century: Part One*, pp. 77-133, here p. 81.

and season the stores it contains, to make our countrymen look to it as a tower of
strength, and to defend it against open and secret enemies.[10]

On the one hand, theology was a closed system which did not allow for critical
thought, and, on the other hand, it was a requirement for all students, whatever
they might be studying. Not surprisingly, given its compulsory status and limited
content, it was not always taken seriously (just like obligatory chapel).

While there were many efforts to improve the status of theology in the 1830s
and 1840s, which led to the foundation of several new professorships, the
compulsory element of theology in all Oxford degrees seemed increasingly
anachronistic, even if it was not finally abolished until 1931.[11] Following the Royal
Commission which reported in 1854 and which led to the Oxford University Act of
the same year, there were huge changes in the ecclesiastical presumptions of
Oxford and a sharp decline in the numbers of graduates entering ministry. The Act
itself, while not completely removing all religious tests, abolished subscription to
the Thirty-Nine Articles on matriculation and graduation. In the Archbishop of
Canterbury's report on *The Supply and Training of Candidates for Holy Orders*
(which eventually led after the First World War to the introduction of the General
Ordination Examination and the requirement for all ordinands to spend a period in
a theological college) Dean Church was cited as evidence of the need for a non-
university theological education:

> It is necessary to remember that the University, as the Commission left it, is
> virtually a secular institution. The Divinity Professorships are still held by Priests,
> but the University is not concerned as such, either with maintaining, or
> developing, or arousing a desire for Holy Orders.[12]

Although Newman, Keble and Pusey had fought to ensure that Oxford University
remained – and here it resembled their model of the apostolic church – a religious
institution subject to its own form of authority and not to an apostate parliament,
the forces of change were inexorable.[13] As late as 1853 in his response to the Royal
Commission on Oxford, Dr Pusey claimed that theology was something quite

[10] Cited in M. G. Brock, "The Oxford of Peel and Gladstone, 1800-33" in M. G. Brock
and M. C. Curthoys, *The History of the University of Oxford*, vi, pp. 7-71, here p. 11.

[11] M. C. Curthoys, "The Examination System" in M. G. Brock and M. C. Curthoys,
The History of the University of Oxford, vii, pp. 339-74, esp. pp. 357-8.

[12] *The Supply and Training of Candidates for Holy Orders: Report of the Committee
appointed by the Archbishop of Canterbury*, 1908, p. 16n.

[13] The decline of the "Anglican" University is described by Peter Nockles in "'Lost
causes and … impossible loyalties': the Oxford Movement and the University" in Brock
and Curthoys, *The History of the University of Oxford*, vi, pp. 195-267.

distinct from other subjects and simply too sacred to be studied academically. He insisted that it was wrong to study the "history of doctrine", because it had no real history, "the faith having been, once for all, made known to the inspired Apostles, and by them inserted in Holy Scripture, and committed to the Church".[14] As the century progressed, however, theology became simply one subject alongside the others, rather than a fundamental aspect of all higher education: the Oxford Honour School of Theology was finally established in 1870. By this time even Pusey had changed his mind, supporting the move in the hope that it might act as a bulwark against a more critical theological method.

The growth of Anglican theological education was in many ways a form of resistance to this gradual secularisation of the universities. It provides an alternative response to the German model which sought instead to accommodate theology to the modern university by redefining its character as a practical and historical discipline.[15] If theology as the science of sacred knowledge and as the presupposition for all other knowledge could no longer find a home in the university, then it had to look elsewhere. By deliberately creating an atmosphere of holiness and withdrawal – virtues which appeared to be moribund in the secular universities – the first theological colleges, pre-eminent among them Cuddesdon, were to assist their students in the complex process of the discernment of God's will through the life of prayer and discipline. Under the influence of the Oxford Movement, high spiritual ideals and independence from the world were consciously adopted as a witness against the decline of the university as a religious institution. While this new form of theological education might be a symptom of the increasing professionalisation of the clergy, which has been noted by many commentators, it should also be noted that the area of professional specialisation was in what might be called "affairs of the chancel", and it comes as little surprise that it was accompanied by widespread architectural and liturgical reform. Where the secular role was declining, the religious became increasingly important.[16]

Henry Parry Liddon, Samuel Wilberforce's choice as first vice-principal of Cuddesdon Theological College (founded in 1854), and later to be Pusey's

[14] E. B. Pusey, *Report and Evidence*, 1853, pp. 102-6. See also Peter Hinchliff, "Religious Issues: 1870-1914" in M. G. Brock and M. C. Curthoys, *The History of the University of Oxford*, Oxford: Clarendon Press, 2000, vol. vii: *The Nineteenth Century: Part Two*, pp. 97-114, esp. p. 97.

[15] See esp. W. R. Ward, "From the Tractarians to the University Commission, 1845-1854" in M. G. Brock and M. C. Curthoys, *The History of the University of Oxford*, vi, pp. 306-38; and W. R. Ward, *Victorian Oxford*, London, 1965, chs 5-7.

[16] On this see Anthony Russell, *The Clerical Profession*, London: SPCK, 1980; Rosemary O'Day, "The Clerical Renaissance" in Gerald Parsons (ed.), *Religion in Victorian Britain*, Manchester: Manchester University Press, vol. i: *Traditions*, 1988, pp. 184-212; Brian Heeney, *A Different Kind of Gentleman*, Hamden Connecticut: Anchor Books, 1976.

biographer, offers a shining example of a second generation Tractarian instilled with the sense of seriousness, and with a high vision of a form of theological education quite distinct from its secular counterparts.[17] The proper study of theology required holiness of life, and simply could not be properly undertaken in what he later described as a "secularized university".[18] Even Cuddesdon's location proclaimed something of these lofty spiritual ideals: where some dioceses had sought to establish theological colleges in the cathedral close in conscious imitation of a medieval ideal,[19] it seemed to Wilberforce far better to build a college in a (relatively) remote country village location. This isolation would serve to instil a sense of spiritual discipline among the graduates of Oxford and Cambridge who might have sullied their minds by dabbling in methods imported from Germany. Clergy were to be educated not among the temptations of the modern city, but in a quiet village dominated by the church – just as it had been in the middle ages, when much of the village was part of the estates of Abingdon Abbey.[20]

In a sermon preached at the Cuddesdon College Festival in 1868, Liddon summarised what he understood to be the purpose of this new form of theological education:

[17] Liddon's part in the shaping of Cuddesdon is described in detail by Owen Chadwick in *The Founding of Cuddesdon*, Oxford: Oxford University Press, 1954. See also below, chapter two.

[18] "The Moral Groundwork of Clerical Training" in *Clerical Life and Work* in *Clerical Life and Work. A Collection of Sermons*, London: Longmans, 1894, pp. 73-92, here p. 84.

[19] Chichester was founded in 1839 and Wells in 1840. See R. S. T. Haslehurst, "A Short History of Chichester Theological College" in *Cicestrian* 10 (Trinity 1939), pp. 82-100; and E. L. Elwes, *The History of Wells Theological College*, London, 1923; and W. M. Jacob, "The Diffusion of Tractarianism: Wells Theological College, 1840-49" in *Southern History* 5 (1983), pp. 189-209. While it is true in part that theological colleges represented an aspect of the "diocesan revival" of the nineteenth century, it is also crucial to see them as reactions to the secularisation of the universities. See Arthur Burns, *The Diocesan Revival in the Church of England c. 1800-1870*, Oxford: Clarendon Press, 1999, pp. 151-6.

[20] The manor had belonged to Abingdon Abbey since before the Norman Conquest. The rectory of Cuddesdon had been appropriated by the Abbey in the thirteenth century. After the Reformation the manor passed into secular hands but the rectory, the advowson to the vicarage, and some glebeland were annexed to the new see of Oxford in 1589. In 1632 John Bancroft, Bishop of Oxford, nominated himself as vicar and built his house in Cuddesdon. The bishops lived in the village until the 1970s. From 1636 the vicarage was also appropriated to the see. This meant that the bishops held the rectory and were also "vicars" of Cuddesdon until 1852, when the post of vicar was separated from the see, with Alfred Pott becoming first incumbent. He became the first principal of the college in 1854.

A theological college endeavours, so far as human agency can do this, to give the tongue of the learned, the power of spiritual instruction to the future ambassadors of Christ. ... It would fain teach them to listen, morning by morning, for the Divine Voice, explaining, deepening, fertilising within them the truth which is thus committed to their guardianship.[21]

On this model, theological education takes place within the broader context of a life committed to prayer and discipline. Here Liddon outlines the goal of theological education by drawing on what he calls the "God-taught wisdom" (*sophia theodidaktos*) tradition of the Greeks. Knowledge was not a matter of the assimilation of facts, but instead was the cultivation of a distinct form of wisdom required for the discernment of the voice of God. Indeed, for Liddon, it is this wisdom to which everything else is subordinated, and it is consequently the acquisition of such wisdom that characterises the goal of theological education. This is not limited to mere doctrine but embraces all aspects of life, thus shaping the very being of the clergyman as he "lives for God".[22] Liddon contrasts this form of education with that offered in the universities, institutions which, he felt, were already ceasing to "yield any public homage or honour to the name of our Lord Jesus Christ".[23] If the universities could no longer be entrusted with the cultivation of the traditional disciplines of knowing God, then the Church would have to develop its own system of education.

In another sermon preached at the College Festival five years later, Liddon further developed his understanding of wisdom as the basis of theological education. The primary task of the theological college, he maintained, was to ensure that theology was undertaken in the context of the Church and under the discipline of the "fear of the Lord". Indeed, he went on:

The absence of [the] fear of the Lord, which is wisdom in the leading Bible sense of the term, is fatal to any living appreciation, if not to any appreciation whatever, of the doctrines of Redemption and Grace. ... Dogmatic wisdom has its root and beginning in the culture of those moral and spiritual sensibilities which Scripture calls the "fear of the Lord".[24]

On Liddon's account, spiritual and theological wisdom required a basis in "conduct, in life, in conscience" which in turn implied both a "system" and an "atmosphere". Against the reduction of theology to simply another form of

---

[21] "The Work and Prospects of Theological Colleges" in *Clerical Life and Work*, pp. 46-72, here pp. 49-50.

[22] Ibid., p. 62.

[23] Ibid., p. 67.

[24] "Moral Groundwork", pp. 82-3.

knowledge, it was impossible "in the case of theology to ignore morals, conduct, life, without the greatest risk".[25] This required living by a "rule of love", which would furnish the future clergy with an ideal pattern for living. Consequently any academic "system" required "a moral and religious atmosphere".[26] This educational model was not easy to express but provided the means by which the sincerest form of friendship might be rooted in "consciously common convictions".[27]

Figure 1.1. Cuddesdon College Reading Room in about 1860

For Liddon, then, education in a theological college was first and foremost education in a disposition of the heart. This meant that its students were to be "men who know something of their own hearts ere they preach to others".[28] In turn, this implied that the context of theological speculation was every bit as important as the speculation itself as part of the cultivation of theological wisdom. It was for this reason that the communal life and spirit were so important in forming the theological disposition. On Liddon's account, a theological college was a community entrusted by the Church to develop theological wisdom in "the

[25] Ibid., p. 84.
[26] Ibid., p. 87.
[27] Ibid., p. 89.
[28] Ibid., p. 92.

ambassadors of Christ", that is, in those who were to be ordained to act in its name, to preach to it and to exhort and admonish it. For Liddon, theological education was far removed from the mere acquisition of a body of academic knowledge and a number of pastoral skills which were later to be put into practice. It was instead rooted in the quest for the knowledge of God.

The Theological Background

Given the educational background of the founders of Cuddesdon and their Tractarian forebears, it is hardly surprising that there was a strong Patristic and more general classical element in their understanding of theology.[29] The picture of a fixed truth which matured into its final doctrinal expression in the fourth and fifth century, combined with a modest study of the great Anglican theologians, Hooker and Pearson,[30] dominated the curriculum in distinction to the critical historical study undertaken on Schleiermacher's model. Indeed the vision of theological education, as centred on the acquisition of a shared corporate mode of existence or form of life, is something akin to the ancient Greek model of *paideia*,[31] that is, education in a continuing tradition borne by the society, in this case, the ecclesial society. Education was thus the process of being fitted for the life one led in society, which in the case of Athens involved the acquisition of the Athenian civic virtues: for the Christian it was by analogy the process of acquiring the virtues for life in the Christian society. Theological education on such a model was not something undertaken simply to acquire skills for the practice of a particular set of ministerial tasks but was the shared pursuit of all Christians who sought to journey through the Christian life.

[29] On the revival of Patristics by the Tractarians in the 1830s, see Peter Nockles, *The Oxford Movement in Context*, Cambridge: Cambridge University Press, 1994, esp. pp. 110-13. More generally on Greek thought in the nineteenth century, see David Newsome, *Two Classes of Men: Platonism and English Romantic Thought*, London: John Murray, 1974. See also Frank Turner, *The Greek Heritage in Victorian Britain*, New Haven: Yale University Press, 1981; Richard Jenkyns, *The Victorians and Ancient Greece*, Cambridge, Mass: Harvard University Press, 1980. Newsome (like F. D. Maurice) points to the importance of Aristotelianism of the Oxford Movement over and against the Platonism of Cambridge (pp. 62-72).

[30] Chadwick, *Founding of Cuddesdon*, pp. 30-2.

[31] On *Paideia* see the magisterial work by Werner Jaeger, *Paideia: The Ideals of Greek Culture*, Oxford: Blackwell, 1939. For its assimilation into early Christianity see Jaeger, *Early Christianity and Greek Paideia*, London: Oxford University Press, 1961. On *Paideia* and the social and tacit character involved in the assimilation of tradition, see Andrew Louth, *Discerning the Mystery*, Oxford: Clarendon Press, 1983, pp. 73-95.

Several of the Greek Fathers pioneered similar models of Christian education:[32] the education of people into their faith was an aspect of Christian life, as central as the discipline of prayer and the practice of Christian ethics. The teachings of the church (or "doctrines") were not usually formulated along systematic lines, but were taught in sermons or expositions of scripture, as part of the very process of Christian living. For some, the goal of education was to get to know the Christian tradition and through this to encounter the divine teacher: theological education, as it was for Liddon many centuries later, was about listening out for the divine teacher. The interaction between educating the mind and the spiritual journey is well put by Gregory of Nazianzus:

> God is light: the highest, the unapproachable, the ineffable, that can neither be conceived in the mind nor uttered in speech, that gives light to every reasoning creature. He is in the world of thought what the sun is in the world of sense; in proportion as we are cleansed, he presents himself to our minds; in proportion as he is presented to our mind he is loved; and again in proportion as we love him, he is conceived; himself contemplating and comprehending himself, and pouring himself out upon what is external to him. I mean that light that is contemplated in the Father and the Son and the Holy Spirit, whose wealth is their unity of nature and the single outburst of their brightness.[33]

Gregory thus suggests that the true theologian has to submit to the prayerful discipline of the contemplation of God; God in turn accommodates himself to the appropriate level of the spiritual ascent of the disciple. Theology, on this model, is no second-order reflection on Christian experience (as it was for Schleiermacher), but is an integral part of the religious life: it is a way of living and thinking in the presence of God which happens as a necessary corollary to prayer and worship. The teacher is God and the process of education is spiritual growth towards union with that God. Frances Young writes:

> The earliest Christians were regarded as atheists because they did not practise recognisable religious rites. Rather they taught a way of life on the basis of a textbook received from the divine *Paidagogus*. That the earliest church was a learning community is borne out by subsequent development. True, more usual religious features crept in as analogies were drawn between Christian activities

[32] Frances Young, "*Paideia* and the Myth of Static Dogma" in Sarah Coakley and David Pailin (eds.), *The Making and Remaking of Christian Doctrine*, Oxford: Clarendon, 1993, esp. pp. 280-2.

[33] *Orat.* 40.5. Cited in Young, "*Paideia* and the Myth of Static Dogma", p. 280.

and mystery-religions, between sacrifice and the Christian Eucharist, and so on. But the aim of the church remained spiritual *paideia*.[34]

At the same time the corporate dimension of learning was central. Christians did not live alone as isolated individuals, but instead entered into a historical tradition, a shared language and a communal way of life which belonged to the church. Some went even as far as suggesting that it was impossible to understand the very word "God" without some prior shared linguistic framework. Experience is nothing without a language to express it and a life to live it: experience thus depended upon language rather than vice versa. Andrew Louth points to a passage in Plotinus, admittedly a non-Christian thinker, which expresses the communal and ethical dimension of knowledge of God:

> For to say "Look to God" is not helpful without some instruction as to what this looking imports: it might very well be said that one can "look" and still sacrifice no pleasure, still be the slave of impulse, repeating the word "God" but held in the grip of every passion and making no effort to master any ... "God" on the lips without a good conduct of life, is but a word.[35]

Similarly, for Augustine, learning, assimilating, reshaping and passing on a tradition are essential human characteristics, which go far beyond the mere emptiness of grammatical rules. Language gains its meaning only in relation to the rules for communal living. Thus before it is possible to tackle the profundities of Christian doctrine, it is first necessary to have mastered the preliminaries of the Christian life:

> When, then, the reader is possessed of the instruction here pointed out, so that unknown signs have ceased to be a hindrance to him; when he is meek and lowly of heart, subject to the easy yoke of Christ, and loaded with his light burden, rooted and grounded and built up in faith, so that knowledge cannot puff him up, let him then approach the consideration and discussion of ambiguous signs in scripture.[36]

Learning and growing together is part of exploring what it means to live in a community of love. Consequently, for Augustine, theological education is the business of learning and teaching within the Christian community (the church). It

---

[34] Frances Young, *"Paideia* – What can we learn from the first four centuries?"* in David Ford and Dennis Stamps (eds), *Essentials of Christian Community*, Edinburgh, T & T Clark, 1996, pp. 229-40, here p. 240.

[35] Plotinus, *Enneads*, II ix 15, cited in Louth, *Discerning the Mystery*, p. 76.

[36] *On Christian Doctrine*, Book II, Ch. XLII.

is the acquisition and assimilation of a Christian culture: it is literally indoctrination.

The Rediscovery of *Paideia*

In recent years there have been many calls for a revival of something resembling this form of theological education: in the United States Edward Farley has dominated the discussion.[37] To counter the tendency in modern universities towards the fragmentation of theology into numerous and only loosely-related sub-disciplines, Farley calls for the recovery of "theologia", where all aspects of theological education are unified around a single purpose. Theology becomes the mode of "ecclesial reflection", the goal of which is the possibility of ensuring a continued ecclesial presence in the world. What unifies theological education, on Farley's phenomenological model, is thus the "comprehensive historical phenomenon, ecclesial existence".[38]

This re-invigoration of theological education with the ideals of *paideia* is perhaps particularly appropriate in Farley's American context with its often sharp division between historical theology and practical theology. Many seminaries from the mid-nineteenth century consciously or unconsciously adopted something similar to Schleiermacher's method, with its emphasis on clerical practice and theoretical knowledge, which stressed the divide between theory and practice.[39] What became more evident as the century wore on, however, was that the traditional sub-disciplines of theology were not necessarily the most appropriate forms of knowledge for the exercise of ministry. Indeed where ministry was increasingly understood in terms of its social and therapeutic functions, the forms of theoretical knowledge required for its practice would also be quite different.

This is perhaps best typified by the Chicago Divinity School, where, as with the university as a whole, sociology, and empirical science more broadly, were to become the chief subjects of study in clergy education. As the President of the University, William Rainey Harper wrote:

A specific amount of laboratory work in science is in our day as necessary for the prospective theological student as a knowledge of Greek, and if the college does

[37] On this see esp. Edward Farley, *Theologia*; and *The Fragility of Knowledge: Theological Education in the Church and the University*, Philadelphia: Fortress, 1988. See also Charles M. Wood, *Vision and Discernment: An Orientation in Theological Study*, Atlanta: Scholars Press, 1985.

[38] *Theologia*, p. 191.

[39] On this see Farley, *Theologia*, ch. 4.

not furnish the student this equipment, the seminary must take the necessary steps
to provide it.

Similarly there would be much to gain if the time devoted to the study of the Bible
could be devoted instead to English literature. In short, Harper claimed, "the day
has come for a broadening of the word minister, and for the cultivation of
specialism in the ministry. ... The ministry stands today in this respect where law
and medicine stood twenty years ago".[40] This understanding of ministerial
expertise and clinical skills became remarkably influential on both sides of the
Atlantic, especially in the development of practically orientated "theological
clinics", and of the suggestion that seminaries and theological colleges should take
more account of the situation of learning (their "context").

The chief problem with both Schleiermacher's model as well as its
development in Chicago is that, by defining theology solely in terms of ministerial
education, or what David Kelsey calls the "clerical paradigm",[41] theology ceases to
have much purpose in a secular academic university, especially when some of the
functions of ministry might be far better performed by professionals in other walks
of life (like doctors and social workers). Theology, like the ministry it is intended
to equip, would thus become simply irrelevant in the modern welfare state.

In contrast to this model, the alternative view of theological education as the
cultivation of the mode of ecclesial existence is quite different from
straightforward "professional education". Theology is neither a body of theory to
be learnt in order to be put into practice, nor a purely academic task, where the
pursuit of scientific research is seen as an end in itself. The primary goal of
ministerial education is not a "technical rationality" which encompasses a number
of scientifically based skills, but is instead the acquisition of theological
understanding or wisdom. Farley's alternative to Schleiermacher makes no clearcut distinction between theory and practice. Theology is not defined in terms of the
functions of ministry, but instead in terms of the acquisition of theological wisdom,
the *habitus* of theology.

Consequently, against a view of theology which is focused primarily on the
practice of ministry, Farley sees theology as necessarily combining theory and
practice, and furthermore as established on the assimilation into the learner's heart
and mind of the historical being of the Church. The unifying feature of theology is
thus first and foremost the acquisition of a tradition, an inheritance, a set of rules
for living the Christian life in prayer, thought and action. Drawing on such a

[40] William Rainey Harper, "Shall the Theological Curriculum be modified, and how?" in
American Journal of Theology 3 (1899), pp. 45-66, here p. 53.
[41] David H. Kelsey, *To Understand God Truly. What's Theological About a Theological
School?*, Louisville: Westminster John Knox, 1992, p. 91.

tradition, and in distinction to Schleiermacher, Farley thereby sees historical theology as something which cannot be divorced from practical theology:

> Historical, thus, is theology itself. It may continue to be knowledge, but if it is the wisdom, the understanding, and insightfulness that occur when the human being is shaped in a redemptive way, it occurs in connection with the believer's or Church's responses to things, and as such it has the character of interpretation. ... It is the shift from theology as a cluster of sciences based on a priori authority to theology as historically situated reflection and interpretation.[42]

Paideia in Anglican Theological Education

The parallels between the model outlined by Farley and that of Liddon are clear: indeed, Liddon's idea of a theological college is perhaps even further removed from the mere acquisition of pastoral and academic skills, mere "theory" to be put into practice, than Farley's. This is principally because the residential and corporate dimension, with the emphasis on "withdrawal" and "fellowship",[43] is of far more significance.[44] What is perhaps surprising, however, given the enormous changes in theological education and higher education more generally in the past 150 years is that Liddon's ideals have survived remarkably intact. Indeed, until very recently, most of the changes to the education of the clergy have served to increase the role of residential theological colleges, particularly the 1921 requirement that all ordinands should spend a period in residential training. Alternative patterns to theological colleges were slow to develop: the residential pattern consequently provided the norm until very recently. It was not until 1960 that the first part-time Course was set up by Mervyn Stockwood and John Robinson

---

[42] Farley, *The Fragility of Knowledge*, p. 128. While not rejecting the *paideia* model, David Kelsey has tried to combine it with the Berlin model: "The goal is to form persons with the *habitus* that capacitate them as agents in a shared public world to apprehend God Christianly, rather than to form only their 'reason' with capacities for disciplined and self-critical inquiry. As in *paideia*, *habitus* that capacitate people to apprehend God are formed only indirectly by study of something else. However, the *range* of things studied and the type of *critical thinking* employed are appropriated from 'Berlin'" (*To Understand God Truly*, p. 236).

[43] See Edward Knapp-Fisher, *Cuddesdon College Lent Letter*, 1960, CCA LL17.

[44] On this see William Jacob, "The Development of the 'Concept of Residence' in Theological Education in the Church of England" in *Residence – An Education*, London: Advisory Council for the Church's Ministry (ACCM), 1990, pp. 68-91. He develops this in D. W. Hardy and P. H. Sedgwick (eds), "An Integrating Theology in Theological Education" in *The Weight of Glory*, Edinburgh: T & T Clark, 1991, pp. 185-94. The Report *Residence – An Education* (esp. p. 58), while on the whole favourable, does not idolize the idea, but is able to offer criticism of the tendency of the community to become over-absorbed with itself.

in Southwark. The next course was not established until 1970, and as late as 1994 courses were training only about one quarter of the clergy of the Church of England, and this was primarily for non-stipendiary ministry.[45] It is only in the past couple of years that numbers of stipendiary clergy on courses have increased significantly, primarily because of severe financial pressure.[46]

Indicative of the persistence of Liddon's ideals, however, is the attention that was paid in the late 1980s to the educational procedure for best ensuring that theological students were able both to learn the tradition but also to assimilate it in their prayer and spirituality. The key-word was "integration" where the many different and complex aspects of theological education and spiritual and personal formation were to be integrated in the light of a coherent vision. There was an anxiety that the increasing fragmentation of the theological disciplines would result in a lack of a sense of overall purpose. Peter Baelz, Chair of ACCM's Committee for Theological Education, (and for a time Chairman of the Ripon College Cuddesdon Governing Body), wrote in his introduction to the influential report, *An Integrating Theology*, of the importance of:

> ... an approach to theological education which would hold together in a creative relationship the formation of a person's own ministerial formation and character, the acquisition of an appropriate and serviceable knowledge of the living tradition, and an understanding of the forces operating in contemporary culture at the individual and at the social level.[47]

Similarly, in the 1987 report *Education for the Church's Ministry* (known as ACCM 22), which has had far reaching effects on the curriculum as well as the academic and personal assessment of students in theological colleges and courses, the approach taken emphasises that "all parts of the educational programme are to be seen in relation to, or 'relativised' by, the central aim of theological education; and no one part should be seen as the heart of the process".[48] The Report goes on to enunciate this "central aim" in some detail. It should:

> ... enable the student to grow in those personal qualities by which, with and through the corporate ministry of the Church, the creative and redemptive activity

[45] On developments in clergy education in the 1980s, see Hugh Melinsky, *The Shape of the Ministry*, Norwich: Canterbury Press, 1992, esp. pp. 249-62.

[46] For statistics, see the recent report, *Structure and Funding of Ordination Training*, London: Church House Publishing, 2002.

[47] Peter Baelz, introduction in *An Integrating Theology*, London: ACCM Occasional Paper 5, 1983.

[48] *Education for the Church's Ministry*, London: ACCM Occasional Paper 22, London, 1987, §57 (1).

of God may be proclaimed and realised in the world. One who is to show God's activity must know of it, respond to it, participate in it, be animated by it in relationships with others and seek to proclaim and realise it in the world. This requires that he/she seek to be conformed to the very form of God's being for mankind in the world, intellectually, spiritually and practically, and into the discipline of thought and life which is implicit in this. He/she must seek to be incorporated into the truth by growing in wisdom and godliness by the grace which God confers.[49]

Theological education is thus not just about learning the tradition, the story of the creative and redemptive activity of God, but also about engaging with that tradition in order to make it live. It is about learning how the tradition is true today, and then making it true today. Peter Baelz wrote in the introduction to the Report:

> If we are to be true to a living tradition, then we dare not separate so-called spiritual experience from so-called theological knowledge. Neither will live and flourish without the other. Indeed, divorced from each other, both become mockeries of their true selves. … A living tradition, with its roots in the past, is one that sets people free to explore the unrealised potentiality of the future.[50]

The spiritual "atmosphere", of which Liddon spoke in the 1870s, was still being breathed deeply by ACCM well over a hundred years later. All this goes to show that Anglican theological education was undoubtedly moulded, at least in its ideals, by the model of *paideia*, and resembles something of the union between the theoretical and practical which characterises Christian life itself. Baelz's colourful idea that theology was something to be worn like comfortable clothes and not left hung up unused in a wardrobe, thus describes both the practice and the goal of theological education: theology is a usable wisdom, a *habitus*, which shapes all aspects of life.

The Dangers of *Paideia*

There are, however, dangers in this model of theological education. Through the history of Ripon College Cuddesdon and its constituent colleges these have emerged at different points. The one over-riding question is whether the acquisition of theological wisdom is in reality little more than the adoption of a fixed closed system of ecclesial existence which allows for no criticism. Its origin

---

[49] Ibid., §45.

[50] See also the introduction by Peter Baelz in *Experience and Authority*, London: ACCM Occasional Paper 19, 1984.

lies in a reaction to critical thought and relies on the myth of static and unchangeable dogma. Dr Pusey's legacy has been large. Whether such an inherently conservative system can be made more open and critical is of central importance. Is it possible to combine something of the critical principles that formed the theological approach of Ripon Hall through much of its history with the integrated pattern of *paideia*? Can ecclesial existence become an open rather than a closed system and thus something which leaves room for, and might even require, constant vigilance and ideological criticism?

It is important to note that in its original usage *paideia* was education for life in a distinct society with a clear pattern of rules and regulations which involved the acquisition of those distinctive virtues which formed the social cement for the polis, or served as a basis for its survival or "immortality" into future generations.[51] As such it appears to have been inherently conservative, and lacked a critical dimension. Similar dangers are evident from a cursory glance at the history of Anglican Colleges. The idealistic language of *paideia*, or something similar, which extols the virtues of fellowship and community can in practice frequently become little more than a cipher for the more or less uncritical assimilation of the ideology of an institution and through it the ideology of a Church party.

This is hardly surprising in that many of the Colleges set up in the second period of the founding of Colleges in the 1870s and 1880s were designed to promulgate a distinct party ethos against the perceived Tractarianism of the diocesan seminaries like Cuddesdon.[52] A Church of England Report on theological education of 1949 went as far as suggesting that the "best theological college is one in which the Chapel, the lecture room and the common room are all working together to make a fellowship of Christian life both natural and supernatural, the power of which shall remain in the memory of the ordinand as a pattern and inspiration for his future work in a congregation".[53] Without due caution, however, the goal of theological education can become little more than that of instilling the party line of the college into the future clergy.[54] Perhaps for reasons of social stability, or at least their religious analogues (for instance, ecumenical co-existence or Anglican "comprehensiveness"),[55] *paideia* as practised by the Church of England is likely to

[51] See Jaeger, *Paideia*, pp. 379-408.

[52] See Andrew Atherstone, "The Founding of Wycliffe Hall, Oxford" (unpublished paper).

[53] *The Purpose and Scope of Clergy Training: An Outline of Current Practice*, London: Central Advisory Council for the Ministry, 1949.

[54] On this see Anthony Dyson, "Theology and the Educational Principles in Ministerial Training: Problems of Collection Codes and Integrated Codes" in *Kairos* 6 (1982), pp. 4-16; and Melinsky, *The Shape of the Ministry*, p. 254.

[55] On this see esp. Stephen Sykes, *The Integrity of Anglicanism*, Oxford: Mowbray, 1978, p. 19.

conform the student to a distinctive form of ecclesial being which lacks much of a critical dimension. It is a common experience that collaboration between colleges, not least those in Oxford, has often been scuppered by students rather than staff. Perhaps the greatest danger of partisan theological education is that of a pride that refuses be open to criticism.[56]

In order to avoid this danger of *paideia* becoming little more than a conservative form of indoctrination, there seems, firstly, to be a vital need to ensure that the particularity of the tradition through which one comes to the Gospel, that is a particular mode of ecclesial existence, is not mistaken for the Gospel itself. As Rowan Williams put it in relation to the early church, but which seems equally applicable to theological education: "The convert enters a new world in which, because conflict, constraint and uncertainty remain, learning and exchange must continue, and progress needs to be checked against original inspiration, individually and collectively."[57]

Secondly, there should always be room within any ecclesial tradition for the critical encounter to take place. There is the need to awaken in the student a suspicion that through history there have been attempts to control the ecclesial tradition: Christ himself, as the ultimate judge, thus stands over against any form of ecclesial existence. Theological integration, Farley's "theologia", should thus be on guard that it does not simply become the passive assimilation of or conformity to a particular form of ecclesial existence or tradition, but always remains a re-invigoration of that tradition through the often painful business of constructive criticism.[58] This requires an understanding of tradition, not as a closed system or "semantic universe" (Lindbeck), but as an open system which is constantly tested. Consequently, the acquisition of tradition is not a passive assimilation of a language but the active response to a critical encounter with that tradition.[59] Despite his clamour for theologia, Farley also recognises the importance of this critical dimension. He sees the clergy's role in the corporate assimilation of ecclesial existence as not simply that of passing on the tradition but as a "situationally oriented dialectic of interpretation", that is, the task of evoking ecclesial presence in the world through a constructive critique of the tradition. In

---

[56] See A. Michael Ramsey, *The Gospel and the Catholic Church*, London: Longmans, Green and Co., 1937, p. 66.

[57] Rowan Williams, "Does it make sense to speak of pre-Nicene orthodoxy?" in Rowan Williams (ed.), *The Making of Orthodoxy*, Cambridge: Cambridge University Press, 1989, pp. 1-23, here p. 15.

[58] On this, see Kelsey, *To Understand God Truly*, ch. 7.

[59] See also John B. Webster, "Locality and Catholicity: Reflections on Theology and the Church" in *Scottish Journal of Theology* 45 (1992), pp. 1-17, esp. p. 5.

this way a more authentic ecclesial existence will be discerned, and theology will not simply be a static and unchanging discipline.[60]

Conclusion

In the educational ethos which lies at the foundation of Cuddesdon, which has been upheld by many recent thinkers both inside and outside the Church of England, there is an inherent tendency towards conservatism and towards the absolutisation of a particular tradition. This does not mean that the residential theological education pioneered in the nineteenth century should be abolished for the sake of something more "modern". This would be to lose its strengths in helping the student develop an integrated approach to theology, prayer and spirituality. But at the same time it is important to be aware of the anti-secularising and anti-critical thrust of the original ethos behind the colleges. Indeed corporate ritual and prayer can easily function to reinforce prejudice and to close off dialogue with those who do things or think differently.

To counter this tendency towards absolutising a particular tradition, it needs to be shown that the tradition or culture into which the Christian is socialised through *paideia* is no closed system, but one founded on what Rowan Williams calls a "permanently disturbing generative event",[61] which defies "schematisation into a plan of salvation that can be reduced to a simple and isomorphic moment of self-recognition in reasons to illumination".[62] Similarly, it is to counter what he calls the "hypostatisation of the traditional context" that Farley ensures that his mode of ecclesial being involves a critical dimension which de-absolutises any particular context in the "purging and sifting of the mythos", with the proviso that criticism is always "truth-oriented", that is, undertaken constructively with the goal of moving ever closer to the kingdom of God.[63] The theologian's task is thus to open up possibilities for the creation of a new situation for faith's dealing with the world, something undertaken in the conscious criticism of all past situations. The Christian "system" is thus at the same time the constant critique of all systems, including its own ecclesial expressions: the 1906 statement of aims at the foundation of Ripon Clergy College is still relevant. The aim of the College was to be:

---

[60] *Theologia*, p. 191.

[61] Rowan Williams, "What is Catholic Orthodoxy?" in Kenneth Leech and Rowan Williams (eds), *Essays Catholic and Radical*, London: Bowardean, 1983, p. 19.

[62] Rowan Williams, "Pre-Nicene Orthodoxy?", p. 16.

[63] *Theologia*, esp. pp. 166-7.

> Love of truth, not a certain set of views received by tradition and labeled "The
> Truth", but of reality, the truth of things as it appears in the sight of God, so far as
> that truth can be ascertained by truthful methods.[64]

In its emphasis on integration and the living assimilation of a tradition and
way of being, the *paideia* model of theological education is attractive, but only
when it is no mere indoctrination into the closed semantic system of a Church
party: it always needs to be coupled with a healthy criticism (which might often
manifest itself as a sense of irony). For the Gospel to continue to speak to future
generations requires that the church at every level from the local congregation,
through the church party, the national church, to the worldwide Anglican
Communion, is always open to judgement. Thus, although theological education
must obviously be concerned with the acquisition and "ownership" of a cherished
tradition, at the same time, if the Gospel is to act as a potent force for the coming
generation, it must also seek to awaken the faculty of critical discernment in the
"ambassadors of Christ", who will be authorised to speak and act in the name of
the Church, enabling them to hear, preach and proclaim the word of God, even
where that word is critical of the ideological distortions introduced by the Church.
In the critical encounter the tradition is transformed as new metaphors and images
communicate the "death and birth of meaning"[65] to the succeeding generation.

The primary task of theological education, it seems to me, is not the
acquisition of "theories" and a "body of knowledge" which will later be put into
practice (even though this is undoubtedly important), but rather involves the far
more painful process of encounter, judgement and conversion through study,
prayer and life together. Indeed one of the most important tasks in the theological
education of the preacher, teacher and leader is the acquisition of the faculty of
critical discernment in order to recognise the "bastard traditions",[66] which are so
easily mistaken for the good news itself. Though a conclusion to such a task is
impossible, in that any tradition that is handed on to future generations will itself
be permeated by our own unrecognised and unvoiced prejudices, it is still
nonetheless the pressing task.[67] Constructive criticism is undertaken for the sake of

---

[64] Cited in Ripon College Cuddesdon Newsletter, 1985, p. 2.

[65] Rowan Williams, "What is Catholic Orthodoxy?", p. 19.

[66] F. J. A. Hort, *The Way, The Truth, The Life* (Hulsean Lectures of 1871), London:
Macmillan, second edition, 1897, p. 91.

[67] On this see, for instance, Nicholas Lash, "Theologies at the Service of a Common
Tradition" in *Theology of the Way to Emmaus*, London: SCM, 1986, pp. 18-33; and "Criticism
or Construction? The Task of the Theologian" in *Theology on the Way to Emmaus*, pp. 3-17.
See also Rowan Williams, "Doctrinal Criticism: Some Questions" in Sarah Coakley and David
Pailin (eds.), *The Making and Remaking of Christian Doctrine*, pp. 239-64.

the future as the liberating power of the life, death and resurrection of Christ is released for the next generation of Christians.

This model of theological education, however, leads to a paradoxical conclusion which derives from the paradox at the heart of the Christian faith: the greater the degree of wisdom the greater the ability to live with doubt; the greater the assimilation of Christian spirituality, the greater the suspicion of our own and every other tradition. This means that theological colleges, like the clergy they educate, exist to ensure the continued encounter with an "image of loss: meaning, hope, and communication (Logos) rejected by the world" which nevertheless becomes the very "image of consummation".[68] *Paideia* without critique, however, usurps this Gospel reality for the more familiar dwelling-place of the community of faith where one "learns how to feel, act, and think in conformity with a religious tradition"[69] but where one all too often forgets that the community itself is part of the crucifying world. Thus although a critical theological education may be no friend of tradition, it might nevertheless allow the Word of God to speak afresh in every generation.

It is fitting to end this chapter by citing the leading principles taken from the latest version of Ripon College Cuddesdon's Validation Document. These aim to express something of the idealism of the founders of Cuddesdon with their vision of a community dwelling in the tradition but at the same time tempered by the open critical assessment of that tradition which marked the theological strength of Ripon Hall:

Ordained ministers are entrusted:
- to be thankful people of deep faith, understanding, and self-awareness who through the practice of prayer and worship listen out day by day for the divine voice in the church and the world.
- to exercise critical and prophetic discernment to ensure that the whole Christian community is reminded of its central focus in the mission of God in the light of the vision of the new world order established in the life, death and resurrection of Jesus Christ.
- to foster the development and nurturing of the Christian community of hope and its renewal in future generations.
- to interpret the world in the light of God, and to demonstrate God's love for all people, so that the whole world might be reconciled with the living God and grow to full maturity.

In turn the educational aims of the College seek to be closely related to this view of Christian ministry.

---

[68] Williams, "What is Catholic Orthodoxy?", p. 19.
[69] Lindbeck, *The Nature of Doctrine*, p. 35.

The College seeks to prepare ordained ministers who are:

- disciplined in the life of prayer, competent and creative leaders of worship, and aware of their own needs and motivations.
- critical and constructive theologians who can draw on and interpret the riches of the Christian tradition in the light of contemporary problems and needs.
- able to understand the nature and purpose of Christian community through the experience of living together and to be leaders in its renewal in future generations.
- able to interpret the world to the church and the church to the world imaginatively and constructively in order to demonstrate the love of God for all people.[70]

It is to be hoped that this vision will still have something to contribute in the changed and financially-straitened conditions faced by the Church of England in the twenty-first century. Without such a vision the Church will be in danger of losing its intellectual credibility and critical cutting edge, and thereby growing increasingly sectarian and irrelevant against the secularised society of modern England. The Church needs ambassadors of Christ who are not afraid of acting in his name, whatever that might do to their cherished tradition.

[70] Ripon College Cuddesdon, Validation Document, 2003. The framework is provided in the Report, *Mission and ministry: the Churches' validation framework for theological education*, London: Ministry Division of the Archbishops' Council by Church House Publishing, second edition, 2003.

Chapter 2

The Founding of Cuddesdon: Liddon, Ritualism and the Forces of Reaction

Andrew Atherstone

The Founding of Cuddesdon[1]

Almost as soon as he had been consecrated bishop of Oxford in 1845, Samuel Wilberforce was making plans to establish a diocesan theological college near his episcopal palace at Cuddesdon.[2] He proclaimed to his clergy that such an institution was in fact "essential" for the welfare of the diocese.[3] Funds were rapidly raised and buildings designed by the diocesan architect, George E. Street (later famous for his work on London's law courts and numerous ecclesiastical buildings). The foundation stone was laid in April 1853 and Cuddesdon College formally opened in June 1854 amidst great celebrations.[4]

One of the concerns raised frequently about small theological colleges was that, isolated from the diverse opinions taught at the Universities, they would breed "party-spirit". Indeed those founded at Chichester (1839) and Wells (1840) had

[1] Thanks are due to the Bodleian Library; the warden and fellows of Keble College, Oxford; the trustees of Lambeth Palace Library; and the principal and chapter of Pusey House, Oxford for permission to publish material from their collections.

[2] A. R. Ashwell and Reginald G. Wilberforce, *Life of the Right Reverend Samuel Wilberforce*, 3 vols, London: John Murray, 1880-82, i. p. 349.

[3] Samuel Wilberforce, *A Charge to the Clergy of the Diocese of Oxford, at his Second Visitation*, London: John Murray, 1851, p. 17.

[4] For details of these events, see Owen Chadwick, *The Founding of Cuddesdon*, Oxford: Oxford University Press, 1954.

quickly gained a Tractarian reputation.[5] When a theological college was proposed for Lichfield in 1852, the local opposition was so vociferous that the scheme was delayed for five years.[6] Similar suspicions surrounded the establishment of Cuddesdon. Before building had even begun, it was said the college would be "more or less under Tractarian influence".[7] William Fremantle (the influential incumbent of Claydon and later Dean of Ripon) wanted publicly to oppose the plan, but kept quiet for the sake of the peace of the diocese.[8] However, the evangelical *Record* was not so considerate. It derided the celebrations at the opening of the college as the "monster show of the month", an "Episcopal gala" which boded much "future evil" for the Church of England. An appeal was made that "lovers of Gospel truth and Protestant simplicity" should combine to establish their own colleges "where something better may be taught than posture, prostrations, and sing song".[9] Another observer rejected Chichester, Wells and Cuddesdon as "nurseries of Anglican Popery" which would "bring forth the deadly fruits of Romish teaching and Romish superstitions under the pretence of Anglicanism ... Let us be quiescent no longer. Peace with these betrayers of our Protestant Christianity is impossible."[10] Suspicion of Wilberforce's motives was fuelled by his family connections. His brothers, Henry and Robert, and his brother-in-law, Henry Manning, had all converted to the Roman Catholic Church in the early 1850s.[11] As one evangelical forcibly put it, they had fallen "into that frightful abyss of spiritual darkness" and all eyes were on the bishop to see if he would follow suit.[12]

From the start Wilberforce was determined to head off such allegations. Again and again he emphasised that Cuddesdon College would represent the mainstream of the Church of England, without bias towards any particular theological party. At the laying of the foundation stone he asked for prayers that the institution would be

[5] William M. Jacob, "The Diffusion of Tractarianism: Wells Theological College, 1840-49", *Southern History* 5 (1983), pp. 189-209; Arthur Burns, *The Diocesan Revival in the Church of England c.1800-1870*, Oxford: Clarendon Press, 1999, pp. 151-6.

[6] James Bateman, *The Tractarian Tendency of Diocesan Theological Colleges*, London: Seeley, 1853; Charles Hebert, *Theological Colleges and the Universities; or, What Special Training Should be Given to the Future Clergy?*, Burslem: Bowering, 1853; *Statement of Facts Connected with the Movement in Opposition to the Establishment of a Diocesan Theological College at Lichfield*, London: Dalton, 1856.

[7] Bateman, *Tractarian Tendency*, p. 25.

[8] Wilberforce to William R. Fremantle, 28 November 1853, in E. K. Pugh (ed.), *The Letter-books of Samuel Wilberforce, 1843-68*, Aylesbury: Buckinghamshire Record Society and Oxfordshire Record Society, vol. 47, 1970, pp. 285-6.

[9] *Record*, 6 July 1854.

[10] *Record*, 18 September 1854.

[11] David H. Newsome, *The Parting of Friends: the Wilberforces and Henry Manning* (1966), reissued, Leominster: Gracewing, 1993.

[12] *Record*, 9 November 1854.

"ever free from party and sectarian disputes; that we may rear therein ripened clergymen with the spirit of Richard Hooker and the temper of Lancelot Andrewes".[13] At the opening of the college Wilberforce proclaimed: "what we are doing here is for the Church of our fathers; for no section of it, for nothing narrower than that true Church of England as God in His providence has planted it in this land".[14] He maintained that theological study, such as that offered by Cuddesdon, would help students to avoid "extreme opinion on any side" and to rid themselves of "Private imaginations, the conceits which are bred of the fancy, narrow mindedness, a set of shallow opinions, self-willed rashness, ignorant obstinacy, party spirit, with its shibboleths and its unchristian judgments, and its uncharitable speeches and all its injuries to souls".[15]

As the first principal of his new institution, Wilberforce chose Alfred Pott, one of his chaplains, his chief clerical secretary and the vicar of Cuddesdon. However, the appointment of a vice-principal presented more of a dilemma. In December 1853 the bishop had offered the post to the young H. P. Liddon, recently ordained to a curacy under William Butler at Wantage.[16] Yet the invitation was soon withdrawn when Wilberforce discovered the extent of Liddon's views on auricular confession and his close relationship with E. B. Pusey. He could not afford to have his college identified so easily in the public mind with Tractarian extremism. He was worried lest students also go to Pusey for counsel and thus the college become "a mere collection of young men under his direction".[17] Nine months of tortured negotiation followed in which Liddon was eventually persuaded to go instead to John Keble for spiritual advice.[18] When his appointment as vice-principal was confirmed, a well-wisher gleefully predicted that Cuddesdon would now fulfil "the worst expectations of its Recordite enemies, & I trust the best anticipations of its friends".[19]

---

[13] *Guardian*, 13 April 1853, p. 245.

[14] George A. Selwyn, *"A Little One Shall Become a Thousand". A Sermon Preached at the Opening of the Cuddesdon Theological Institution ... to which is added, an Appendix, Containing an Account of the Proceedings, and the Speeches Delivered by the Bishops Present*, Oxford: Vincent, 1854, p. 19.

[15] Samuel Wilberforce, *A Charge to the Diocese of Oxford, at his Third Visitation*, London: Parker, 1854, p. 11.

[16] John O. Johnston, *Life and Letters of Henry Parry Liddon*, London: Longmans, 1904; Michael J. Chandler, *The Life and Work of Henry Parry Liddon*, Leominster: Gracewing, 2000.

[17] Wilberforce to Liddon, 7 June 1854, Bodl. MS Wilberforce d.40, fo. 149.

[18] Liddon – Wilberforce, 28 December 1853 – 19 June 1854, Bodl. MS Wilberforce d. 40, fos 139-51; Butler to Wilberforce, 1 February and 26 March 1854, MS Wilberforce c.20, fos 151-4; Keble to Wilberforce, 24 June and 7 July 1854, MS Wilberforce d.39, fos 151-6; Wilberforce to Liddon, 24 July 1854, PHL LHP; Pusey to Liddon, 19 June and 26 July 1854, PHL LBV67/29 and 32; Wilberforce to Keble, 3 July 1854, in *Letter-books*, p. 305.

[19] A. Newdigate to Liddon, 15 August 1854, PHL LP, box 2/13.

Figure 2.1. Alfred Pott

Figure 2.2. Henry Liddon

It was not long before Cuddesdon attracted attention for its ritualist practices. Supporters of the institution began to complain against the ornate decoration of the chapel, the Gregorian chants and singing of the Nicene creed.[20] One said the altar was "very like another part of the Vineyard", while less friendly observers called the college "dangerous".[21] At the first annual festival in June 1855 visitors were shocked to see vergers carrying poles surmounted by gilt crosses during a procession through the village.[22] This procession had been organised by a student, Frederick Lee, who was soon appointed curate at Kennington, near Oxford, where he won early notoriety for introducing incense, reredos, cross, candles, stole and a choir in surplices and red cassocks (donated by Sir George Bowyer of Radley Park, a convert to Roman Catholicism). Lee was dismissed from his curacy by Wilberforce after only a year.[23]

In January 1856 a small group of bishops were staying with Wilberforce at Cuddesdon Palace and had a tour of his new theological institution. Liddon noted in his diary that they objected to nothing, although the cross in chapel may have caused "some secret dissatisfaction".[24] During the following summer vacation Wilberforce asked for changes to be made in the style of music, ritual washing and content of the service-book.[25] Nevertheless, visitors to the chapel a few months later were still shocked at its decoration and made "a series of very vulgar remarks about Popery".[26] During another episcopal party at Cuddesdon Palace in early 1857, A. C. Tait (Bishop of London) and W. J. Trower (Bishop of Glasgow and Galloway) remonstrated with Wilberforce and advised that the college chapel be made less "gaudy". So the cross was removed, the white and green altar cloths forbidden, the painted figures on the wall covered over, and use of the eastward position at the eucharist ceased. Walter Hamilton (Bishop of Salisbury) tried to explain to Liddon that it hindered a bishop if he became identified with a distinctive theological party, yet Liddon felt "aggrieved" at the enforced changes and saw them as "lost ground".[27] A fortnight later he wrote: "The chapel is beginning to look terribly bare. ... Nor is there the consolation of hoping that these

---

[20] Liddon diary, 21 January, 7, 22 and 30 March, 6 August 1856, at CCA VP1/2.

[21] Liddon diary, 30 May and 4 June 1855.

[22] Liddon diary, 5 June 1855; *Guardian*, 13 June 1855, p. 459; *Bucks Herald*, 5 February 1859, p. 4; T. W. Perry – Liddon, 16-17 February 1859, KCL LP.

[23] Henry R. T. Brandreth, *Dr Lee of Lambeth: a Chapter in Parenthesis in the History of the Oxford Movement*, London: SPCK, 1951, pp. 13-5; Peter Maurice, *The Ritualism of Oxford Popery, a Letter to Dr Macbride*, London: Shaw, 1867, pp. 24-5.

[24] Liddon diary, 30 January 1856.

[25] Liddon diary, 27 July 1856.

[26] Liddon diary, 23 October 1856. See Liddon – Henry A. Tyndale, 24-28 October 1856, CCA VP1/12-14.

[27] Liddon diary, 2-3 February 1857; Liddon to Wilberforce, 8 February 1858, Bodl. MS Wilberforce d.40, fo. 155. See Keble to Wilberforce, 6 February 1857, Bodl. MS Wilberforce d.39, fos 186-7.

concessions will go any great way towards pacifying the Puritan mind. The chapel will be thought Jesuitical if it is not condemned as Popish."[28]

In September 1857, further private pressure was put on Wilberforce by Charles Golightly, notorious in the diocese as an anti-Tractarian polemicist.[29] He had sprung to prominence in the early 1840s as a vociferous opponent of J. H. Newman and the Oxford Movement, campaigning energetically on many different occasions in defence of the Church of England's Protestant heritage. Having been informed by his friend Trower about the nature of training at Cuddesdon, Golightly wrote to Wilberforce to express his concerns about Liddon's influence. Immediately the bishop tried to play down the issue:

> Oh how I value people for speaking out to me with love & plainness instead of growling behind my back. ... There are it is true *little* things I should myself wish otherwise; but men must work by instruments & when you have instruments of the greatest possible excellence in fundamentals it would in my judgement be very wrong to cast them away for non essentials. I think my Vice Principal eminently endued with the power of leading men to earnest devoted piety: with such a man I do not think I ought to interfere except as to any thing substantially important. Hence in trifles I do not meddle. I have a strong conviction that Cuddesdon college *is* doing God's works for men's souls mightily.[30]

Later Wilberforce reiterated his confidence in Liddon:

> There may be shades of difference as to things on which members of the Church of England may lawfully differ between us. But I have ever found him most loyally ready to act in such matters on my judgement when he knew it: & I have rarely met with any man living who had equal gifts for stirring up the spark of good in a young man's heart into a flame. Now my *first* & greatest object in founding the college was to get under God's blessing a more earnestly religious *young* clergy – & I thought it *far* better to get such a real man than one who might agree with me in every thing & be less real.[31]

Nonetheless, Wilberforce agreed to change anything at the college which Golightly thought tended to Roman doctrine or ritual.[32] Liddon reflected to Pott: "Probably the Bishop thinks it right to silence an eccentric controversialist at the outset. ...

---

[28] Liddon diary, 17 February 1857.

[29] Andrew C. Atherstone, "Charles Golightly (1807-1885), Church Parties and University Politics in Victorian Oxford", D.Phil. thesis, Oxford University, 2000.

[30] Wilberforce to Golightly, 23 September 1857, LPL MS 1811, fos 211-12.

[31] Wilberforce to Golightly, 4 October 1857, LPL MS 1811, fo. 217.

[32] Wilberforce to Golightly, 26 September 1857, LPL MS 1811, fos 213-14.

Figure 2.3. Charles Portales Golightly

Golightly does not require much of a stimulant to write a pamphlet on any subject which he had better leave alone."[33]

Further private complaints came from Wilberforce's friend, Charles Anderson, who warned against the music of Thomas Helmore and flower decorations which "have the look of effeminacy".[34] He advised the bishop to "hold them in at Cuddesdon, for I think it a pity that young Clergy sh[oul]d be encouraged in what might if injudiciously begun, destroy all their usefulness in a new Parish. ... Extreme ritualism & frippery ornament are most repugnant to the English mind."[35] Perhaps with these tendencies in mind, John Sandford (Archdeacon of Coventry)

[33] Liddon to Pott, 3 October 1857, in Chadwick, *Founding of Cuddesdon*, p. 69.
[34] Anderson to Wilberforce, nd, Bodl. MS Wilberforce d.28, fo. 41.
[35] Anderson to Wilberforce, 8 November 1857, ibid., fo. 69.

exhorted ordinands at the college festival of June 1857 to "drink deep at the fountain-head, instead of borrowing your views from ephemeral and party writings, which are the bane of our age and country".[36] Meanwhile Wilberforce reassured the diocese via his triennial charge that he had noticed in students at Cuddesdon "an increased quietness and moderation of tone on things doubtful", and he invited any local clergy to visit the college and observe its practice.[37]

The Public Outcry

In January 1858 the dispute went public. The *Quarterly Review*, in an article on "Church Extension", criticised the establishment of theological colleges and their tendency to breed "party spirit":

> It is the nature of all such institutions to go further than was intended in the line of the impulsion first given, whatever that may be; and there is nothing that we should deprecate more than the foundation of rival colleges by hostile parties in the Church to vie with each other in sectarian bigotry and perpetuate our unhappy divisions. ... the utmost vigilance on the part of their superiors is necessary to correct their inherent tendency to extravagance, and to obtain the confidence of the public by the most rigid forbearance from all sectarian teaching, and all external badges of party.[38]

Cuddesdon College was specifically named. According to the *Quarterly* it had lost its "indispensable neutrality of character" and instead showed signs of an "exclusive, partisan spirit". The college chapel was described as "fitted up with every fantastic decoration to which a party-meaning has been assigned"; the altar as "adorned with flowers, surmounted with lights, covered with a lace-bordered napkin, and in every particular affecting the closest approximation to a Popish model"; the eucharist as conducted "with rinsings of cups in the newly-revived piscina, with genuflexions, and other ceremonial acts which are foreign to our ritual and usages"; and the service-book as "concocted from the 'seven canonical hours' of the Romish Church". The reviewer asked: "what effect must this ostentatious playing at Romanism have on the Protestant public?"[39]

Golightly saw his opportunity. He circulated excerpts from the *Quarterly* throughout Oxford diocese, adding that according to one Cuddesdon student

---

[36] John Sandford, *Clerical Training. A Sermon, Preached on the Anniversary of the Theological College for the Diocese of Oxford*, Oxford: Parker, 1857, p. 20.

[37] Samuel Wilberforce, *A Charge Delivered at the Triennial Visitation of the Diocese*, Oxford: Parker, 1857, p. 29.

[38] Robert H. Cheney, "Church Extension", *Quarterly Review* 103 (January 1858), p. 162.

[39] Ibid., pp. 162-3.

"nobody can pass through the Institution, and continue a Protestant". The tendency of the college, Golightly claimed, was "to sow broad cast the seeds of Romish perversion in the counties of Oxfordshire, Berkshire, and Buckinghamshire".[40] At a meeting of the Church Pastoral Aid Society in Manchester, Hugh Stowell (a leading evangelical) took up the cry, declaring that

> a large number of the younger clergy were preparing to be the voices of the Church of Rome in the Church of England, and some of our Bishops were caught in the snare, and were either dupes or designers in the matter. ... It was high time these things were exposed, for we had been asleep too long.[41]

These charges against Cuddesdon were promptly rejected as "a barefaced lie", "utterly false and ungrounded", and "malicious and wicked".[42] The *Quarterly's* article was called "slipshod stuff" which "savours not a little of malice aforethought" and it was chastised for "the vulgar intemperance of personal animosity and moral guilt".[43] Yet the sternest criticism was reserved for Golightly himself. He was rebuked for "uncharitable meddling", "illiberal zeal" and "pertinacious bigotry".[44] He was called "a great busybody and mischief-maker", and "a Recordite leader and anti-Tractarian martyr" with "exuberant zeal which appears to consume him".[45] The *Clerical Journal* pronounced:

> Mr Golightly's cowardice was quite equal to his ignorant and mischievous prejudices, for he seized the moment when he thought Cuddesdon was fallen to give it a kick and sink it still lower. The *Quarterly Review* had spoken – an undoubted oracle had pronounced the sentence – and it only remained that the pious and evangelic Mr Golightly should hasten on its execution.[46]

Wilberforce spoke of "busy gossip", "evil surmises" and "malicious misrepresentation".[47] He termed Golightly his "gossiping friend" and condemned him for attempting to "excite a storm by appealing to the prevalent suspicions of the hour". The bishop reassured Pott: "the habits of his mind make him unable to form an unbiased judgment on any matter which appeals to his inveterate

---

[40] Alfred Pott, *Correspondence Relating to Cuddesdon Theological College, in Answer to the Charges of the Rev. C. P. Golightly, and the Report of the Commissioners Thereon*, Oxford: Vincent, 1858, p. 3.

[41] *Manchester Examiner* quoted in *Record*, 5 February 1858.

[42] Pott, *Correspondence*, pp. 13, 15, 18.

[43] *Guardian*, 3 March 1858, p. 182; Pott, *Correspondence*, p. 13.

[44] *Clerical Journal*, 8 March 1858, p. 99.

[45] *English Churchman*, 4 February and 11 March 1858, pp. 105, 227.

[46] *Clerical Journal*, 8 March 1858, p. 99.

[47] *Guardian*, 3 March 1858, p. 183.

prejudices – I doubt whether any Diocesan College could satisfy him".[48] Meanwhile Golightly received a direct episcopal rebuke:

> I think you were blinded by party spirit: or you must have felt that the charge of spreading Romanism &c, a charge as poisonous to their character as if you had charged them with adultery … with not a particle of sifted evidence to support it … as gross a violation of the ninth commandment & of St Paul's law of Christian charity as could easily be committed. Nothing in the administration of my Diocese has ever wounded my heart so deeply.[49]

William Butler expressed his "deep regret, that Mr Golightly in his old age has not learnt wisdom, and that, as in days of old, he should still spend his time in the possibly exciting, but assuredly profitless and unedifying occupation of hunting for mare's nests".[50] Anderson, though, saw this Protestant cleric being used as a tool for more sinister purposes:

> The Devil is ready enough to enter into any one even Churchmen in the guise of an Angel of Light, and the more the Church of England lifts her truthful head the more the Papist & the Puritan will fight their several ways against her: and I have no doubt that they combine at Oxford through the medium of the rationalistic people, who are liberal and farsighted enough to be friends with both in order to undermine the Christian Faith, and that if poor Portcullis [Golightly] knew how he was made a tool of by others he would be ready to rush like the herd of swine and drown himself in the Cherwell.[51]

Similarly, the *Union* viewed Golightly as just a pawn in the game:

> Poor Mr Golightly is known to have been the cats paw of a clever and narrow-minded clique at Oxford, headed by a Germanising Evangelical; and, therefore, his false and badly patched-up gossip may be forgiven. If this "not very judicious" parson would attend to the poor people of Headington, and not rake up groundless charges against those of his brother-clergymen who are doing a more effectual and successful work than himself, he would gain more respect from straightforward people generally, if he lost the praises of the low-minded Puritans at Oxford.[52]

Despite this caustic abuse, Golightly's friends came to his defence. One declared: "The Public does not want a railing accusation against the person who

---

[48] Wilberforce to Pott, 1 and 15 February 1858 in Pott, *Correspondence*, pp. 4, 9.

[49] Wilberforce to Golightly, 24 April 1858, LPL MS 1811, fo. 223.

[50] Handbill, 2 February 1858, Bodl. MS Wilberforce c.20, fo. 158. For Butler's authorship, see Liddon diary, 1 February 1858, at PHL.

[51] Anderson to Wilberforce, 3 February 1858, Bodl. MS Wilberforce d.28, fos 76-7.

[52] *Union*, 26 February 1858, p. 136.

makes a charge; but proof that the charge is unfounded."[53] The *National Standard* called Golightly "true-hearted honest, and resolute", a man whose "zeal as a faithful minister of the Gospel never slumbers" and who had "done nothing but what it was his duty to do … the whole community owes him a debt of gratitude".[54] Likewise Bishop Trower encouraged his friend to persevere: "after the experiences of the last 20 years, I see not how it is possible with a safe conscience to stand aloof, while the principles of the Church of England and the Reformation are undermined, & a totally different ἦθος is being insidiously wrought into the Clergy".[55]

Those inclined to view the affair as altogether less serious poked fun at both Cuddesdon and its critics. The following ditty by some local wag circulated Oxford:

> Go lightly when you make a charge
> Against a Christian brother,
> Nor with the bigot's pen enlarge
> The failings of another.
> 'Tis true, in Cuddesdon's priestly home
> Hard is the student's lot;
> But still, he is not sent to *Rome* –
> He simply "goes to Pott".[56]

The Archdeacons' Inquiry and College Concessions

Liddon was confident that increased interest in Cuddesdon College could only be beneficial:

> All that I hear in Oxford makes me think that this Golightly explosion will in the end, by God's mercy, do us great good. It will dissipate reports which may have been prevalent, or anyhow it will relegate them to those strongholds of Ultra-Low Church prejudice, where belief in these matters in no way depends on fact.[57]

At Pott's request, and with what Golightly termed "Napoleonic rapidity", Wilberforce appointed his three archdeacons to hold a Commission of inquiry.[58]

---

[53] Richard Twopeny, *Some Remarks Upon the Visitation of Cuddesdon College, and the State of the Church in the Diocese of Oxford*, London: Wertheim, Macintosh and Hunt, 1858, p. 16.

[54] *National Standard*, 13 and 27 March 1858, pp. 41, 89.

[55] Trower to Golightly, 10 February 1858, LPL MS 1810, fo. 51.

[56] *Jackson's Oxford Journal*, 27 March 1858.

[57] Liddon to Wilberforce, 8 February 1858, Bodl. MS Wilberforce d.40, fo. 154.

[58] Golightly to Tait, 9 February 1858, LPL Tait Papers 79, fo. 161.

Liddon later complained that this "gave a fictitious importance to charges against the college which were either groundless or absurd; – unless indeed the opinions of the Puritanical party were to be made the rule of faith and practice in the diocese."[59] Yet the *Record* put all the authorities in the dock: "It is not so much the Principal and Vice-Principal who are on their defence before the Bishop and the three Archdeacons. It is all these parties who are collectively on their trial in the face of the Church of England."[60]

The Commissioners met at Cuddesdon on 6 February 1858. Golightly was invited to attend and Liddon thought his contributions "exceedingly amusing".[61] It was agreed by the archdeacons that the chapel had "too lavish a display of ornaments" which encouraged "a disproportionate regard for the accessories of Public Worship". However, the candles near the altar were said never to be lit unless the whole chapel was lit, and use of a lace cloth had been discontinued as a result of the recent "Westerton Judgment" (concerning the ritualistic practices of Robert Liddell at St Paul's, Knightsbridge). "Genuflexions" were hard to define but Pott and Liddon denied they were practised, and rinsing of the sacramental vessels in the piscina had been abandoned. Furthermore, the archdeacons concluded there was "no reason for imputing a party meaning to any of these decorations".[62] Richard Twopeny (vicar of North Stoke, between Oxford and Reading) strongly disagreed. He rejected such "excessive ornamentation" as "a badge of party, a display of colours", belonging to those who wished the Church of England to resemble the Church of Rome. Even the cross, he thought, which ought to be a symbol "of peace and unity, has been perverted to become the badge of a party".[63] Likewise Joseph Wilson (a local magistrate) declared:

> There is not much, probably, in a lace cloth and a metal cross; no indication of party was intended; but this is a poor reason for the use of toys and fripperies to satisfy morbid tastes at the risk of creating prejudice in many minds, of causing serious offence, and by a continued series of such trifling practices, unavoidably creating a party, and affixing to it its own characteristics.[64]

[59] Liddon to Golightly, 24 November 1875, LPL MS 1808, fo. 55.

[60] *Record*, 26 February 1858.

[61] Liddon diary, 6 February 1858. For Golightly's account of the commission, see Golightly to Tait, 9 February 1858, LPL Tait Papers 79, fos 161-2; Charles P. Golightly, *A Letter to the Very Reverend the Dean of Ripon, Containing Strictures on the Life of Bishop Wilberforce, Vol.II with Special Reference to the Cuddesdon College Enquiry and the Pamphlet "Facts and Documents"*, London: Simpkin, Marshall, 1881, pp. 34-5.

[62] Pott, *Correspondence*, pp. 7-8.

[63] Twopeny, *Some Remarks*, pp. 6, 8.

[64] Joseph H. Wilson, *Thoughts on Church Matters in the Diocese of Oxford. By a Layman and Magistrate for that County*, London: Saunders and Otley, 1858, p. 27.

Upon investigation, the three archdeacons found the Cuddesdon service-book to be "not only unexceptionable, but highly valuable", although they recommended it be remodelled because of its "unfortunate resemblance" to the Roman Breviary.[65] The prayers were said to be taken from the same source as those in the Book of Common Prayer, to which the *Christian Observer* retorted: "So the slime and mud in which worms crawl and insects are engendered, are taken from the same source as the purest spring water; – one rivulet supplies them both!"[66] A defender of the college, however, thought such abuse of the service-book merely prejudiced:

> Truly "unfortunate" it is that it was not so disguised and wrapped up as to suit the Protestant palate; the contents may be the same – that is not the question. Call your Antiphons "The Golden Treasury", and your book itself, "Gospel Manna, or Crumbs of Comfort for Starving Souls"; date it Clapham instead of Cuddesdon, and let Seeley publish it, and in the "portfolio" of the "Record" you may hope for a Protestant canonization.[67]

When the archdeacons' inquiry was complete, Wilberforce boldly declared (with what the *Record* thought "complacency" and "quiet arrogance") that their report completely refuted every charge brought against Cuddesdon. He reaffirmed his belief that the college intended "to foster no party spirit, but to nourish in young men going into Orders habits of self-denial and true earnest piety on the simplest Church of England model".[68] The *Guardian* too was satisfied: "We had very little doubt at the time, judging from the well-known antecedents of the personage who appeared as the accuser of his brother clergy and of his Bishop, that on inquiry it would turn out that he had found what is popularly called a mare's nest."[69] Likewise the *English Churchman* proclaimed: "the report of the Commissioners proves that upon this, as upon former occasions, Mr Golightly's party-zeal has led him to commit a manifest breach of the ninth Commandment".[70]

By no means all were pacified, however. Even the Roman Catholic *Rambler* sarcastically congratulated the authorities for their "equivocation and suppression of truth".[71] Arthur Isham (a rural dean) thought that far from disproving the

---

[65] Pott, *Correspondence*, p. 8.

[66] "State of the Diocese of Oxford", *Christian Observer* (July 1859), p. 467.

[67] *Counter-thoughts on Church Matters in the Diocese of Oxford. A Letter, Addressed by a Clergyman of that Diocese to a Layman & Magistrate of that County*, London: Hayes, 1858, p. 40.

[68] Wilberforce to Pott, 15 February 1858, in Pott, *Correspondence*, p. 9; *Record*, 17 March 1858.

[69] *Guardian*, 3 March 1858, p. 181.

[70] *English Churchman*, 25 February 1858, p. 179.

[71] Richard Simpson, "Cuddesdon Casuistry", *Rambler* 9 (April 1858), p. 285.

charges, the archdeacons' report "exhibits a complete justification for the attack". To the principal he protested:

> You make ceremonialism an important adjunct. This I consider to be full of danger, as likely to alloy the very doctrine of Christ. Gorgeousness in ritualism, and simplicity of faith, cannot stand together. ... Mr Golightly is not the only objector. There is a deep uneasiness in many minds about the College, which will not be allayed by the Report of the Commissioners.[72]

In reply, Pott lamented: "The Church of England must be indeed given over to a spirit of schism, when a shelf behind the Communion Table, or a fringe on Communion linen, are alleged as reasons for suspicion and separation."[73]

Golightly, of course, thought his charges confirmed rather than contradicted by the archdeacons and circulated excerpts from their report, announcing his intention "to leave the diocese to judge".[74] The *Guardian* was surprised that he had not "at once frankly acknowledged his mistake and apologised for spreading the slander".[75] Yet the *English Churchman* thought this typical of Golightly's character:

> he seems to possess some of the tastes and instincts of the fabled salamander which lives in the fire. ... We cannot conceive what pleasure any Christian man can feel in this perpetual hunt after the presumed faults and transgressions of his neighbours. The gusto with which such a discovery of a "leaning to Tractarianism" is eagerly ferreted out by Mr Golightly's confederates is a painful exhibition, to our minds, and we think both he and his Recordite friends might employ their time and pens to much better effect by concentrating their attention and their powers on some other subjects to which they are solicited both by duty and by the law of charity.[76]

In the light of the archdeacons' report, the *Quarterly Review* came under pressure to withdraw its charges against Cuddesdon. The author of the article remained silent, but Whitwell Elwin (the *Quarterly*'s editor) was prepared to defend its remarks. He wrote to John Murray (the review's publisher): "I am sure I can make good our position, and show the danger of the Cuddesdon system. ... There is no doubt it is a semi Roman Catholic College. ... I think we can crush the

---

[72] *Jackson's Oxford Journal*, 6 March 1858.

[73] *Jackson's Oxford Journal*, 13 March 1858.

[74] Handbill, 20 February 1858, Bodl. MS Wilberforce c.20, fo. 160.

[75] *Guardian*, 3 March 1858, p. 181.

[76] *English Churchman*, 11 March 1858, p. 226.

Bishop of Oxford."[77] Nevertheless with private pressure brought to bear by Bishop Phillpotts of Exeter and by William Gladstone (on Wilberforce's behalf), the *Quarterly* eventually issued a grudging statement that it had not meant to imply Roman Catholic doctrine was taught at Cuddesdon College:

> The questions were purely questions of ritual, upon which there is, and always has been, great difference of opinion within the English Church; and though we retain the same sentiments that we expressed in the Article, we entirely acquit the authorities of entertaining any ulterior or covert designs.[78]

Ironically, Elwin later sent two of his sons to Cuddesdon.

Although his college had been publicly vindicated, when the furore died down Wilberforce urged quiet alteration in the nature of chapel worship. Bishop Trower was not alone in viewing Cuddesdon as evidence that its founder had thrown his weight "into the side of a new, ornate, symbolical, Ritual".[79] John W. Burgon (Fellow of Oriel College) also cautioned Wilberforce: "Like Caesar's wife, Cuddesdon must be *unsuspected*. There must be a *studied* inoffensiveness. What is tolerable elsewhere, is intolerable there."[80] Some, like Hardwick Shute (who had lectured at Cuddesdon), warned that to concede any ground would be seized on by Protestant critics "as a confession of weakness or worse", but Wilberforce went ahead with his changes.[81]

At the start of the crisis Liddon had agreed to any necessary alterations:

> I shall joyfully acquiesce. ... I fear that you may, from time to time have sacrificed your better judgment to your kind consideration for my individual prejudices. Of course I *do* rejoice in the external expression of religious worship; and believe it to be abstractedly right and desirable. But under the circumstances I would gladly prefer to reduce everything to the minimum of the τὸ πρέπον [what is fitting] rather than again hazard the greater – infinitely greater – interests at stake.[82]

Therefore, following the advice of the archdeacons' report, the silk hangings from the walls of the chapel were replaced by plain oak panelling and the service-book

---

[77] Elwin to Murray, 27 February 1858, in *Some xviii Century Men of Letters: Biographical Essays by the Rev. Whitwell Elwin, Some Time Editor of the Quarterly Review, with a Memoir* edited by Warwick Elwin, 2 vols, London: John Murray, 1902, i. p. 190.

[78] *Quarterly Review* 103 (April 1858), p. 574. See W. E. Gladstone to Wilberforce, 2 March – 16 April 1858, Bodl. MS Wilberforce d.36, fos 149-58; Golightly, *Letter to Dean of Ripon*, pp. 38-45.

[79] Trower to Golightly, 1 February 1858, LPL MS 1810, fo. 48.

[80] Burgon to Wilberforce, 20 March 1858, Bodl. MS Wilberforce d.47, fo. 193.

[81] Hardwick Shute, *Cuddesdon College. By One Who Knows It*, Oxford: Parker, 1858, p. 17.

[82] Liddon to Wilberforce, 8 February 1858, Bodl. MS Wilberforce d.40, fos 155-6.

was remodelled,[83] although if it had been Liddon's decision he would rather have met this "outbreak of silly fanaticism by civil but unyielding resistance".[84] He acknowledged that these changes dealt only with surface issues:

> That we shall be exposed to such onslaughts hereafter – I can hardly doubt. Golightly's objection lay against a moral & intellectual atmosphere: his attack was directed against the accidental tokens of that atmosphere, because from want of address & penetration, he was unable to analize its characteristic life. ... But he & those who think with him must understand as well as we do, that a religious tone though it may express itself in this or that phrase or ornamentation does not (God forbid) depend upon it; and he will not be satisfied with a Panelled Chapel, and our revised Service Book.[85]

Naturally, such concessions to Protestants in the diocese only infuriated those in the ritualist vanguard. The *Union* sarcastically jibed:

> One half gallon of whitewash judiciously applied, and the sanctuary might, perhaps, present an appearance even still more in accordance with the "customary simplicity of our beloved Church". ... Sad, indeed, was the hour when compromise gained the day at Cuddesdon ... If Cuddesdon College is to be moulded after the type of the ancient Church of Laodicea, the sooner it is shut up the better; or turned into a home for decayed needlewomen; or made a storehouse for apostate priests.[86]

Later in the month it continued to round on what it saw as the weak compromising of the college authorities:

> such pitiable subterfuges as these will only lower the place in the estimation of all people who profess Catholic principles, and never be the means of satisfying the carping Protestants who make Mr Golightly their cats-paw, and who are now glorying over their present success. ... Such an onslaught was to have been looked for; and would that it had been met manfully, resolutely, uncompromisingly, and without any equivocation! ... Compromises in cases of this character are nothing less than deliberate sins – the old story of "Pilate satisfying the people".[87]

---

[83] Pott to Wilberforce, 5 April 1858, Bodl. MS Wilberforce c.20, fo. 175. See correspondence on "Litany of our blessed Saviour", May 1858, PHL LHP and Bodl. MS Wilberforce d.40, fos 158-63.

[84] *Spectator*, 13 November 1875, pp. 1421-2.

[85] Liddon to Wilberforce, 19 June 1858, Bodl. MS Wilberforce d.40, fos 165-6.

[86] *Union*, 8 April 1859, p. 210.

[87] *Union*, 23 April 1858, p. 258.

The annual festival of June 1858 was shorn of its usual ceremony, without cross, flowers, banners, Gregorian music or procession through the village.[88] Again the *Union* lamented: "Upon the whole there was a visible lack of heartiness and spirit; and the most earnest supporters of the College are distressed at the spirit of compromise which broods over the place."[89]

Student Idiosyncrasies and Secessions

One supporter of Cuddesdon argued that its distinctive theological position was an asset: "Individuality of character is indispensable to living success. ... There is plenty of room in the Church of England for many Colleges of every shade of opinion."[90] Nevertheless the authorities tried to show that the institution lay firmly within the Anglican mainstream. Throughout the troubles, Wilberforce insisted there was "no party bias" at Cuddesdon.[91] In September 1858 he rejoiced that he could say of his ordinands: "No party, no pamphlets, no Roman postures or imitations rule my Candidates."[92]

There was certainly a breadth of opinion amongst the early Cuddesdon students. Some had an abhorrence of the ritualism they found there. Amongst Liddon's private notes on ordinands are found verdicts such as: "Puritan tendencies – great aversion to aesthetics – corrected during his residence here"; "joined in taking in the Record, and in active opposition to the Spirit of the place"; "gave greater trouble than any man we have yet had. Organised opposition (i) to choral services (ii) to doctr[ine] of sacraments (iii) to fasting." On the other hand, some did not think the ritualism at Cuddesdon went far enough. For instance, Liddon noted that one student had "*twice* spoken of the college as a 'Protestant' affair" and another was "Disappointed in Cuddesdon: was looking out for a mediaeval ideal".[93] This second group did the college most damage by unhelpful publicity.

When the controversy first broke over Cuddesdon in February 1858, Charles Anderson wrote to Wilberforce:

> it is some of those silly aesthetical people that have raised this dust by what may
> be called trifles in themselves but which become serious evils in times of

---

[88] Liddon diary, 1 June 1858; *Guardian*, 2 June 1858, p. 446.

[89] *Union*, 4 June 1858, p. 362.

[90] *Further Thoughts Upon the Diocese of Oxford, with Especial Reference to Cuddesdon College, in Reply to Mr Twopeny. Pamphlet, no. II by an Oxfordshire Idler*, London: Bell and Daldy, 1858, p. 14.

[91] Wilberforce to Pott, 1 February 1858 in Pott, *Correspondence*, p. 4.

[92] Wilberforce to Anderson, 18 September 1858, Bodl. MS Wilberforce d.28, fos 155-6.

[93] CCA VP1/1, fos 315, 319-21, 327.

suspicion, distrust, and malignity – and common sense which is so scarce an article, becomes invaluable in managing an Institution like Cuddesdon, and which has been somewhat wanting in your subordinates, or at least in some of the Students ... I am very sorry that aesthetics were not checked at the outset because I think they have got into too full swing.[94]

Some months later he again warned: "Depend on it, ritualism after having been greatly neglected is beginning to want a pruning knife." Curates, Anderson wrote, needed to be taught that helping people in their "everyday struggles" was of "tenfold more importance than the cut of a surplice, or bow at the altar or even the medieval inch".[95] The students' distinctive dress was raising eyebrows in the neighbourhood and even supporters of the college had to encourage the public to look beyond appearances: "if they wear long coats and eschew shirt-collars, I, who have more collar and less coat, should no more judge a man by his dress, than a book by its binding, or title".[96] One ordinand, Francis Burnand (future editor of *Punch*), was surprised by Liddon's unusual appearance. At Cambridge he had been used to clerical dons "attired in the ordinary black suit and white tie, with college cap and M.A. gown, and, as a rule, with a fine head of hair and full whiskers", but at Cuddesdon he was greeted by "an Italian-looking ecclesiastic, glittering-eyed, clean-shaved, and closely-cropped, wearing a white band for a collar, and a black cassock with a broad belt".[97] To his vice-principal, Wilberforce complained at length about such idiosyncrasies:

> Our men are too *peculiar*, especially some at least of our best men. I shall never consider that we have succeeded until a Cuddesdon man can be known from a non-Cuddesdon man only by his loving more, working more & praying more. I consider it a heavy affliction that they should wear neckclothes of peculiar construction, coats of peculiar cut, whiskers of peculiar dimensions: that they should walk with a peculiar step; carry their heads at a peculiar angle to the body, & read in a peculiar tone. I consider all this as a heavy affliction, first because it implies to me a want of vigour, virility & self-expressing vitality of the religious life in the young men. It shews that they come out too much cut out by a machine & not enough indued with living influences, & secondly because it greatly limits their usefulness, & ours, by the natural prejudice it excites. Then there are things in our actual life I wish changed. 1. The tendency to crowd their walls with pictures of the mater dolorosa &c, their chimney piece with crosses, their studies with saints – all offend me, & all do incalculable injury to the college in the eye of chance visitors. 2. The habit of some of our men of kneeling in a sort of rapt prayer on the steps of the communion table when they cannot be *alone* there:

[94] Anderson to Wilberforce, 3 February 1858, Bodl. MS Wilberforce d.28, fos 75-6.
[95] Anderson to Wilberforce, 28 November 1858, ibid., fos 168-9.
[96] *Counter-thoughts*, p. 48.
[97] Francis C. Burnand, *Records and Reminiscences Personal and General*, London: Methuen, revised edition, 1905, p. 184.

when visitors are coming in & going out & talking around them: such prayers should be "in the closet" with "the door shut" – and setting apart their grave danger as I apprehend them to the young men they really force on visitors the feeling of the strict resemblance to what they see in Belgium &c, & never in Church of England churches. ... Pinder has not at Wells; Curt[e]is has not at Lichfield this effect on the pupils. Why should Cuddesdon have it?[98]

Several of theses idiosyncrasies could be traced directly back to Liddon. For instance, the bishop lamented, one student "walks, holds his head, speaks as if he had just practised your modes before a glass. He has not a manly individuality."[99]

It had never been intended that Liddon should have such a strong role in determining the direction of the college. Wilberforce had originally hoped to offer close supervision, aiming to see and pray with his ordinands "day by day".[100] Yet in the midst of an episcopate of legendary activity this proved impossible to sustain. In 1857, for instance, he spent only 85 days of the year at Cuddesdon.[101] Nor was Pott able to work closely with the students. He lived off site and his attention was absorbed by his responsibilities as vicar of the parish, as a husband with a growing family and as the one in charge of the college's financial and administrative affairs. Pott was absent through illness for Lent and Trinity terms 1857, so Liddon in effect became acting-principal.

Liddon was prepared to admit that to a certain extent Cuddesdon "reflects the idiosyncrasies of my personal character", but he nonetheless insisted that "the outline and structure of our system is emphatically that of the Church".[102] Several were concerned by his heavy influence. Edward King (who began as chaplain in November 1858) warned that the college's problems stemmed from the vice-principal's "determination, *on principle*, to fit the Cuddesdon shoe on every foot". Liddon's strong will, he wrote, was a "prominent evil".[103] Similarly Burgon remonstrated: "If he likes to file a notch in a sovereign which belongs to *him*, *that* is *his* affair: but if he makes a notch in *the die*, & so *coins my* sovereigns with a flaw in them, – then I grow savage."[104]

The isolated nature of Cuddesdon was partly blamed for creating an environment in which Liddon was able to hold sway. With his eye clearly on the college, Bishop Sumner of Winchester explained why he was opposed to theological education detached from the Universities:

[98] Wilberforce to Liddon, 20 November 1858, Bodl. MS Wilberforce d.40, fos 196-9.
[99] Ibid., fo. 203.
[100] Selwyn, *A Little One*, p. 17.
[101] Ashwell and Wilberforce, *Wilberforce*, ii. p. 358.
[102] Liddon to Laurence C. Cure, 22 May 1858, CCA VP1/25.
[103] King to Wilberforce, 27 November 1858, Bodl. MS Wilberforce d.40, fo. 78.
[104] Burgon to Wilberforce, 20 March 1858, Bodl. MS Wilberforce d.47, fo. 193.

It is the characteristic merit of an University that its teaching is affected by the peculiarities of no particular school. If the individual colleges have their idiosyncrasies, the harm is counteracted by their mutual relation to the general body, – the common centre round which all revolve, and where they lose their shibboleths, if they have any. The eclectic institution, on the contrary, wears the colours of its single presiding head, sees with his eye, listens with his ear, speaks with his voice, walks with his gait, and in the very path in which he himself has trodden. Under such exclusive influence independent opinion has scarcely power to act, the character is moulded after one uniform type, and the mind of the student, like the habit he wears, is shaped into a distinctive cut and fashion.[105]

Likewise Bishop Tait proclaimed that at the Universities, unlike at theological colleges, "the very number of teachers must be the best safeguard against the exclusiveness of narrow sects".[106] In June 1859 Bishop Jackson of Lincoln again warned Cuddesdon students that without the diversity natural in a large University, a small and isolated college had "a tendency to narrow and exclusive views", particularly if under "a single presiding mind". They were thus in danger of suffering from "that curse of our time, under which Christian charity seems withering away, – party spirit, with its jealousies, and miserable suspicions, and lying accusations, – Satan's triumphant substitute for godly zeal".[107]

Reflecting on the ritualism promoted at Cuddesdon by Liddon, the *Record* asked:

What must be the effect on the students but to teach them that God is best honoured by a full amount of hangings, pictures, gilding, and Church ornaments; that the Church of England, even where her liberty on this side is strained to the utmost, is a harsh stepmother, who grudges them these innocent helps to devotion, and that they must step over to the Mother Church, if ever their devotional instincts are to have their full play, and find their natural home?[108]

Although the vice-principal himself was said to be "as likely to become a 'Romanist' as to become a 'Mormon'",[109] conversions to the Church of Rome from amongst his students dogged the college. When Pott assured the archdeacons' commission in February 1858 that no student had seceded to Rome, Golightly retorted: "Early days yet, Mr Principal. ... You are now sowing; hereafter you will

---

[105] Charles R. Sumner, *Church Progress. A Charge Delivered to the Clergy of the Diocese of Winchester*, London: Hatchard, 1858, p. 18.

[106] A. C. Tait, *A Charge Delivered in November, MDCCCLVIII to the Clergy of the Diocese of London, at his Primary Visitation*, London: Rivington, 1858, p. 28.

[107] John Jackson, *Rest before Labour: the Advantages and Dangers of Theological Colleges*, London: Skeffington, 1859, pp. 13-14.

[108] *Record*, 26 February 1858.

[109] Shute, *Cuddesdon College*, p. 11.

reap."[110] In fact one student, John Flesher, had already become a Roman Catholic the previous November, a step viewed by Liddon as a "disaster".[111] At the same time Arthur Alleyne was in need of counsel, suffering from similar doubts and ready to pull out of his ordination.[112]

In September 1858, J. A. Maude (whose father was a prominent anti-ritualist) became the second Cuddesdon student to secede.[113] Ironically, Maude attributed his conversion partly to the concessions over ritual made by the college the previous spring: "I was considerably shaken in my respect for High-Church principles by the mode in which Mr Pott replied to the accusations of Mr Golightly; I felt that his reply was wanting in firmness and clearness, and that it was certainly not calculated to strengthen or restore an already weakened confidence."[114] At the Brompton Oratory he prayed "daily for many old Cuddesden [sic] friends, whom I know to have *no sort of business* to be in Anglican orders".[115]

Pott insisted the secessions of Flesher and Maude had nothing to do with Cuddesdon, since both were at the college for only a few weeks and had arrived with doubts.[116] However, more students were to follow suit. In December 1858 Francis Burnand was caught with a book entitled *Mariologia* in his room and was asked to leave the next day.[117] He became the third to secede, upon which Liddon reflected: "How utterly humbled before God I feel at this miserable fruit of my ministry!"[118] Arthur Cumberlege was the fourth ordinand to secede in November 1859.[119]

---

[110] *Record*, 24 December 1858.

[111] CCA VP1/1, fo. 327. See John H. Flesher to Liddon, 21 January – 20 February 1857; Susan Foster to Liddon, 2 January 1857, KCL LP; Wilberforce to Liddon, 8 January 1857, PHL LHP.

[112] Arthur O. Alleyne – Liddon, 12 October – 19 November 1857, KCL LP; Alleyne – Liddon, 30 July 1857 – 11 April 1858, PHL LP, box 1/10.

[113] *Record*, 24 and 27 September, 1 and 6 October 1858; Liddon to J. Arthur Maude, 26 September and 9 November 1858, CCA VP1/2, fos 168-71; Maude to Liddon, 7 November 1858, VP1/27; Maude – Liddon, 24 September – 26 December 1858, KCL LP; Wilberforce to Francis Maude, nd, Bodl. MS Wilberforce c.20, fo. 186; Liddon to Wilberforce, 24 June and 29 December 1858, MS Wilberforce d.40, fos 168-9, 220-5.

[114] *Record*, 6 October 1858.

[115] Maude to Liddon, 16 December 1858, KCL LP.

[116] *Record*, 27 September and 1 October 1858.

[117] Burnand, *Records and Reminiscences*, pp. 188-93; Liddon diary, 3-18 December 1858; Liddon to Wilberforce, 4 December 1858, Bodl. MS Wilberforce d.40, fos 209-10.

[118] CCA VP1/1, fo. 335.

[119] Liddon to Wilberforce, 12 November 1859, Bodl. MS Wilberforce d.40, fos 248-55; Arthur Cumberlege to Liddon, 12 November 1859; Alleyne to Liddon, 11 November 1859; Charles Cumberlege to Liddon, 15 November 1859, KCL LP; C. Cumberlege to Liddon, 21 November 1859, PHL LHP.

A Change of Staff

In December 1858 the *Record* asked: "Ought not the College to be closed, or, at all events, the College officers dismissed, and the Institution put upon another footing?"[120] By then this process had already quietly begun. The previous March the chaplain, Albert Barff, had been an early casualty of the Protestant attack upon the college.[121] In October Pott had resigned as principal due to continued ill-health, though he was to remain in post until Easter 1859.[122] A variety of men were considered to replace him, such as E. H. Plumptre (Professor of Pastoral Theology at King's College, London), R. W. Church (Rector of Whatley in Somerset), Frederick Meyrick (Fellow of Trinity College, Oxford), Arthur Purey-Cust (a rural dean) and Burgon.[123] Liddon wanted Robert Milman (Vicar of Lambourn and a future Bishop of Calcutta) as someone with similar views to his own, but Wilberforce felt strongly that the new principal needed to counter-balance his vice-principal. He explained:

> I do not feel that our Theological standing place is *identical*. ... You have not *intended* to teach beyond our standing point and I have always felt that *un*-intentional deviations whether in lecture, conversation, example or ritual were modified & as I should of course say corrected by Pott's connection with the College as Principal. ... if I now appoint a Principal who exactly represents *your* standing point the colour & character of the College must be altered and the alteration will be a removing of it further from what appears to me to be the most exact line of Church of England life.[124]

King advised Wilberforce: "there should be a Principal whom the students would regard as their head – one who would clearly put the Vice Principal in his right place – which is the *second*".[125] The bishop hoped that the new man would be able "to correct our evils, to counter act our peculiarities, & to widen our sympathies",[126] but Liddon wanted as little change as possible:

> We cannot afford, my dear Lord, to make any changes in our System however trivial, for a long time to come. Our past concessions have been invariably interpreted, not as a charitable deference to prejudice, but as a confession of

---

[120] *Record*, 24 December 1858.

[121] Liddon diary, 18 February – 10 March 1858.

[122] Liddon diary, 23 October and 2 November 1858.

[123] For discussion between Liddon and Wilberforce of various candidates, see Bodl. MS Wilberforce d.40, fos 176-219.

[124] Wilberforce to Liddon, 20 November 1858, ibid., fos 194-5.

[125] King to Wilberforce, 27 November 1858, ibid., fos 78-9.

[126] Wilberforce to Liddon, 20 November 1858, ibid., fo. 199.

weakness or as a confession of error. ... There is in fact no choice *now* between a complete Revolution and the most Rigid Conservativism.[127]

As Pott later observed: "Liddon was not a man ready in any way to compromise his own judgment, or to give way to clamour. His error lay rather in the other direction."[128]

First Burgon was offered the principalship, as someone who might satisfy both Liddon and old-fashioned Protestants like Golightly. Yet Liddon was far from confident that they could work together:

> I cannot doubt that if he came here he would turn things upside down. Perhaps such a change may be thought well. But I could not be a party to it. I could not bear to be in a state of chronic visitation & ill-concealed opposition of thought and action towards the man whom I ought to try by God's grace to second and obey.[129]

Burgon for his part refused to take the post unless Liddon was removed,[130] and he would insist on radically transforming Cuddesdon: "I should have, singlehanded, to revolutionize, – calmly and gently, but with the whole determination of my nature to revolutionize – *the entire system of the College*, as well as *to create a fresh atmosphere within it.*"[131] In the end Burgon turned down the offer, primarily because of financial considerations.[132] Instead, in late December 1858, Henry H. Swinny (Vicar of Wargrave) was appointed principal. Golightly thought him "a Protestant, and a good and pious man",[133] while Wilberforce hoped his influence would "prevent idiosyncrasies of manner &c being acquired by our men".[134] Not surprisingly, Swinny acknowledged that he and Liddon "would never be in harmony".[135]

The change of principal brought into question Liddon's own position at the college. On several occasions during 1858 he had offered his resignation and now Wilberforce began to take the suggestion more seriously.[136] The bishop became

[127] Liddon to Wilberforce, 24 November 1858, ibid., fos 192-3.

[128] Johnston, *Liddon*, p. 33.

[129] Liddon to Wilberforce, 19 November 1858, Bodl. MS Wilberforce d.40, fo. 180.

[130] Liddon dairy, 8 December 1858.

[131] Burgon to Wilberforce, 9 December 1858, Bodl. MS Wilberforce d.47, fo. 197.

[132] Liddon diary, 10-11 December 1858.

[133] Charles P. Golightly, *The Position of the Right Rev. Samuel Wilberforce, D.D., Lord Bishop of Oxford, in Reference to Ritualism*, London: Hatchard, 1867, p. 19.

[134] Wilberforce to Liddon, 20 November 1858, Bodl. MS Wilberforce d.40, fo. 200.

[135] Swinny to Liddon, 11 February 1859, KCL LP.

[136] Liddon to Wilberforce, 8 February, 18-19 November, 29 December 1858, Bodl. MS Wilberforce d.40, fos 156, 179, 183, 224; Liddon diary, 6 November 1858.

Figure 2.4. H. H. Swinny

Figure 2.5. Edward King as Principal

increasingly aware of the extent of their disagreement and realised that they were working to opposing agendas:

> I want to turn out the Established English clergyman with a more awakened heart, quickened self-devotion & better furnished Theology: you want to get *more* of a reformed Seminary Priest. I believe that resemblance to that type will spoil our men's usefulness & ruin us.[137]

According to Burgon, it was "as reasonable to expect that a chronometer could keep time while half the mechanism was defective" as to hope Cuddesdon College could function effectively with Liddon on the staff. He advised Wilberforce:

> if you wish to restore health in that quarter, you must employ, *not* healing plaster, but the knife: & you must cut deep: & you must cut *now*; – or the mischief will go too far. It will indeed! You are chivalrous, & unwilling to part with Liddon. ... But he has had his trial. He has proved his method, & it has failed *egregiously*. Amiable, & excellent, learned as he is, he has been the ruin of the College. Is *he* then to be alone considered? – to the disadvantage of yourself – the men – the neighbourhood – the diocese – the Church![138]

Matters came to a head at Christmas 1858 when Edward Elton (Vicar of neighbouring Wheatley) warned Wilberforce that he had heard it said at the Brompton Oratory "that if any one went to Cuddesdon with the *slightest* Roman tendency, under the V. P. he would be sure to go to Rome".[139] As a result the bishop laid down new rules concerning celebration of the eucharist, books of devotion and auricular confession.[140] He asked Liddon not to teach his personal views on eucharistic consecration, which put the vice-principal in "a most painful dilemma – I must be either insincere or disobedient".[141] These scruples came as a revelation to Wilberforce who had assumed Liddon never publicly went beyond his own teaching.[142] He further discovered that Liddon had been giving Pusey's adaptations of Roman Catholic books of devotion to students, despite his express disapproval.[143]

Liddon was depressed: "The Bishop is yielding everything to its enemies. He clearly *suspects* me: and Pott who is weak sides with the assailants – or almost so."[144] Yet Butler encouraged him that Wilberforce must be taught "that some of us

---

[137] Wilberforce to Liddon, 20 November 1858, Bodl. MS Wilberforce d.40, fo. 203.

[138] Burgon to Wilberforce, 9 December 1858, Bodl. MS Wilberforce d.47, fo. 202.

[139] Elton to Wilberforce, 25 December 1858, PHL LP, box 2/13.

[140] "Rules for next Term", 27 December 1858, ibid.

[141] Liddon to Wilberforce, 7 January 1859, Bodl. MS Wilberforce d.40, fo. 230.

[142] Wilberforce to Liddon, 15 January 1859, PHL LP, box 2/13.

[143] Wilberforce to Butler, 5 February 1859, Bodl. MS Wilberforce d.33, fo. 81.

[144] Liddon diary, 1 January 1859.

believe certain things too deeply ... to give them up for the sake of ἀρέσκεια [gaining favour]".[145] He lamented that there seemed to be "a resolute determination to prevent a higher life than 'the parsonage & pony-carriage' from taking root in the Church of England".[146] Meanwhile Wilberforce was also using Butler as a confidant:

> You at Wantage have as much right to teach your shade of the common teaching & be considered a loyal son of the Church as I have mine here: & I with no compromise can as Bishop wholly support & maintain you – maintaining my own proper claims to my own views ... But when I come to the College here the case is different – I am judged of in my secret intention for the Diocese by the exact Shade imparted here to the men sent out. ... if from Cuddesdon go out as the best men, men of the most sacerdotal type it cannot it seems to me but happen that I am counted for a deceiver, professing one thing in my own words & conduct to the Diocese & then sending out from my own training College men of a different Shade.[147]

Since Liddon would not change, Wilberforce gradually realised that the only way to save his college and his own reputation was to sacrifice his young associate:

> there is in him a strength of Will – an ardour – a restlessness a dominant imagination which makes him unable to give to the young men any tone save exactly his own tone. Under this conviction I have from my hearing of this diversity of ritual been drifting with a really heart tearing pain to the conviction that I *must* accept *his* tendered resignation to act myself with honesty to the Diocese.[148]

He wrote again to Butler a few days later:

> Doctrinally L. might hold all he holds & work happily with me. It is that He is fit only to be absolute, great as is his love & tenderness & forbearance, he *must* re-impress his *exact* self ... I always hoped that I could have influenced L. enough to keep down the "tinting" process to such a pitch that I could quite honestly retain him & that a few years hence the difficulty would be mellowed out – I come to the opposite conclusion with a torn heart.[149]

At the end of January 1859, a full year after the charges in the *Quarterly Review*, Wilberforce finally accepted his vice-principal's resignation.[150] He

[145] Butler to Liddon, 8 January 1859, PHL LP, box 2/13.

[146] Butler to Liddon, 10 January 1859, KCL LP.

[147] Wilberforce to Butler, 22 January 1859, Bodl. MS Wilberforce d.33, fos 75-6.

[148] Ibid., fo. 77.

[149] Wilberforce to Butler, 26 January 1859, ibid., fos 79-80.

[150] Liddon to Wilberforce, 29 January 1859, Bodl. MS Wilberforce d.40, fos 244-5.

lamented to Liddon: "nothing can more grieve me than that we should part at this time when it will seem like a triumph to Golightly & Co., & yet what can I do?"[151] Meanwhile Burgon encouraged him: "Liddon's resignation, believe me, *was inevitable*. I mean, the days of your College were numbered else."[152] Liddon continued in post until Easter and was replaced by W. H. Davey, previously vice-principal of Chichester Theological College. Liddon's friends saw his departure as a major set back for Cuddesdon:

"The Bishop has made a false move ... under its new trammels the College will take the position of a High Church Seminary of a very low standard, and what can well be worse than that."[153]
"Perhaps England is not yet ripe for the old Cuddesdon teaching and practice."[154]
"Cuddesdon College can never prosper now!"[155]
"[Cuddesdon] will sink to the same level as Wells or Chichester."[156]
"Looking at the quarter from whence the pressure has come which has produced this change, the prospect of Religion in England looks gloomy indeed."[157]

Liddon himself concluded: "My first great attempt at work in life has failed. This no doubt is good for my character."[158]

In November 1858, due to the constant bad publicity surrounding Cuddesdon, Wilberforce had feared "the falling off of all save *extreme* men".[159] In a vain attempt to prevent this, Liddon had been pushed out. Yet by May 1860 the *Union* was lamenting that the staff changes had "utterly ruined" the college:

Of old, there were always more than *twenty students*: now (after every attempt to hook them in has been made and failed) there are but *seven*! And the very truth is that the polite dismissal of the very man, Mr Liddon, who stamped an impress upon Cuddesdon College, and made it a success, has turned out a more fatal mistake and a greater loss than was ever anticipated. Many enrolled themselves as *alumni* for the single and simple privilege of sitting at his feet; for he is verily a Tractarian "Gamaliel". ... When, as we are credibly informed, fourteen sets of chambers are vacant and dusty in his lordship's pet institution, and no fresh names are on the books for next term, the simple and very practical consideration of £. *s. d.* may effectually prove to him that the reformation at Cuddesdon College – intended to hoodwink the High and Dry Anglicans and keep quiet the troublesome

[151] Wilberforce to Liddon, 26 January 1859, PHL LP, box 2/13.
[152] Burgon to Wilberforce, 11 February 1859, Bodl. MS Wilberforce d.47, fo. 204.
[153] Henry Lanphier to Liddon, 19 February 1859, KCL LP.
[154] Albert Barff to Liddon, 10 February 1859, KCL LP.
[155] Maria E. Austis to Liddon, 11 February 1859, KCL LP.
[156] Verney C. B. Cave to Liddon, 10 February 1859, KCL LP.
[157] John H. Burgess to Liddon, 9 February 1859, KCL LP.
[158] Liddon diary, 9 February 1859.
[159] Wilberforce to Liddon, 20 November 1858, Bodl. MS Wilberforce d.40, fo. 202.

Puritans – was a great and grievous mistake, and that the only people who really gained by the alteration were Messrs. Litton and Golightly, who did so well and effectively the dirty work of their party – the lowest type of miscalled Evangelicals.[160]

With Liddon at the helm, Wilberforce's institution would probably have sunk without trace, a brief but failed experiment in theological education. Without Liddon it managed to stay afloat, though only just. Despite the damaging campaign of the college's Protestant critics it kept its doors open and, once out of the spotlight, slowly but surely began to attract students again. Cuddesdon College had survived its first and sternest test.

[160] *Union*, 25 May 1860, pp. 321-2.

Chapter 3

Wilberforce and Pastoral Theology

Alastair Redfern

Samuel Wilberforce lived in the Bishop's Palace at Cuddesdon from 1845 to December 1869, providing a pervasive presence during the time of the first three principals of the College. The foundations which were laid in terms of training for ordination were rooted not simply in his initial vision,[1] but in the ongoing presence of his own ministry and teaching. By 1870 he had become "the chief ornament" [2] of the English Church, and it is important to note Chadwick's comment that, despite long absences from Cuddesdon as his Diocesan and national responsibilities developed, his correspondence confirms his deep involvement with staff and students in the detailed running of the college.[3]

Pastoral Theology

It may seem odd to associate Wilberforce with pastoral theology. Modern textbooks assert that, even in the early twentieth century, pastoral theology was "mainly a matter of instructing those training for ministry in the skills and aptitudes that they needed for practical tasks such as visiting people in their homes...".[4] The narrative then traces the development of a serious theological discipline within which "contemporary experience and the resources of the religious tradition meet in a critical dialogue that is mutually and practically transforming".[5] Probably the best known tool of this discipline is the pastoral

---

[1] Owen Chadwick, *The Founding of Cuddesdon*, Oxford: Oxford University Press, 1954, pp. 12-18, 29.

[2] *The Times*, 26 July 1873.

[3] Chadwick, *The Founding of Cuddesdon*, p. 50.

[4] James Woodward and Stephen Pattison (eds), *The Blackwell Reader in Pastoral and Practical Theology*, Oxford: Blackwell, 2000, p. 1.

[5] Ibid., p. xiii.

cycle, linking experience, analysis, reflection and action.[6] John Elford, for instance, describes pastoral theology as beginning with reflection on pastoral need, under God, in an ever developing tradition.[7] There are many variations, and the editors of the *Blackwell Reader in Pastoral and Practical Theology* readily admit that this area is not easy to define.[8]

The key point is that contemporary pastoral theology, which has become a backbone to both ordination and post ordination training, begins and ends with the agenda of human being, and draws upon the resources of faith/religion for the enhancement of both elements. The methodology tends to be rational, empirical, focused: there is a ready embrace of "scientific" disciplines such as sociology and psychology. The seeds of this development are often traced to Schleiermacher, who provided theology "with academic credibility in the modern rationalistic university".[9] A second strand of development has been the shift from pastoral theology being seen as a tool for the clergy, towards it becoming a professional discipline for all Christian living – a basic resource for the whole people of God.[10]

Wilberforce was equally convinced that theology was essentially a practical discipline – and the fruits of his own teaching and preaching are generally regarded as monumental, for individuals, institutions, social justice and national politics.[11] However, his understanding of method in terms of pastoral theology was radically different from the tradition which was to evolve from Schleiermacher. It underscores the holiness and humility, "the pre-eminence of heart over head", which gives such an attractive flavour to the founding of Cuddesdon in the accounts of Chadwick[12] and the *Record and Memorial* of 1930[13] and it provides an interesting measuring rod for all who respond positively to that narrative and feel somewhat ambivalent about the ecclesiology and apologetics being shaped by the current emphasis upon a very different understanding of practical and pastoral theology.

[6] Paul Ballard and John Pritchard, *Practical Theology in Action*, London: SPCK, 1996, pp. 74-82.

[7] R. John Elford, *The Pastoral Nature of Theology*, London: Cassell, 1999, pp. 3-10.

[8] Woodward and Pattison (eds), *The Blackwell Reader*, p. 4

[9] Ibid., p. 24; see also Ballard and Pritchard, *Practical Theology in Action*, p. 59.

[10] Ballard and Pritchard, *Practical Theology in Action*, p. 3; Woodward and Pattison (eds), *The Blackwell Reader*, pp. 62, 79.

[11] See Arthur Burns, *The Diocesan Revival in the Church of England c. 1800-1870*, Oxford: Clarendon Press, 1999, p. 11; see also Maurice Reckitt, *The Church and The World*, London: George Allen and Unwin, 1940, iii, p. 102.

[12] Chadwick, *The Founding of Cuddesdon*.

[13] *Cuddesdon College 1854-1929: A Record and Memorial*, Oxford: Oxford University Press, 1930.

Wilberforce as Pastoral Theologian

Wilberforce was primarily a practitioner, as parish priest, rural dean and bishop. Yet he became one of the foremost teachers and preachers of the nineteenth century. He did not produce works of systematic theology; rather his publications were in the form of sermons and articles: that crucial Anglican tradition of doing theology in relation to particular issues and events. Nevertheless in 1860 he published a book of *Addresses to Candidates for Ordination*,[14] and these provide the basis of a fairly comprehensive view of his ideas about training and formation for ordained ministry. They also offer an outline of an alternative, and classically Anglican, approach to Pastoral Theology as the exercise of ensuring engagement between "contemporary experience and the resources of the religious tradition".

Theology and Practice

Wilberforce was formed for ordained ministry in the accustomed manner of the beginning of the nineteenth century: he studied at Oriel College, Oxford; he read widely, interacted with his peers, and learned his craft as a priest and practical theologian on the job – in a series of ministerial appointments. He participated in this model by having ordinands to work with him in Alverstoke, and by forming a society for clerical discussion and support.[15] Debate raged throughout the nineteenth century about the respective merits of this model (university plus practical experience) as opposed to a special time of formation at a theological college.[16] However the fact that by the time he became Bishop of Oxford in 1845 Wilberforce recognised the need for a Diocesan Theological College as a priority, points to a very significant development in his understanding of the pastoral nature of theology, and thus the most effective and faithful approach to the practice of Christian ministry.[17] Similarly, the manner in which he revolutionised the immediate preparation for ordination in terms of a residential retreat with devotional addresses,[18] highlights the whole notion of spiritual formation as being the core of ministry and Christian practice. This chapter will explore his work as a pastoral theologian in this context – as a model for ministry and for basic Christian witness. It is especially important to note that Wilberforce was opposed to theology

[14] Samuel Wilberforce, *Addresses to the Candidates for Ordination*, Oxford: Parker, seventh edition, 1878.

[15] See A. R. Ashwell and R. G. Wilberforce, *The Life of Samuel Wilberforce*, London: John Murray, 1880-1883, i, pp. 63, 173; Chadwick, *The Founding of Cuddesdon*, p. 9.

[16] D. A. Dowland, *Nineteenth-Century Anglican Theological Education: The Redbrick Challenge*, Oxford: Clarendon Press, 1997, p. 177; F. W. B. Bullock, *A History of Training for the Ministry of the Church of England, 1800-1874*, London: Home Words, 1955, pp. 52-4.

[17] Chadwick, *The Founding of Cuddesdon*, p. 12.

[18] A. R. Ashwell and R. G. Wilberforce, *The Life of Samuel Wilberforce*, i, pp. 330-39.

becoming a "subject-matter of examination upon which honours can be received": the pastoral nature of the theology for the working priest, in his understanding, required a very different kind of exploration and learning.[19]

The Priest as Pastoral Theologian

Wilberforce gives an important clue to his understanding of the clerical task and the nature of a properly pastoral theology in the memorandum he wrote to outline the purpose of his foundation: "Threefold object of residence here – 1. Devotion. 2. Parochial Work. 3. Theological Reading."[20] The primary emphasis was upon Devotion from which sprang practical pastoral engagement; from both of these activities would come an engagement with theological study. Crucial to formation in this approach was the element of residence, a feature which made Cuddesdon unique as a theological college at the time of its foundation.[21] He emphasised the notion of a common life of prayer, practice and study: participation in the corporation of the ministerial priesthood.

The key issue was the relation of learning to holiness: "an ignorant clergy is a reproach to any church, and must injure its efficiency; but an ungodly clergy threatens the removal of its candlestick and the extinction of its life".[22] Wilberforce was a minister of enormous efficiency and practical achievement, but he recognised that the bedrock of all ministerial activity must be "the possession of a true and living faith in Christ our Lord, both for your own salvation, and for all the work of His ministry to be committed to you".[23] Ministry belonged to God, and was offered and achieved in Him. Thus those called and commissioned were graced with particular powers and responsibilities: "Your words cannot be unsaid; your ministerial character is indelible."[24] The ordained are set apart from the laity, and have a function in the divine economy alongside the other key resources given by God – scripture, sacraments and creeds.[25]

The task of the ordained minister is "to win souls to Christ, not to produce a certain general decency and amendment in the face of society around you".[26] The agenda is spiritual; the key area that of devotion. Indeed this sets the tone for pastoral engagement and theological study. The resource is "simply to exalt before

---

[19] *Report of the Proceedings of the Church Congress*, Oxford: Parker, 1862, p. 35.

[20] A. R. Ashwell and R. G. Wilberforce, *The Life of Samuel Wilberforce*, ii, p. 245.

[21] Chadwick, *The Founding of Cuddesdon*, p. 49.

[22] Wilberforce, *Addresses to the Candidates for Ordination*, p. 3.

[23] Ibid., p. 3.

[24] Ibid., p. 4.

[25] Wilberforce, *Essays Contributed to the Quarterly Review*, London: John Murray, 1874, i, p. 247.

[26] Wilberforce, *Addresses to the Candidates for Ordination*, p. 12.

your people Christ crucified".[27] For Wilberforce the atonement is the basic, objective event and transaction which is the only measure and model of encounter between the human soul and God. He recognised an increasing tendency in Anglican theology to emphasise a theology of incarnation, and this was prophetic of the influence of his disciple Charles Gore with the publication of *Lux Mundi* in 1889.[28] Wilberforce was keen to focus upon the atonement as signifying all that was distinctive about the Christian gospel, and thus providing a tone of dependence, humility and gratitude in fallen humanity.

Yet the priest was in no way superior. He was, "as a ransomed sinner, minister to ransomed sinners".[29] The currency is not that of human affection, but divine atonement. The priest operates with "a deep inward love of souls learned beneath the cross of Christ".[30] The crucified one is not a useful model, but an objective and essential reference point for the minister doing pastoral theology – a transaction which embraces priest and people together, and a public truth about the mechanism of the kingdom and the calling of the church.

Thus, for Wilberforce, holiness and devotion are essential to any theological enterprise. In a University Sermon of 1837,[31] Wilberforce used the story of Moses and the burning bush to argue that human curiosity – "I will turn aside and see" – must always give way to the primary need to "draw not nigh hither: put off thy shoes". This was the "Teaching that reverence and adoration, rather than the sharpness of observing scrutiny, were the attributes with which it became the creature to enter his Creator's presence". The inquisitiveness and speculativeness of the intellect must be shaped by "the cultivation of a habitual reverence for holy things".[32]

In another sermon on this story, preached at Buckingham Palace in 1846, Wilberforce argued that the highest human wisdom imbibed from Egypt, alongside the Hebrew religious nurturing of his mother/nursemaid, seemed to give Moses every equipment to deliver his people: and yet when he acts, by killing the Egyptian, the whole project is put back by forty years. Moses needs to spend time in the wilderness, "as a foreigner"[33] to the civilised world, to be taught by "silence, separation, loneliness and thought", a process of formation which comes to a focus through a "summative sign", given by God, to yield clarity and an experience of "being called by name".[34] The discipline of formation by going apart – to

[27] Ibid.

[28] Charles Gore, *Lux Mundi*, London: John Murray, 1889.

[29] Wilberforce, *Addresses to the Candidates for Ordination*, p. 15.

[30] Ibid., p. 93.

[31] Wilberforce, *Sermons Preached Before the University of Oxford, 1837-1839*, Oxford: Parker, 1839, pp. 66-94.

[32] Ibid., p. 71.

[33] Wilberforce, *Sermons Preached on Various Occasions*, Oxford: Parker, 1877, p. 40.

[34] Ibid., p. 44.

Cuddesdon, on retreat prior to ordination, or daily in ministerial life – was the foundational ingredient to becoming equipped by God to be a pastoral theologian, enabling proper connection between human experience and the Divine purposes.

Being a priest – one called and set apart to put devotion and an habitual reverence for holy things at the centre of life – laid the foundational perspective for pastoral theology. This emanated from engagement with human living in the context of the grace offered through the miracle of atonement, which was God's key summative sign.[35]

Context

For Wilberforce, the context which should be determinative for pastoral theology was not the agenda of human kind, but scripture and creeds: "the great truths which the blessed God has taught us of Himself". By contrast, the priest must "beware of always tarrying amongst the graves and corruption of our own fallen and tempted state".[36] Since Darwin, the human agenda has become the stuff of pastoral theology – focusing upon the desire to develop human life and secure its flourishing and progress. As Woodward and Pattison write:

> The twentieth century has seen a decisive turn to the human in theology. If traditional theology was tempted to focus on the nature of God and a world and life beyond this one, twentieth century theology has located itself as a firmly human activity situated within human-created language and so focusing on the human condition.[37]

Scripture and doctrine have been increasingly measured against this more tangible and empirical concern. By contrast, Wilberforce recognised in his review of Darwin's work, that the crucial issue was the role of the human "verifying faculty":[38] to him this "faculty" would be always suspect and subject to the fallenness of the human state. What he came to call "the morbid anatomy of humanity"[39] must be recognised as penultimate and dependent upon a greater and prior, given framework, the mighty atonement wrought in Jesus Christ and held in Scripture, tradition and the commission of the church.

The priest was set apart, and graced specifically, to handle this framework, for the better ordering of the practice of human life. The role was representative: "rise

---

[35] Wilberforce, *Words of Counsel*, Oxford: Parker, 1854, p. 122.

[36] Wilberforce, *Addresses to the Candidates for Ordination*, p. 13.

[37] Woodward and Pattison (eds), *The Blackwell Reader*, p. 65.

[38] Wilberforce, *Essays Contributed to the Quarterly Review*, i, p. 114.

[39] Wilberforce, *Addresses to the Candidates for Ordination*, p. 49.

up to God and Christ and the Holy Ghost and bear your flock with you there".[40] Thus devotion, and the discipline of going apart, taking off the shoes which carry one about the everyday world, and thereby receiving a revelation from the very different and always challenging perspective of the living God – this activity was primary, for the priest as well as for the people thereby represented. The tenor was one of trust, dependence, humility before a greater mystery; humankind as receiver of grace and love through moments of encounter and God-given signs.

By contrast, Wilberforce saw the danger for "the academical clergyman" to be one of "self-confidence, fondness for speculation, love of singularity, separation from brethren ... undoubted scepticism".[41] Theology for practical living will come from the spiritual transaction which cures souls and offers signs of salvation and transcendence and not from intellectual endeavours to measure and master the immediate human situation: the latter leads only to division and narrowness.

Preaching before the University of Oxford, Wilberforce pointed to an especial danger:

> it is not safe for us to smooth down by our refinements such difficulties as those presented to us by the great doctrine of the Atonement: in doing so we run a fearful risk of trying to improve the message Christ has brought from the Father, and failing in our probation. We must take it in its simplicity.[42]

The ministerial concern is "to awaken and define in the hearer's heart the natural sense of distance from God, and enmity against him" and then to declare the great act of God in Jesus Christ "this bearing of sinners' punishment, ... His rising again as Head of a new kingdom." Thus "we shall explain to men the enigma of their own nature by casting on it the light of God's countenance".[43] Theology is the seed of spiritual encounter rather than any kind of sociological analysis.

This meant that the later notion of contextuality might be positively misleading. Wilberforce wrote:

> Things present, felt, seen, handled, which address themselves to the appetites of the body, which promise to give immediate satisfaction to the lower impulses of the soul, these have so vast an influence on us, their voice is so loud, their instancy so urgent, their promises so high, that they cloud over all sight of our true blessedness.

---

[40] Ibid., p. 14.

[41] Ibid., p. 15.

[42] Wilberforce, *Sermons Preached Before the University of Oxford 1847-1862*, Oxford: Parker, 1863, p. 218.

[43] Wilberforce, *Addresses to the Candidates for Ordination*, pp. 43-4.

Figure 3.1. Samuel Wilberforce as Bishop of Oxford

Figure 3.2. Cuddesdon College in about 1860

The Human condition, he went on, is "this disturbed state".[44] Consequently, true theology is based upon a very different context: "a declaration of God concerning Himself".[45]

The Method of Pastoral Theology

Wilberforce recognised that there was a strong temptation for the church to offer "morality" and "a dangerous subjectivism"[46] – both tailored to the apparent presenting issues of human living. The burning bush requires humble contemplation before any analytical action. The nub of his understanding of method in pastoral theology is expressed thus:

> it may begin and end with man, and only speak of God as a general power, generally; instead of beginning with God, and ending with God, and thus in declaring the persons of the ever-blessed God-head throwing light upon man's inmost motives.[47]

Here is the contrast with, and challenge to, the methodology of pastoral theology which has flowed from Schleiermacher to the present day. Instead of placing the emphasis upon experience, analysis, reflection and action, that is, beginning and ending with the human agenda, and looking to God and the resources of the faith for guidance and help, Wilberforce is clear that pastoral theology begins with God in devotion and spiritual encounter, and ends in theological reflection to deepen devotion – thus providing a "framework" within which human living can be not simply interpreted, but more significantly, transformed and saved from sin and deathliness.

As in his debate with Darwin, Wilberforce refused to accept an optimistic, progressive understanding of human being, without the transforming intervention of atonement; the human condition, in the language of the *Book of Common Prayer*, was that of "miserable sinners": this was the inmost reality of our basic and constant state. Salvation was the grace and gift of God through the supernatural society of the Church in word and sacrament, ministered by specially called and commissioned officers who were distinctive and real agents of God's new life, using as tools the special divine gifts of creeds, scripture and sacraments.[48]

---

[44] Wilberforce, *Sermons Preached Before the University of Oxford 1847-1862*, p. 263.

[45] Ibid., p. 262.

[46] Wilberforce, *Addresses to the Candidates for Ordination*, p. 49.

[47] Ibid., p. 50.

[48] Wilberforce, *Charge to the Diocese of Oxford 1866*, Oxford: Parker, 1866, p. 66. He fixed the identity of the Church of England in four marks: "in the written word, in creeds, in

The role of the priest, and of pastoral theology, is "the preservation of the truth in the holy severity of its own fixed proportions".[49] Wilberforce recognised the importance of tolerating a wide range of theological views and pastoral practices in relation to this basic framework,[50] but the task of the ordained minister was to maintain the discipline, priority and God-given core ingredients of the framework – thus enabling a range of explorations and expressions within it.[51] Fifty years later, Charles Gore was to develop this notion of the church and her officers holding a "mould" within which Christian life could be lived.[52]

Moreover, the "pastoral" element of theology needed a hard edge: truth was rarely popular and there was always a tendency amongst the church's public ministers "to lower down the truth that we may please those to whom we minister".[53] Once again, the danger was that of starting and ending with the human agenda. The framework of God's acts and designated resources constantly confronts humanity with the need to give priority to devotion. In this sense Wilberforce tells his ordinands "you are to be yourselves not merely religious men but theologians". They were to base their ministry upon "sound, strong doctrine, ... deep, constant, practical praying, ... study of scripture, ... under the guidance of, and obedience to the church".[54] Here we have a clear sense of the ingredients for the pastoral theologian – God first and last. This established the framework for helping others interpret and engage in the practical project of existence, held by the church and her appointed ministers.

Pastoral Theology as more than a Human Enterprise

In distinction to this notion of a divinely appointed framework and resources for transforming human life, Wilberforce was keenly aware of "that general tendency to a disbelief in all fixed eternal dogmas": the gathering momentum of a hermeneutics of suspicion and subjectivity. In contrast, Wilberforce held, the church was charged with a counter-cultural task – to "build up beforehand our people in the full range of Christian truth and doctrine".[55] Like his mentor, Bishop

sacraments, in Apostolic Ministry" – a quadrilateral which anticipated the Lambeth Conference declaration in 1888.

[49] Wilberforce, *Addresses to the Candidates for Ordination*, p. 61.

[50] Wilberforce, *Charge to the Diocese of Oxford, 1851*, Oxford: Parker, 1851, p. 45.

[51] Wilberforce, *Sermons Preached Before the University of Oxford 1847-1862*, pp. 64-9.

[52] Charles Gore, *Orders and Unity*, London: John Murray, 1909, p. 73.

[53] Wilberforce, *Addresses to the Candidates for Ordination*, p. 68.

[54] Ibid., p. 70.

[55] Ibid., pp. 83-6.

Butler,[56] Wilberforce was keen to emphasise the necessity of the "wholeness" of Christian doctrine and practice, and the fatal danger of taking parts which seem to suit a particular situation, and thereby detaching them from the full scheme and from the determining doctrine of atonement.[57] This constant emphasis upon atonement and the completeness of the Christian scheme is in marked contrast to the methodology of the pastoral cycle and the more modern tendency to ransack the resources of the faith to fit the apparent demands of a particular human context.

In one of his addresses, Wilberforce offers a syllabus for ministerial education, and an indication of the whole package of the Gospel:

Especially must we labour to work into the very texture of their souls those master truths:

- the personality of the all-holy, all-mighty God;
- the mystery of the ever blessed Trinity;
- the fall of man and his corruption;
- the misery and defilement wrought in him by sin;
- the eternal counsels of the Father's love in the Gospel scheme of salvation;
- the incarnation of the ever-blessed Son our Lord;
- His perfect life, His spotless death, His all-sufficient atonement;
- the gift of the Holy Spirit;
- the calling and grace of the Church;
- the presence of Christ in the sacraments;
- the need of individual renewal unto holiness.[58]

This outline of the framework of pastoral theology provides the priest with a particular agenda from which to start in any pastoral encounter, and the whole endeavour is to be rooted in the minister's own devotional discipline, and desire to involve others in the worship and waiting and watching of the church, before the signs and structures given by God to focus and administer His grace.

The pastor thus invites people to enter into a consecrated relationship, whereby the framework of public, universal truth provides a context for the exploration of individual, personal or more local searchings for grace and guidance. Hence there is always an element of negotiation and "immediate contextuality" – but always as referenced to public, catholic truth, held by the church and administered by her appointed officers.[59]

---

[56] Ibid., p. 202.

[57] Wilberforce, *The Ministry of Reconciliation: a sermon, preached in the Chapel of Farnham Castle, at the general Ordination held by the Lord Bishop of Winchester, December 15, 1839*, London: James Burns, 1840, p. 14.

[58] Wilberforce, *Addresses to the Candidates for Ordination*, p. 88.

[59] Ibid., p. 127.

This understanding of pastoral theology and practice safeguards the minister from generalities which give the impression of relevance while in fact connecting with no-one in particular: at the same time it prevents a narrow concentration upon a very limited concern. The encounter must always have the hard edge of challenge, and resist the temptation "to substitute ordinary kindly intercourse".[60] As an experienced parish priest, Wilberforce knew that these encounters worked through particular "moments", in which the Gospel could be offered and impressed. The aim of doing pastoral theology was always the imparting of spiritual direction. This required priests to be confident in their commission and authority to minister God's agenda and resources in this way.

Wilberforce consequently encouraged the priest to plan visiting, keep records, and review encounters and situations regularly. The pastoral task was targeted and specific,[61] and preparation for a particular encounter should bring to light "a definite aim". Yet the key, as always, was the exhortation: "prepare yourself by secret prayer". Thus the pastor will have confidence not simply to negotiate, but also

> to bring your people indeed to Christ, be content with nothing less than making them feel their sinfulness and utter loss without Him ... evermore seek to raise Him before the eyes of men, to lift up His cross, to bring them under His hands for healing.[62]

The key is the Christ of the church: it is His atonement and His healing which ministers grace and salvation and nourishes an indwelling spirit. The marks of human flourishing are only assessed and measured within this given scheme of salvation. It is in this sense that the minister is distinctive from the laity. He "really does wield the powers of the world to come", since

> God acts through His ministers upon the souls and spirits of those to whom they minister... for He uses His servants not merely as simple instruments for doing certain actions ... but He employs also the powers of their minds and souls to affect the minds and souls of the brethren.[63]

The exercise of the office of priest thereby "secures the cooperation of the Holy Sprit". This is based not upon any personal qualities, but upon devoted use of the resources given specifically by God for this task – scripture, sacraments, creeds and articles. These resources for revelation and salvation "are to be reproduced as a

---

[60] Ibid., p. 107.
[61] Ibid., p. 130
[62] Ibid., pp. 112, 138.
[63] Ibid., pp. 174-5, 209.

new thing for others".[64] This is the heart of the task of pastoral theology – an enabling of what is essentially a spiritual transaction to place human living within the framework of God's purposes and particular presence.

Wilberforce contrasts this delicate task of interlinking public truth with personal needs, with the tendency so often for the priest to offer

> cold professional decency, comfortable worldly maxims ... the flesh betrays us, personal religion decreases, vanity and self-seeking spring up, secret prayers become few and cold, interior communion with the Lord is interrupted, the work of the Spirit is stayed.[65]

Pastoral engagement depends upon a deep and real devotional discipline in the one who is empowered to minister the ingredients of catholic truth, so that those who thus engage are similarly embraced in a spiritual exercise, which begins and ends in God, and thus provides a framework for salvation. The pastoral theologian's work cannot be measured by competencies, but depends upon an inner and prior spiritual discipline. Hence the importance for Wilberforce of a theological college set apart from the university – a space for withdrawal and preparation, to encourage humility and holiness before the signs God has given. This spirit of devotion, and a sense of the common corporation of the priesthood as holding for the church the key ingredients for ministering God's grace, were essential to the formation of priests and to their understanding of their peculiar and precious tasks as pastoral theologians. It was a discipline Wilberforce himself practised throughout his ministry, by his daily drawing apart to pray; by the discipline of launching each new Diocesan enterprise with an act of Holy Communion;[66] and by his annual birthday discipline of prayerful review and reflections.

The outcome of this devotional discipline was an outpouring of practical engagements, each fuelled by serious theological reflection and wrestling – well known examples were his involvement in the unsuccessful efforts to prevent the liberal, R. D. Hampden, becoming Regius Professor of Divinity in Oxford in 1836, the debate over Darwin's *Origin of Species*, the establishment of creative structures and organisations in the Diocese of Oxford, as well as innumerable personal encounters of deep significance for those he advised.[67]

---

[64] Ibid., p. 177.

[65] Ibid., p. 185.

[66] E. K. Pugh (ed.), *The Letter-books of Samuel Wilberforce, 1843-68*, Aylesbury: Buckinghamshire Record Society and Oxfordshire Record Society, vol. 47, 1970, p. 284.

[67] Ibid.

The Pastoral Theologian as Priest and Prophet

The pastor as theologian thereby exercised a prophetical office, convincing the world of sin, righteousness and judgement. Wilberforce could therefore stress that the minister needed to be "diligent in prayer, in reading Holy Scripture, in studies as help in knowledge of Scripture, and in laying aside the study of the world and the flesh".[68] Here is the sharpest challenge to the tradition of pastoral theology stemming from Schleiermacher. For Wilberforce pastoral *theology* needs to be done by ministers set apart, who, with others, provide the key framework for all theology, which begins and ends with God. In turn, the human agenda can be a hindrance and a diversion, and will always need to be put in this greater perspective. Otherwise, Wilberforce claimed,

> the cardinal doctrines of the faith ... are explained away without a scruple: the atonement wrought out for us by the sacrifice of Our Lord and Saviour Jesus Christ, the inspiration of Holy Scripture, the grace of sacraments, the whole objective truth of everything in the church.[69]

This provides a challenging and prophetic list of the four corners of Wilberforce's framework for pastoral theology, which over the years have all become much less significant, and have tended to be reshaped according to human needs and interests.[70] He recognised the persistent tendency to "reduce (these elements) to the most natural proportions":

> A habit is formed in the mind, of subjecting the written word and the authoritative declarations of the faith to the scrutiny of each man's intellectual faculties, and according to their decisions, of his accepting, modifying or rejecting them.[71]

In distinction, Wilberforce emphasised "the objective truth of creeds and articles"[72] and the priority of Scripture and Sacraments. There should be a proper humility before these gifts, since we "learn the truth on our knees".[73] Revelation, he held, is "concerned with matters beyond our observation, and must be received, if received at all, on the authority of the giver".[74] The essence of the human journey is thus one of probation, of

---

[68] Wilberforce, *Addresses to the Candidates for Ordination*, p. 185.

[69] Ibid., p. 198.

[70] Woodward and Pattison (eds), *The Blackwell Reader*, pp. 62-7.

[71] Wilberforce, *Sermons Preached Before the University of Oxford, 1847-1862*, p. 281.

[72] Wilberforce, *Sermons Preached Before the University of Oxford, 1837-1839*, p. 87.

[73] Ibid., p. 13.

[74] Wilberforce, *Sermons Preached Before the University of Oxford, 1847-1862*, p. 282.

whether he will submit his will to the will of God ... to receive His revelation as the Truth; not to modify or adjust it according to their notions of what is true, or what is good, or what is befitting.[75]

Revelation is thus given "for the sake of training the heart, not of gratifying the intellect".[76]

As a pastoral theologian the priest does not depend upon intellectual capacity,[77] but upon a spirituality of dependence and yielding of self-will to the divine message and invitation. The human view in this life will be always partial, and involve the need to live with contradictions and incompleteness. Hence the pastor as theologian calls people into an engagement with a spiritual state rather than an intellectual position. Wilberforce consequently issues a warning against the tendency to seek salvation in systematic theology.[78]

Pastoral theology offers engagement with the livingness of God, a faith to receive grace as a gift, and courage to focus on a cross which "does contradict the preconceived notions of the worldly wise, and the whole system of self-righteousness".[79] As an experienced pastor Wilberforce recognised that in times of testing people want to offer the cry of a child to its Father, "coming with boldness through the blood of Jesus".[80] The pastoral theologian responds as priest and prophet, modelling and inviting devotion. This provides a trusting engagement with the full framework provided for the church to focus God's gracious revelation of new life, and enabling a range of theological and practical tasks as particular people and situations respond with thanks and a sense of confident application of the grace thus received. God's will is thus worked "in common things ... daily contacts".[81] In turn, from the "declaring of God" in such dogmatic teaching, "all else may follow; intellectual advancement, moral obligation, the renewing of affections, when their truest object is set before them".[82]

---

[75] Wilberforce, *Sermons Preached Before the University of Oxford, 1837-1839*, p. 207.

[76] Wilberforce, *Sermons Preached Before the University of Oxford, 1847-1862*, p. 285.

[77] Wilberforce, *Sermons Preached Before the University of Oxford, 1837-1839*, p. 208.

[78] Wilberforce, *Sermons Preached Before the University of Oxford, 1847-1862*, pp. 268-73.

[79] Wilberforce, *Sermons Preached Before the University of Oxford, 1837-1839*, p. 218.

[80] Wilberforce, *Sermons Preached Before the University of Oxford, 1847-1862*, p. 289.

[81] Wilberforce, *Words of Counsel*, p. 31.

[82] Ibid., p. 120.

An Enduring Foundation?

During his time at Cuddesdon Wilberforce was keenly aware that he was fighting a battle for the essence of an Anglican tradition which he felt was being undermined by the forces of science and subjectivism. This reflects the shift in the eighteenth and early nineteenth centuries, enunciated by Jürgen Habermas, from a worldview "founded on authority received passively" to one based on "rational argument".[83] Certainly the whole thrust of biblical criticism and scientific discovery enhanced the ethos of optimism about the continued progress of human civilisation. Schleiermacher caught this mood and provided a method of pastoral theology which has proved to be serviceable and attractive. Wilberforce held to a notion of boundaries, roles and human sinfulness which seem anachronistic to modern tastes, but which he nevertheless held to be foundational to the nature and working of the Christian gospel. Pastoral theology – that "critical dialogue between contemporary experience and the resources of the religious tradition"[84] – depended upon set-apart resources (Scripture, Sacraments, Creed) and their handling by a set-apart ministry. It also required negotiation between the Gospel and human being through the discipline of devotion, which drew on a dogmatic theology and thereby opened up people and situations to an encounter with the livingness of God which was always transformative and grace-bearing. Cuddesdon Theological College was founded to give renewed focus to this approach to pastoral theology. As has been discussed in chapter one, the universities could no longer provide the necessary spiritual formation and the move towards a system of competitive examination was seen to be counter to the entire tone and corporateness of the theological enterprise which were required to provide the resources for pastoral engagement.

Such pastoral theology was both priestly and prophetic. It was not systematic, but instead unfolded through moments of engagement with all the vagaries of human living. The basic transaction, however, was simple, and was founded on the miracle of the atonement. In relation to this, both priest and people joined in humble devotion. Authority was in the Giver and the Gifts of grace: pastoral theologians helped in the recognition and acceptance of what had been freely offered. Amidst the ever shifting foundations of twenty-first century pastoral theology and theological institutions, it might be suggested, such an approach may hold the germ of something more enduring.

[83] T. C. W. Blanning, *The Culture of Power and the Power of Culture: Old Regime Europe, 1660-1789*, Oxford: Oxford University Press, 2002, p. 8; see Jürgen Habermas, *The Structural Transformation of the Public Sphere: an Inquiry into a Category of Bourgeois Society*, Cambridge, Mass.: MIT Press, 1989.

[84] Woodward and Pattison (eds), *The Blackwell Reader*, p. xiii.

Chapter 4

Controversy Renewed:
Partisan Polemic and
the Great Ritualist "Conspiracy"

Andrew Atherstone

"Cuddesdon College has been continually in hot water,
although we greatly fear *never clean*" (The *Rock*).[1]

Cuddesdon and Partisan Rivalry

The late 1850s and 60s witnessed the founding of several militant organisations in
the Church of England, each competing to reform the church according to its own
distinctive theological principles. For instance, the English Church Union (ECU)
and the Church Association were directly antithetical and existed partly to oppose
each other. The ECU, established in 1859, aimed "to defend and maintain
unimpaired the doctrine, discipline and ritual of the Church of England against
Erastianism, Rationalism and Puritanism". In contrast the Church Association,
established in 1865, aimed "to counteract the efforts now being made to pervert the
teaching of the Church of England on essential points of the Christian faith, or
assimilate her services to those of the Church of Rome". The aggressive work of
societies such as these resulted in much of the agitation between ritualists and
Protestants which was a marked feature of the late-Victorian period. Theological
opinion became further polarised within the church and opponents became more
deeply entrenched, as is witnessed in the renewed attacks which fell upon
Cuddesdon College in 1877-79.

After the dismissal of Liddon, Cuddesdon had enjoyed almost two decades of
peace and quiet. When Henry Swinny took over in May 1859 there were just seven
ordinands on the books, but gradually public confidence in the college began to

[1] *Rock*, 11 October 1878, p. 814.

return, as did the students. Wilberforce was soon embroiled in new controversies surrounding Darwin's *Origin of Species* (1859) and the liberal theology of *Essays and Reviews* (1860). Yet now he came forward as a champion of orthodoxy, which won him widespread favour even amongst erstwhile evangelical critics. This in turn revived sympathy for his theological institution. Swinny collapsed and died in December 1862, aged just 49, and Edward King agreed reluctantly to promotion from chaplain to principal.[2] During the decade under his leadership the college continued to avoid public attention and so was free to get on quietly with its task of training clergymen. This was a period of much needed stability and consolidation. King managed to form friendships across a wide theological spectrum and even Golightly became "sincerely attached" to him. Cuddesdon's arch-opponent later admitted that although he and the principal differed widely, "in long conversations … we have found so much in which we agreed, that we never got on to the points in which we differed".[3] When King was appointed Professor of Pastoral Theology at Oxford in 1873, he left behind a college more firmly established and better able to withstand future storms.

The renewed Protestant attacks upon Cuddesdon were reserved for King's successor, Charles Wellington Furse.[4] Owen Chadwick suggests that this fresh round of controversy was simply "laughed at" by most observers and that even the Cuddesdon staff thought it "more frivolous than vexatious".[5] Certainly the college was not now in danger of folding, as it had been when Liddon was dismissed twenty years before. Nevertheless these renewed criticisms were treated with deadly seriousness and did the college real damage. Cuddesdon's quiet life was replaced by months of intensive and hostile scrutiny, through which it emerged battered but not beaten.

---

[2] On King, see George W. E. Russell, *Edward King: Sixtieth Bishop of Lincoln*, London: Smith, Elder, 1912; Lord Elton, *Edward King and Our Times*, London: G. Bles, 1958; John A. Newton, *Search for a Saint: Edward King*, London: Epworth, 1977; Geoffrey Rowell, *The Vision Glorious: Themes and Personalities of the Catholic Revival in Anglicanism*, Oxford: Clarendon Press, 1983, ch. 7; Owen Chadwick, *The Spirit of the Oxford Movement: Tractarian Essays*, Cambridge: Cambridge University Press, 1990, ch. 13.

[3] Charles P. Golightly, *A Letter to the Very Reverend the Dean of Ripon, Containing Strictures on the Life of Bishop Wilberforce, Vol. II with Special Reference to the Cuddesdon College Enquiry and the Pamphlet "Facts and Documents"*, London: Simpkin, Marshall, 1881, p. 73. See, however, Golightly's criticisms of King's connection with the ECU: *The Position of the Right Rev. Samuel Wilberforce, D.D., Lord Bishop of Oxford, in Reference to Ritualism*, third edition, London: Hatchard, 1867, pp. 98-100.

[4] On Furse, see Michael B. Furse, *Stand Therefore! A Bishop's Testimony of Faith in the Church of our Fathers*, London: SPCK, 1953, ch. 1.

[5] Owen Chadwick, *The Founding of Cuddesdon*, Oxford: Oxford University Press, 1954, p. 129.

Figure 4.1. Charles Wellington Furse

Figure 4.2. Edward Willis

The troubles began when it was discovered in July 1877 that Edward Willis, Cuddesdon's vice-principal, was a member of the Society of the Holy Cross (SSC). The SSC, exclusively for clergymen, was considered more extreme than the ECU. It had been founded by Charles Lowder and other ritualists in 1855 but obtained widespread notoriety in 1877 when Lord Redesdale exposed in the House of Lords a work entitled *The Priest in Absolution*, an SSC translation of a French Roman Catholic manual for confessors.[6] Protestants across the country, always deeply suspicious of "auricular" confession, were shocked and outraged that Anglican clergymen should dare to propagate such a book.[7] The bishops led the denunciations, with Archbishop Tait of Canterbury describing the SSC as part of a "conspiracy" to undermine the doctrine and discipline of the Reformed Church.[8] Soon the national press began to hunt out SSC adherents. As a result of the controversy membership of the organisation fell from an all-time high of 397 in 1877 to just 227 in 1879.[9] Within Oxford, the Bodleian Library banned undergraduates from reading *The Priest in Absolution*, due to its "obscene" content.[10] The Church Association also launched an Oxford branch in mid-1877, heralded by a series of events in the Town Hall at which prominent evangelical clergymen spoke passionately against ritualism.[11]

When Willis' SSC connections were found out, the spotlight fell back on Cuddesdon College. At first Furse was approached in his capacity as vicar of Cuddesdon by his churchwardens and other local laymen, who requested that Willis be banned from ministering in the parish church. Furse dismissed their appeal, surprised that anyone could "harbour a suspicion against so upright and spotless a Christian man ... a more pure, and holy, and temperate-minded man I cannot reckon among my friends". However, his parishioners were not to be thus pacified and when Willis next entered the church pulpit in August 1877, many walked out in protest.[12]

Soon Bishop John Mackarness (Wilberforce's successor) was embroiled in the controversy. He was asked how the SSC was allowed to operate under his very nose, in his own parish, in a church which his own family attended. His diocese was described as "priest-ridden", "a safe haven for Rome-bound vessels, liable to

---

[6] *Hansard*, 14 June 1877, pp. 1741-53.

[7] L. E. Ellsworth, *Charles Lowder and the Ritualist Movement*, London: DLT, 1982, pp. 138-46; Nigel Yates, "'Jesuits in Disguise'? Ritualist Confessors and their Critics in the 1870s", *Journal of Ecclesiastical History* 39 (1988), pp. 202-16; Walter Walsh, *The Secret History of the Oxford Movement*, London: Swan Sonnenschein, 1897, ch. 4.

[8] *Chronicle of Convocation*, 6 July 1877, p. 315.

[9] J. Embry, *The Catholic Movement and the Society of the Holy Cross*, London: Faith Press, 1931, p. 128.

[10] *Oxford Chronicle*, 1 September 1877.

[11] *Oxford Times*, 26 May, 30 June, 15 September & 20 October 1877.

[12] *Oxford Chronicle*, 1 September 1877.

suffer serious damage in the free and open sea of English public opinion".[13] Although Mackarness quickly tried to distance himself from the SSC, the *Record* still protested that no other bishop on the bench had approached the issue "in such a trimming, undecided manner".[14] One observer remarked on "the utter inconsistency between Episcopal words and Episcopal actions", declaring that "while brilliant memories [of Wilberforce] hang about Cuddesdon Palace, the damp and mildewy odour of insincerity has not yet departed from its walls".[15] Another queried, "Will our Episcopal rulers be much longer blind to the forecast of the coming storm? ... if the Church of England is to be saved it must be done in the next five years or never".[16]

Willis was forced to withdraw from the SSC at his bishop's insistence and it seemed that the college might escape further bad publicity. Yet the Cuddesdon parishioners who had refused to listen to his preaching were raised up in the local press as a proud example to emulate. Calls were made for "a steady persevering agitation" which would show the ritualists "that a strong and resolute will is possessed by sturdy laymen as well as by meek priests". One prophesied, "The farmers of Cuddesdon ... have been the first to resist; the fire has now been lighted, and it will blaze throughout the whole diocese".[17] The only surprise is that it was a full year before the college was caught up in the conflagration.

Not until September 1878 did the aged Golightly issue *A Solemn Warning Against Cuddesdon College*. He argued that Cuddesdon was one of the "chief nurseries" of that "conspiracy" to subvert the principles of the Reformation outlined by Archbishop Tait.[18] He called Furse "a very marked party man" and warned that Willis' withdrawal from the SSC did not prove any change in his sentiments. Golightly calculated that of Cuddesdon's 350 alumni, several had become Roman Catholics, or were members of the SSC or the Confraternity of the Blessed Sacrament, and at least 145 were members of the ECU.[19] To illustrate attempts to overthrow the doctrines of the Church of England, he quoted from the works of two ex-students, Orby Shipley (a Roman Catholic from November 1878)

---

[13] *Oxford Times*, 8 September 1877.

[14] *Record*, 7 & 14 September 1877.

[15] *Oxford Times*, 15 September 1877.

[16] *Record*, 7 September 1877.

[17] *Oxford Times*, 8 September 1877.

[18] Charles P. Golightly, *A Solemn Warning Against Cuddesdon College. Addressed to the Laity, and more Particularly to the Lay Members of the Oxford Diocesan Conference*, London: Hatchard, 1878, p. 3.

[19] Ibid., pp. 5-6.

and Frederick Lee (who had been secretly consecrated bishop in 1877 in the bizarre Order of Corporate Reunion).[20]

Golightly's pamphlet re-lit the touchpaper. Alfred Pott (now Archdeacon of Berkshire) declared:

> I do not think hard words any help in controversy. "Conspiracy", "party man", "secret society", "paralysis of the clergy", are words which ought not to be used by any clergyman of his brethren. This kind of stone-throwing can only issue in the recoil of the missile on him who casts it: according to the wise proverb, "Curses, like chickens, come home to roost".

He thought Golightly's account of the Cuddesdon Affair of 1858-59 "a tissue of inaccuracies", "calculated to mislead" and "utterly unhistorical",[21] and Liddon also entered the fray with his version of events.[22] Golightly was called "an inveterate 'accuser of the brethren'",[23] and was mocked in a parody by "the Unreverend Gohitagain" about "the bile of Mr Gone Slightly".[24] Nevertheless he remained unmoved: "Those who engage in controversy must make up their minds to rough handling."[25]

By others Golightly was praised as a "veteran champion of Church of England orthodoxy" and "one of the few who from the first withstood the Romish movement".[26] He was applauded for drawing the nation's attention to the influence of Cuddesdon by his "brave and powerful onslaught on ... one of the plague-spots of the Church of England".[27] After reading Golightly's *Solemn Warning*, one observer asked: "Are the bishops slumbering while treason is hatching?"[28] The *Oxford Times* similarly protested:

> The spectacle of professing ministers of the Church of England going forth from Cuddesdon College, under the very shadow of the Bishop's Palace, to proclaim their assent to the dogmas of Rome, and asserting the consistency of this belief with the continued exercise of their ministerial functions, is immoral and offensive.[29]

[20] On the OCR see H. R. T. Brandreth, *Dr Lee of Lambeth: a Chapter in Parenthesis in the History of the Oxford Movement*, London: SPCK, 1951, ch. 6; Walsh, *Secret History*, ch. 5; Embry, *Catholic Movement*, pp. 136-45.

[21] *Guardian*, 13 November 1878, p. 1578.

[22] *Guardian*, 20 November 1878, p. 1610.

[23] *Church Times*, 18 October 1878, p. 579.

[24] *An Image of Cuddesdon College, as Reflected in the Bile of Mr Gone Slightly ... by the Unreverend Gohitagain* (np, 1878) (copy at CCA, X1/44).

[25] *Guardian*, 13 November 1878, p. 1578.

[26] *Oxford Times*, 21 December 1878; *Rock*, 18 October 1878, p. 829.

[27] *Rock*, 4 October 1878, p. 802.

[28] *Times*, 8 October 1878, p. 8.

[29] *Oxford Times*, 28 September 1878.

Figure 4.3. Ordination Group 1880

Figure 4.4. Cuddesdon Chapel in 1883

The Oxford Diocesan Conference

In his first charge as Bishop of Oxford, Mackarness deplored the "want of active and cordial co-operation" between clergy and laity in the diocese, and announced his intention to establish a diocesan conference, a development which Wilberforce had consistently opposed.[30] In October 1872 the diocesan clergy met together, followed in subsequent years by meetings of a mixed body of clergy and laity.[31] Nigel Yates argues that all sections of the Church of England were divided over ritual and that it is "a gross over-simplification" to suggest advanced ritual was supported primarily by the clergy and opposed primarily by the laity.[32] Nevertheless, it was said of Wilberforce that he left Oxford diocese "with nine out of ten of the clergy High Churchmen, and nine out of ten of the laity the other way".[33] The first diocesan conference of 1873, with its debates on Parochial Church Councils and the Public Worship Facilities Bill, was said to reveal "the rising impatience, the overflowing indignation" of the laity at the ritualism of the clergy.[34] As has been seen, it was the lay parishioners of Cuddesdon who first blew the whistle on Willis. This tension was harnessed by Golightly, who addressed his *Solemn Warning* exclusively to the laity, particularly the lay members of the Oxford diocesan conference:

> Because in this Diocese at all events the Clergy are paralysed. Some of the more excellent of my Clerical brethren are so absorbed in their parishes, as hardly to have time or inclination to attend to anything else; some are indifferent; and others, moderate High Churchmen with no Ritualistic inclinations, – a class of Clergy of whose supineness the Archbishop of Canterbury has more than once publicly complained, – lament over the widespread mischief, but do nothing; only whispering one to another that nothing should induce them to take a Curate from Cuddesdon.[35]

Golightly asked the young E. A. Knox (later Bishop of Manchester) to initiate a debate at the diocesan conference of 1878 about Cuddesdon College. Knox

---

[30] John F. Mackarness, *A Charge Delivered to the Diocese of Oxford, at his Primary Visitation*, Oxford: Parker, 1872, pp. 37-9. See Arthur Burns, *The Diocesan Revival in the Church of England c.1800-1870*, Oxford: Clarendon Press, 1999, ch. 9.

[31] *Oxford Diocesan Conference Minutes*; C. C. Mackarness, *Memorials of the Episcopate of John Fielder Mackarness*, Oxford: Parker, 1892, pp. 12-17.

[32] Nigel Yates, *Anglican Ritualism in Victorian Britain, 1830-1910*, Oxford: Clarendon Press, 1999, p. 152.

[33] "Life of Bishop Wilberforce", *Edinburgh Review* 157 (April 1883), p. 557.

[34] John W. Burgon, *The Oxford Diocesan Conference; and Romanizing within the Church of England*, Oxford: Parker, 1873, p. 17.

[35] Golightly, *Solemn Warning*, p. 8.

agreed to broach the issue out of "a plain sense of duty and nothing else",[36] and tabled a motion that the teaching at Cuddesdon did not "deserve the confidence of members of the Church of England".[37] Professor Montagu Burrows (who had been chairman of the Oxford branch of the ECU but who had resigned because of its extremism[38]) refused to second Knox's motion, despite his own concerns about Cuddesdon, because he thought it "a vote of censure".[39] Instead Alfred Christopher (chairman of the Oxford branch of the Church Association) agreed to do so, observing: "Now that persecution has ceased I think that one of the greatest trials to which Christ's servants are exposed is to be required by faithfulness to oppose publicly an extreme party, towards some of whom ... one feels a sincere regard."[40] Before the conference began letters in the *Record* and the *Times* encouraged those alarmed at "Mediaeval Romanism" or "the present Romeward movement" to attend the debate.[41] In reply Knox and his supporters were challenged whether they could

> in the face of Oxford immorality and Oxford free thought, afford to throw a stumbling block in the way of a diocesan college (patronized, be it remembered, by your own Bishop) which at least trains her sons to go out into the world like valiant soldiers of the Cross, and combat these two crying evils of the day?[42]

In his opening address to the conference in Oxford's Sheldonian Theatre on 9 October 1878, Bishop Mackarness tried to defuse the situation. He announced his pleasure that the assembly had never been "divided into parties" and hoped they had better things to do than attack one another.[43] As one observer later wrote: "Diocesan conferences are not courts of heresy; directly you allow votes of censure and declarations of want of confidence to be discussed in them their death-warrant is sealed. They must need become a simple nuisance to the Church."[44] The debate on Knox's motion was set for the afternoon of 10 October.[45] As delegates left the Sheldonian after the morning session they were handed an article from the *Rock*

---

[36] E. A. Knox, *An Address Respecting Cuddesdon College, Intended to have been Delivered at the Oxford Diocesan Conference, October 10th, 1878*, London: Simpkin, Marshall, 1878, p. 4.

[37] *Times*, 24 September 1878, p. 9.

[38] *Autobiography of Montagu Burrows*, edited by S. M. Burrows, London: Macmillan, 1908, pp. 210, 218-20.

[39] *Record*, 11 October 1878.

[40] Christopher to G. N. Freeling, nd, in John S. Reynolds, *Canon Christopher of St Aldate's, Oxford*, Abingdon: Abbey Press, 1967, p. 214.

[41] *Record*, 7 October 1878; *Times*, 8 October 1878, p. 4.

[42] *Times*, 9 October 1878, p. 9.

[43] *Record*, 16 October 1878.

[44] *Guardian*, 23 October 1878, p. 1470.

[45] For details of the debate, see *Record*, 11 October 1878.

(an evangelical newspaper) exhibiting two coloured woodcuts of the "altar" in Cuddesdon College chapel, purporting to show "the striking progress made by Cuddesdon in the race to Rome". This showed that the simple altar cross ("itself illegal") had been replaced by a triptych; the altar cloth now displayed a chalice and host ("Nothing can be more detestable"); and two golden angels were suspended over the altar ("doubtless designed to suggest the notion of cherubim overshadowing and protecting – as in the Holy of Holies – the ark of GOD").[46]

The Sheldonian Theatre was crowded for the afternoon session. Before Knox could speak, however, Sir Robert Phillimore rose to denounce the "irrelevancy and impropriety" of his motion. He considered it "unjust to the individuals intercated ... discourteous and unfair to the Lord Bishop ... very injurious to the Conference itself". Mackarness agreed that if Knox were heard it would be difficult to refuse any censorious motion in the future. John Hubbard (later Baron Addington), John Mowbray (MP for Oxford University) and the three archdeacons of the diocese spoke in support of Phillimore, one of them mocking Golightly's pamphlet as not worth its price of thrupence.[47] Arthur Purey-Cust (Archdeacon of Buckingham) appeared to be in "a paroxysm of rage" and "in a state approaching frenzy".[48] He claimed the conference was too heated to consider the question and rejected the *Rock*'s handbill on the two altars as "a disgrace even to that disgraceful periodical". Knox recalled that Purey-Cust waved the handbill "with wild gesticulations" and denounced him "with passionate fervour".[49] The archdeacon concluded his diatribe: "There is a right way and a wrong way of bringing every matter forward. Mr Golightly has gone to work the wrong way – he has mistaken his time, he has mistaken his instruments, he has made a mess of the whole thing. (Laughter.) Do not allow him to make a mess of this Conference. (Cheers.)" Phillimore's motion that Knox be not heard, described as "a deplorably shuffling, Jesuitical mode of evading the matter", was carried by 252 votes to 75.[50] The appeals of Christopher and Sir Harry Verney (a vice-president of the Church Association) for open discussion fell on deaf ears and the bishop pronounced his pleasure at the result.

During the course of the debate Knox had referred to Mackarness' dismissal of complaints against M. H. Noel (the ritualist vicar of St Barnabas', Oxford) because Noel worked hard. The bishop sarcastically apologised for

> the offence of saying that somebody was a hard-working man. (Laughter.) ... I frankly confess that whenever I see any brother in the diocese who is really

[46] *Rock*, 11 October 1878, pp. 814-15.

[47] *Record*, 14 October 1878.

[48] *Rock*, 18 October 1878, pp. 829, 832.

[49] E. A. Knox, *Reminiscences of an Octogenarian, 1847-1934*, London: Hutchinson, 1934, p. 116.

[50] *Truth*, 24 October 1878, p. 465.

devoting all his energies, his time, and his money to the welfare, as he believes, of his flock ... I feel inclined not to be too nicely curious as to some matters which, perhaps, if he were a mere trifler, I should be inclined to notice with much more severity. (Cheers.)

Such toleration, according to Handley Moule (later Bishop of Durham), dispensed with the Bible as "the one infallible instrument for forming and testing belief and teaching". He lamented:

such is now the length which toleration goes in the direction of Rome, of Jesuit Rome, the Rome of the Curia, that under an English Bishop, firm in his own personal allegiance to the Bible, the disciples of thorough-going mediaeval and post-mediaeval tradition can teach nearly what they like, if they will only do it like men in right earnest.[51]

While acknowledging his duty as Visitor of Cuddesdon, Mackarness played down the seriousness of the charges levelled at the institution:

no one has a deeper interest in its welfare and in its conduct than I have, but I do not write to the newspapers whenever I see something which I do not entirely approve of. (A laugh.) Perhaps if I happen to see anything which I do not entirely approve of, I have a few minutes quiet talk with a dear old friend about it, and he may take a hint from me without laying the matter before his visitor in solemn court. (A laugh.) I hope this is not wrong. (Cheers.)

And so the conference closed in what the *Oxford Times* called "a barren victory for the Ritualists".[52]

Golightly's work for that day, however, was not yet finished. Having calculated that Knox would be silenced, he had positioned helpers at each door of the Sheldonian Theatre with printed copies of Knox's speech, resulting in its wide circulation. Knox reflected: "The old tactician had once more out-manoeuvred his adversaries."[53] Golightly was rebuked by the *Church Review* for his "inconceivable folly". The newspaper proclaimed:

This is the end, we should suppose, of "the Oxford spy", and foreshadows the end of all the conspiracy-mongers. We do not regret the miserable attempt. It has cleared the air, and the stupid party in the Church of England are a league nearer common sense.[54]

---

[51] *Record*, 21 October 1878.

[52] *Oxford Times*, 12 October 1878.

[53] Knox, *Reminiscences*, p. 116.

[54] *Church Review*, 19 October 1878, p. 501.

This was far from the end of the affair, however. Many objected to Golightly and Knox's methods, but did not want the subject "quietly quashed as an unpleasant subject".[55] Even Edward Elton of Wheatley, a long-time supporter of Cuddesdon College, would have welcomed formal investigation:

> Had Mr Golightly, instead of writing an inflammatory pamphlet, manfully grappled with the question whether the teaching of the college exceeded that of the great Anglican divines, he would have been listened to with interest, and good might have come out of the inquiry. ... Had Mr Knox, instead of listening to mere newspaper gossip, and like sources of information, come over to Cuddesdon, mixed with the students, as I have, I am sure his testimony would have been different.[56]

There were growing calls for an open inquiry, perhaps even a Royal Commission established by Parliament.[57] The *Oxford Times* declared that a theological college "can afford, less than Caesar's wife, to bear for an hour the shadow even of stain upon its fair name".[58] Another observer stated: "It is no mere 'Evangelical craze' that is at work to make men disquieted. There is really and truly, perhaps groundlessly, but no less actually, a very uneasy feeling about Cuddesdon among many High Churchmen in the diocese of Oxford."[59] Further fuel was added to the fire by John Burgon (now Dean of Chichester), who preached at the University Church three days after the diocesan conference against

> a miserable endeavour to familiarize our people with Romish dresses, Romish gestures, Romish practices, Romish phraseology, Romish doctrines; as if *this* were the legitimate aim of English Divines in these last days; instead of being as it is, nothing else but a crime. ... O do ye beware of this miserable counterfeit, this pitiful caricature rather, of true Religion, "pure and undefiled", – this unhealthy yearning after the corrupt method of a Church which is branded in the Apocalypse with infamy and a most tremendous doom.[60]

[55] *Standard*, 12 October 1878.

[56] *Guardian*, 16 October 1878, p. 1452.

[57] Church Association Committee Minutes, 25 October 1878, p. 21 (at LPL); *Rock*, 13 December 1878, p. 995.

[58] *Oxford Times*, 21 December 1878.

[59] *Guardian*, 23 October 1878, p. 1470.

[60] John W. Burgon, *Nehemiah, a Pattern to Builders: Counsels on the Recommencement of the Academical Year*, Oxford: Parker, 1878, pp. 18-19.

Cuddesdon Teaching and Secessions

More than a month after his *Solemn Warning*, Golightly wrote to Mackarness reiterating his charges. He reminded the bishop of his duty "to banish and drive away all erroneous and strange doctrine", and implored him to dismiss the teaching staff at Cuddesdon and close the college until suitable replacements could be found.[61] The *Oxford Times* agreed: "Excision is now the only remedy equal to the emergency."[62] Likewise the *Rock* wrote: "At present Cuddesdon College is infected with sacerdotal fever in its most virulent form; therefore the sooner it is fumigated the better for the spiritual health of the Church of England."[63]

One of the chief complaints against Cuddesdon was that the staff were "members of disloyal, discreditable and Romish Societies".[64] Furse, Willis, and Herbert Barnett (the chaplain) were all members of the ECU. Meanwhile Willis was forced to defend his former links with the SSC: "I joined it with no party aims, still less with any shadow of a thought of disloyalty to the Church of England, but with a view to my own life before God. I have never been able to understand by what right outsiders have interfered with my personal and religious liberty."[65] He assured his critics that none had "a more profound horror of Romanism" than himself, and his aim was to make his students "on the one hand, intelligent, uncompromising opponents of the encroachments and unauthorised developments of the Roman Church, and, on the other, steadfast, hearty, and loyal members of the Church of England".[66] Willis' friend, H. T. Morgan (a former chaplain at Cuddesdon), defended him as "entirely moderate and sound is his teaching", with no tendency "to lay stress on externals, or to encourage Romanism in any way" but rather to "discourage men from party strife".[67] Likewise the *Church Times* defended Furse as "a very moderate, not to say cautious, Anglican Churchman".[68]

In order to explain publicly the nature of teaching and discipline at Cuddesdon, Furse published a report on his five years as principal.[69] Yet the *Rock* remained dissatisfied with such self-justification: "They have not a single independent witness to place in the box, nor a tittle of evidence to disprove the charge."[70] Similarly the *Record* wanted an open inquiry rather than this vain

---

[61] *Record*, 25 October 1878.

[62] *Oxford Times*, 21 December 1878.

[63] *Rock*, 4 October 1878, p. 802.

[64] *Oxford Times*, 30 November 1878.

[65] *Guardian*, 23 October 1878, p. 1470.

[66] *Guardian*, 6 November 1878, p. 1548.

[67] *Guardian*, 30 October 1878, p. 1503.

[68] *Church Times*, 13 December 1878, p. 706.

[69] C. W. Furse, *Cuddesdon College. A Report for the Five Years Ending Trinity Term, 1878*, Oxford: Parker, 1878.

[70] *Rock*, 6 December 1878, p. 957.

attempt with a "little handful of dust ... to still the angry buzzing". It warned that Mackarness was

> surrounded by a knot of shrewd, unscrupulous intriguers who, in a spirit of ultra-partisanship, are managing the diocese with the comfortable assurance that if these proceedings are questioned they will simply have to give any account they please of themselves, and that the Bishop will assure the public that they are all honourable men.[71]

Nevertheless, Furse received encouragement from Liddon. In the light of the debacle surrounding Golightly's attacks in 1858-59, he urged Furse to ensure

> no changes whatever will be so made as to give an appearance of yielding to pressure. There may of course be changes, which, on consideration, *are* desirable; none of us pretends to be practically infallible. But they should be carried out, if at all, in utter independence of forms of opinion which in reality are hostile, not to the accidents, but to the substance, of all true Church work, & which never will be satisfied by partial concessions. As for the Puritan temper ... you do it no kindness by teaching it to think itself reasonable & right.[72]

The *Record* advised that Cuddesdon's teaching should be "a prophylactic against Romanism".[73] However, there were concerns about instruction on auricular confession and that the *Cuddesdon Manual of Intercession for Missions* included prayers "for the fuller restoration of the religious life" and for God's blessing in "hearing confessions" and "exorcising evil spirits".[74] When the *Rock*'s "special correspondent" visited Cuddesdon village, he found in the parish church an altar "of the most repulsive and Popish kind" and a stone reredos with a striking portrait: "*It was that of a Pope in full Pontifical garments, and with the unmistakable Papal tiara on his head!!!* Therefore when a Ritualistic worshipper bends before the 'altar' in Cuddesdon Church he actually bows before the image of a Pope which a former principal of Cuddesdon has set up!" On infiltrating the college chapel the correspondent found a stained glass window representing fourteen saints: "It will be observed that all the male 'saints' were thorough-going *Papists*. ... Dominick the murderer, Xavier the Jesuit, and Bonaventura the blasphemer – these are the men whom Cuddesdon delighteth to honour!" He also spotted a processional cross inscribed with the letters A. M. D. G. (the motto of the Jesuits), "stations of the

---

[71] *Record*, 9 December 1878.

[72] Liddon to Furse, 15 October 1878, LPL MS 4122, fo. 15.

[73] *Record*, 1 November 1878.

[74] *The Cuddesdon Manual of Intercession for Missions*, Oxford: Bowden, 1876, pp. 31, 42-3 (copy at CCA, C1/12); *Rock*, 13 December 1878, p. 990; *Guardian*, 4 & 24 December 1878, pp. 1677, 1803.

cross", and the college prayer book with "canonical hours" given Roman names such as prime, terce, sext, none and compline.[75]

Another major complaint against Cuddesdon was that approximately twenty ex-students had seceded to Roman Catholicism.[76] Willis thought such secessions "simply irrelevant" since the same could be said of Balliol College or Exeter College, to which came the predictable retort: "Mr Willis forgets that Cuddesdon is distinctly a *theological* college."[77] Supporters of Cuddesdon argued that some students arrived on the brink of secession, so the college could not be held responsible for failing to keep them all within the Anglican Communion. Pott explained that four of the first seven seceders were judged unfit for ordination, a fifth never proceeded beyond deacon's orders, and the other two converted after many years working within the Church of England. This satisfied Bishop Mackarness that there was not "a tittle of evidence" to connect Cuddesdon with the secessions.[78] The teachers could not be blamed simply for failing to cure student errors: "When patients die in a hospital during the prevalence of an epidemic, we do not lay their deaths to the charge of the hospital staff."[79]

Others defended the college in like manner. For instance, Elton stated: "Those who went from us were mostly weak and ill-instructed minds, who brought their Romanism to Cuddesdon, and did not find it there."[80] Similarly Morgan argued:

> A theological college has to deal, not with machines, but with human minds, which often refuse to be moulded after a given type. Some young men came to us, from time to time, of an unquiet, restless spirit, often full of devotion, but with little intellectual power or grasp of facts, longing for a peace, or a reverence, or seeming certainty, which they could not find in the Church of England. ... Who will, in these troubled days, give a specific for scrupulous conscience? If Mr Knox or his friends are able to provide a perfectly satisfactory cure for persons troubled with Romanizing fears and doubts, let them tell it to us, and we shall be too glad to apply it.[81]

[75] *Rock*, 13 December 1878, p. 997. On the stained glass and processional cross, see *Cuddesdon College Annual Record* (1877), pp. 33-4.

[76] Knox, *Address*, pp. 7-8. Knox had to apologise for errors in his list of seceders: *Oxford Times*, 19 October 1878; *Guardian*, 6 November 1878, p. 1548.

[77] *Guardian*, 23 & 30 October 1878, pp. 1470, 1504.

[78] Furse, *Cuddesdon College*, p. iii. See *Cuddesdon College, 1878. Address of Old Students to the Right Rev. the Lord Bishop of Oxford, Visitor, on the Subject of Recent Charges Brought Against the College: Together with his Lordship's Reply*, Oxford: Parker, 1878, pp. 5, 15.

[79] *Guardian*, 24 December 1878, p. 1796.

[80] *Guardian*, 20 November 1878, p. 1610.

[81] *Guardian*, 30 October 1878, p. 1503.

With similar logic, another observer asked: "Is then the Evangelical party to be cast out because such a very large per-centage of Roman perverts were originally Evangelicals?"[82] In a variation on this theme, a correspondent in the *Church Times* declared that the Church Association, "that most disgraceful caucus", was itself to blame for conversions to Rome.[83] It is one of the ironies of family life that Knox's own son, Ronald, was to become an influential Roman Catholic.

With less than twenty secessions from Cuddesdon to Rome in 24 years, the *Guardian* thought that "the evil is absurdly exaggerated". Likewise Mackarness wrote: "For one recruit to Rome, there have probably been fifty deserters from the Church of England to the forces of unbelief, and a still larger number, alas! of victims to the fatal seductions of immorality and vice. Here are our greatest perils, our most serious losses."[84] Unlike other theological colleges, he proclaimed, Cuddesdon did not "admit only the straitest adherents of a special system of theology", but rather "men of wide and varied sympathies, who would have refused to be bound by party tests of any kind". He believed that residence at Cuddesdon always produced a change for the better.[85] The bishop was addressed by 284 ex-students who repudiated "with indignation, the imputations of unfaithfulness and disloyalty to the Church of England" which had been cast upon them and their college tutors.[86] Another irony was that at least six of these signatories were themselves to secede to the Church of Rome in later years.

Address from the Laity

At a lecture against ritualism in Oxford in early November 1878 given by Walter Walsh (a representative of the Protestant Reformation Society, now notorious for his *Secret History of the Oxford Movement*), it was announced on Golightly's authority that a large demonstration against Cuddesdon College was being arranged, at which Lord Macclesfield, a major landowner in the village, would take the chair.[87] This planned demonstration was soon replaced by an Address to the bishop. After the diocesan conference, Golightly had asked the council of the

---

[82] Ibid.

[83] *Church Times*, 18 October 1878, p. 581.

[84] *Guardian*, 24 December 1878, pp. 1793, 1796.

[85] Furse, *Cuddesdon College*, p. iv. For praise of Cuddesdon curates, see *Guardian*, 16, 23, and 30 October 1878, pp. 1452, 1470, 1503.

[86] *Cuddesdon College, 1878*, p. 5.

[87] *Oxford Times*, 16 November 1878. See Walter Walsh, *"Is Ritualism Loyal to the Church of England?" Report of a Lecture and Discussion*, Oxford: Hall, 1879.

Church Association whether an appeal to the Queen might be organised, but was advised to address Mackarness as Cuddesdon College's Visitor.[88]

The Address was headed by Lord Jersey, but was said to have originated with the Oxford branch of the Church Association and Christopher was involved in co-ordinating it.[89] It complained that Golightly and Knox's charges had been ignored, expressed concern that the teaching staff at Cuddesdon were members of the ECU, and appealed to the bishop to find "a remedy to the serious evil".[90] At Christopher's request, the Church Association helped to generate support for the Address by distributing to all JPs and churchwardens in Oxford diocese pamphlets entitled *The English Church Union Proved to be a Romanizing Confederacy* and *Twelve Reasons for Not Joining the English Church Union*.[91] The protest was eventually signed by 827 peers, JPs, churchwardens and lay members of the diocesan conference.[92] The *Rock* concluded that the affair was "a turning-point in the history of the great struggle between lay endurance and ecclesiastical tyranny and assumption".[93]

The signatories were said to be mostly from "the old moderate High Church party",[94] but were dismissed as neither "leaders in religious opinion" nor "peculiarly conversant with Anglican theology".[95] The *Church Review* remarked: "it would be interesting to know how many are not communicants, how many of the ordinary aggrieved parishioner sort, how many members of the Church Association, how many liturgical revisionists, how many not even Churchmen".[96] The wide spectrum of opinion represented by the Address was freely acknowledged by the *Church Times*:

> Its signatories are partly men of such notorious character that a little more discretion would have prompted the suppression of their names; partly old-fashioned Evangelicals who cannot bear to think that their hey-day is over, and would like to deal a blow at the competition who is driving them out of the field; and partly of country peers and squires who find that the High Church parson is the only one who does not treat them as petty kings, with supreme jurisdiction

[88] Church Association Committee Minutes, 11 October 1878, pp. 10-11; W. C. Palmer to Golightly, 14 October 1878, LPL MS 1808, fos 206-7.

[89] *Guardian*, 18 December 1878, p. 1766; Mackarness to Christopher, 18 December 1878, in Reynolds, *Canon Christopher*, p. 215; *Record*, 23 December 1878.

[90] *An address to the Right Reverend the Lord Bishop of Oxford, from Peers, Magistrates, Lay Members of the Diocesan Conference, and Churchwardens, Resident within his Lordship's Diocese, concerning Cuddesdon College*, Oxford: Baxter, 1878, p. 4.

[91] Church Association Committee Minutes, 13 December 1878, pp. 68-9.

[92] *Record*, 23 December 1878.

[93] *Rock*, 3 January 1879, p. 2.

[94] *Record*, 2 December 1878.

[95] *Guardian*, 1 January 1879, p. 7.

[96] *Church Review*, 28 December 1878, p. 626.

over ecclesiastical as well as temporal causes within their domains; whereas a Low or Broad Churchman is usually far more docile, obsequious, and squeezable.[97]

In reply to the Address, Mackarness expressed sorrow that the laity had chosen to act alone, without the advice of the clergy of the diocese. He announced that Furse, Willis and Barnett had all withdrawn from the ECU of their own volition and therefore the memorialists' only charge against the college had been removed. Unless more than "vague imputations" were put forward, with specific charges and citations of laws allegedly broken, no case could be heard in the visitorial court "without absurdity".[98] The *Oxford Times* thought the bishop's response "disengenuous [sic] and superficial ... a dodge and an artifice ... Why not face the question like a man?"[99] Some suggested the laity should press the matter further, but Lord Jersey decided the correspondence should cease.[100]

The English Church Union and the Church Association

Members of the ECU and the Church Association played a prominent part throughout the Cuddesdon controversy. The local branches of these organisations continued to stoke the fire at their rival meetings. In November 1878 T. H. Gill of Manchester spoke at the Oxford branch of the Church Association, criticising Pusey's recent adaptation of the Abbé Gaume's *Manual for Confessors*.[101] Three days later C. L. Wood (national president of the ECU and later Viscount Halifax) told ECU's Oxford branch that the Cuddesdon furore was about "no mere question of ritual ... but the whole principle of the sacramental system".[102] The *Church Times* asked why the ECU, with approximately 3,000 clerical members and 15,000 lay members, should not have one theological college out of twenty which was sympathetic to its aims, "on mere grounds of demand and supply".[103] Likewise the *Guardian* thought that if colleges with Low Church sympathies were allowed, such

---

[97] *Church Times*, 13 December 1878, p. 705.

[98] *Guardian*, 24 December 1878, p. 1796.

[99] *Oxford Times*, 4 January 1879.

[100] See letters between Hubbard and Jersey, *Oxford Times*, 18 January & 1 February 1879.

[101] T. H. Gill, *Dr Pusey and the Abbé Gaume: or, the Latest Development of the Confessional in the Church of England*, London: Hatchard, 1878. See correspondence between Christopher, Liddon and Pusey: Reynolds, *Canon Christopher*, pp. 380-93; Bodl. MS St Edmund Hall 88, fos 1-27.

[102] *Oxford Times*, 30 November 1878.

[103] *Church Times*, 13 December 1878, p. 706.

as St John's, Highbury and St Aidan's, Birkenhead, then a High Church tendency at Cuddesdon should be tolerated.[104]

The debate was characterised by heated polemics, and after only a couple of months one observer appealed: "I really think it is time to cry truce."[105] Another concluded: "There is ample room for both parties to work side by side with charity and with mutual trust; the present want of this is the great evil of the day. If it is not too late, let all parties agree to pursue their work in their own way, and to cease cutting one another's throats, or we know what the result will be."[106] A plea for tolerance was issued: "The heathen of old was able to say, 'See how these Christians love one another!' The English infidel of to-day is able to say the same, but, alas! with a large qualification if he is unfortunate enough to observe the spirit of the Church Association, the *Rock*, or the *Church Times*."[107] The *Guardian* went further and encouraged the dissolution of both the ECU and the Church Association: "It would be a happy and hopeful Christmas for the Church of England if both parties were disbanded. Parties in the Church there always have been. Organisations for party purposes exclusively, and for party warfare, are an unhappy and disastrous novelty of these days of ours."[108]

Numerous other appeals were issued for an end to such conflict. For instance, in October 1878 William Ince (Regius Professor of Divinity) asked an Oxford congregation:

If men are deep-rooted in the love of God and imitation of Jesus Christ, why should they bite and devour one another? ... Surely, in the presence of a blighting infidelity, and a despairing scepticism all around us, we who profess the faith of Christ are bound, above all things to abstain from internecine controversy.[109]

In December Purey-Cust preached what the *Rock* called a "peace-at-any-price sermon",[110] on *Harmony in Spite of Differences*, lamenting the prevalence of "rabid and savage strife", "mutual insinuations and imprecations" and "hereditary prejudices and watchwords".[111] He appealed for mutual toleration:

My brethren, I believe that one crying need in our day, that in a Church, *where parties must be tolerated*, party spirit on all sides should be discouraged and

---

[104] *Guardian*, 24 December 1878, p. 1793.

[105] *Guardian*, 20 November 1878, p. 1610.

[106] *Church Times*, 18 October 1878, p. 581.

[107] *Guardian*, 30 October 1878, p. 1503.

[108] *Guardian*, 24 December 1878, p. 1793.

[109] William Ince, *The Internal Duties of the University in Prospect of External Changes*, Oxford: Parker, 1878, p. 16.

[110] *Rock*, 3 January 1879, p. 9.

[111] Arthur P. Purey-Cust, *Harmony in Spite of Differences*, London: Allen, 1878, pp. 6, 8.

frowned down. Such hateful imputations are condemned in politics, why are they tolerated and encouraged in religion, until weak men are driven out, and thoughtful men are rendered sick at heart, and the love which might, and I believe would, redress many of the evils which the law cannot touch, and restrain those whom the law only goads into mad rebellion, is evaporated in the crucible of controversy and mutual recrimination?[112]

Purey-Cust further advised the clergy of Buckinghamshire archdeaconry:

My friends, if we are ever to have peace in our distracted Church, our first step must be to relinquish and set our face against the use of hateful party names. ... Party cries have been the bane of the seventeenth and eighteenth centuries, – are they to be the bane of the nineteenth also? ... Are we so stupid? Have we learned nothing by experience? Must history ever repeat itself to our shame?[113]

He described the ECU and the Church Association as "grinding millstones, between which the very heart of our Holy Faith will be inevitably crushed out".[114] Yet the *Rock* objected that "Religion itself sinks to the level of a 'cat's concert' if Romish and Reformed tunes are to be played simultaneously in the National Church".[115]

Bishop Mackarness' attitude to the ECU and the Church Association came under close scrutiny during the controversy. Some praised his "impartial conduct, tact and temper",[116] but the *Record* thought him at best guilty of weak leadership:

Bishop MACKARNESS has the reputation of being a very kindly, genial man, who would be very anxious, if he possibly could, to make all things pleasant for everybody all round, probably even for Mr GOLIGHTLY himself if he could. His notion seems to be that the Church of England is well able to take care of herself without any intervention on the part of Bishops.[117]

By others Mackarness was seen as strongly biased towards the ritualists. It was discovered that he had himself once been a member of the ECU, resigning in 1869 shortly before his consecration as bishop.[118] This explained why he had appointed more than twenty members of the ECU to livings of which he held the patronage,

[112] Ibid., p. 9. Cf. Arthur P. Purey-Cust, *Unity with Division in the Established Church Possible and Essential*, London: Rivington, 1874.
[113] Arthur P. Purey-Cust, *A Charge Delivered at His Third Visitation of the Archdeaconry of Buckingham*, London: Rivington, 1879, pp. 37-9.
[114] Ibid., p. 40.
[115] *Rock*, 3 January 1879, p. 9.
[116] *Oxford Times*, 12 October 1878.
[117] *Record*, 9 December 1878.
[118] *Guardian*, 8 January 1879, p. 45.

but few evangelicals.[119] He had also written prefaces to "Romeward-propelling books" and prevented prosecutions of ritualistic clergy at Clewer, Reading and Dorchester.[120]

However, in his reply to the Address of the laity concerning Cuddesdon College, Mackarness publicly assailed both the ECU and the Church Association:

> As to the English Church Union, if they [the memorialists] regret its methods of action, I go further, and regret that it exists. Excellent as were the purposes of its foundation twenty years or more ago, it has resulted in a state of things injurious to the welfare of the Church. Stirring up rival organisations, it has divided Churchmen into hostile camps, and has brought many good men, who have no real share in its counsels, though they are counted among its 17,000 members, into indiscriminate and unmerited obloquy. Fruitless litigation has been encouraged, charity grievously impaired. The heaviest indictment against the Church Union is, that it called the Church Association into life. Until both societies are dissolved there will be, in my judgment, small hope of peace for the Church.[121]

Predictably, such statements produced a stern reaction from both organisations. G. A. Denison, one of the original founders of the ECU and a former curate of Cuddesdon, thought the claim that it had stirred up rival organisations was "historically ludicrous".[122] Meanwhile Thomas Andrews (chairman of the Church Association) argued that "A truce with the enemy while within the walls (actually daily sustained by the supplies and wearing the uniform of our Church) is not 'peace', but a shameful surrender from which true Churchmen cannot but shrink with the deepest aversion". To this Mackarness responded:

> I have no sympathy with your appetite for condemnations. Too often they do but provoke men to revolt. In things indifferent liberty, and neutral toleration, are more to my taste. In things really objectionable, as ministering to superstition, we might have trusted the good sense and sound feeling of Churchmen to prevail, if polemical confederacies had not almost banished reason and charity from the sphere of their discussion.[123]

By the end of January 1879, the controversy over Cuddesdon College had died down. The attention of Oxford diocese moved instead to the ritualistic practices of T. T. Carter at Clewer, where the ECU and the Church Association were again prominently involved.[124] Only briefly did Cuddesdon regain the limelight when

---

[119] *Record*, 13 November 1878.

[120] *Rock*, 6 December 1878, p. 981.

[121] *Guardian*, 24 December 1878, p. 1796.

[122] Quoted in *Oxford Times*, 18 January 1879.

[123] *Church Association Monthly Intelligencer* 13 (February 1879), pp. 46-7.

[124] W. H. Hutchings, *Life and Letters of Thomas Thellusson Carter*, London: Longmans, 1903, pp. 150-79; Mackarness, *Memorials*, pp. 86-98.

Charles Elliott (Vicar of Winkfield, near Bracknell) attacked *The Communicant's Manual*, a book "tainted with Roman error" to which King had contributed a preface when principal.[125] The *Rock* immediately proclaimed once more that Cuddesdon had "no right whatever to call itself in any true sense a Church of England institution", and concluded that if Mackarness were a man of honour he would resign his see and secede to Rome.[126]

Unlike with their attacks upon Liddon and Pott in the 1850s, Golightly and his allies failed to provoke substantial changes in the teaching at Cuddesdon during the affair of 1878-79. Willis remained until 1880 when he became a founding member of the Oxford Mission to Calcutta, and was replaced as vice-principal by Charles Gore. Furse continued in charge until 1883 when he was appointed a canon of Westminster. Nevertheless the controversy received nationwide attention and its outcome was seen as of vital import to the future direction of Anglicanism. The *Rock* described it as "a struggle which – despite all attempts to localize it – is rapidly assuming an importance co-extensive with the Church of England".[127] The achievement of Oxford's Protestants was assessed differently by observers from the various camps. The *Guardian* maintained: "Mr Golightly and his henchman Mr Knox have led their too credulous followers – as the former gentleman has more than once done before – into something very like 'a mare's nest'."[128] In contrast the *Record* judged that they had gained "a substantial victory" because of the extensive publicity: "Forewarned is to be forearmed, and parishes which receive Cuddesdon curates will know what to expect."[129] From no matter what theological perspective, one thing was now certain: the college's influential role within Anglican theological education could not be ignored. Cuddesdon College was able to celebrate its twenty-fifth anniversary in the sure knowledge that it was there to stay.

[125] Charles J. Elliott, *Some Strictures on a Book Entitled "The Communicant's Manual"*, London: John Murray, 1879, p. 29. See also Edward King, *A Letter to the Rev. Charles J. Elliott*, Oxford: Parker, 1879; Elliott, *Some Remarks Upon a Letter to the Rev. C. J. Elliott*, London: John Murray, 1879.

[126] *Rock*, 14 March 1879, p. 206.

[127] *Rock*, 6 December 1878, p. 957.

[128] *Guardian*, 24 December 1878, p. 1793.

[129] *Record*, 8 January 1879.

Chapter 5

Ripon Hall, Henry Major and the Shaping of English Liberal Theology

Michael W. Brierley

Introduction[1]

> I never quite understand what the position of Ripon Hall is in the system of the National Church. Is it a recognised Training College for the Clergy, and do the Bishops sanction the training of candidates there?[2]

There must be at least a hint of sarcasm in these words of Herbert Hensley Henson, written at the age of 83 in 1947, the year in which he died. His words echo some of the contemptuousness which the very name "Ripon Hall" evoked in some circles.[3] Yet bishops not only sent ordinands to Ripon Hall, Ripon Hall itself produced a number of diocesan bishops: of Derby, Durham, Sheffield, Ely, Newcastle, Leicester, and Ripon and Leeds.[4] It also educated Bishops of Hull, Dorking,

---

[1] I am grateful to Mark Chapman and Clive Pearson for comments on a draft of this chapter. Some of the material used is part of current doctoral research with the University of Birmingham.

[2] E. F. Braley, *Letters of Herbert Hensley Henson*, London: SPCK, 1951, p. 205.

[3] Cf. the comments of Frank Weston cited in Alan M. G. Stephenson, *The Rise and Decline of English Modernism: The Hulsean Lectures 1979-80*, London: SPCK, 1984, p. 10; the episcopal opposition to Ripon Hall alluded to in Clive R. Pearson, *H. D. A. Major and English Modernism 1911-1948*, University of Cambridge: unpublished Ph. D. thesis, 1989, p. 154; and the opposition mentioned in Henry D. A. Major (subsequently Major), "An Appeal to Modern Churchmen", *Modern Churchman* 20 (1930), pp. 98-9 at 99.

[4] Geoffrey Allen, Bishop of Derby (1959-69), trained at Ripon Hall 1924-27 (and was Chaplain 1928-30 and Principal 1952-59); Ian Ramsey, Bishop of Durham (1966-72), trained at Ripon Hall 1939-40; Gordon Fallows, Bishop of Sheffield (1971-79), trained at Ripon Hall 1935-36 (and was Principal 1959-68); Stephen Sykes, Bishop of Ely (1990-99), trained at Ripon Hall 1963-64; Martin Wharton, Bishop of Newcastle from 1997, trained at Ripon Hall 1969-72; Tim Stevens, Bishop of Leicester from 1999, trained at Ripon Hall

Swindon, Hulme, Edmonton and Gippsland.[5] Ripon Hall can even claim to have produced its own "saint".[6]

Ripon Hall, which merged with Cuddesdon College to become Ripon College Cuddesdon, in 1975, is so named because it began life in Ripon. Its history falls neatly into distinct phases: its life in Ripon (1898-1915); its life under Henry Major in Parks Road, Oxford (1919-33); and its life at Boars Hill, Oxford, under the principalships of Major (1933-48), Douglas Richardson (1948-52), Geoffrey Allen (1952-59), Gordon Fallows (1959-68), and Tony Dyson (1968-74).[7]

> [I]t is definitely said – by a sympathiser – that the Ripon College goes to Oxford
> as a protest against Cuddesdon: and if so, it will, to my mind be doing infinite
> harm. Whatever the faults & excesses & narrowness of the Cuddesdon point of
> view, Cuddesdon is turning out some of the most faithful manly & efficient
> pastors of their flocks.[8]

The move of Ripon Clergy College to Oxford in 1919 was in fact in no way connected to Cuddesdon. The college did, however, by this time have a very definite perspective which it wished to bring to theological education. This perspective, a "modernist" one, and the story of how the college came to assume it, hold the key to understanding the significance of the college in shaping English

1973-75; and John Packer, Bishop of Ripon and Leeds from 2000, trained at Ripon Hall 1967-70 (and was Tutor 1973-75).

[5] George Townley, Bishop of Hull (1957-65), trained at Ripon Hall 1921-22; Kenneth Evans, Bishop of Dorking (1968-85), trained at Ripon Hall 1937-38; Michael Doe, Bishop of Swindon from 1994, trained at Ripon Hall 1969-72; Stephen Lowe, Bishop of Hulme from 1999, trained at Ripon Hall 1966-69; Peter Wheatley, Bishop of Edmonton from 1999, trained at Ripon Hall 1972-74; and David Garnsey, Bishop of Gippsland, Australia (1959-74), trained at Ripon Hall 1933-34.

[6] Geoffrey Studdert Kennedy (1883-1929) trained at Ripon Clergy College 1907-08, and appeared as a "priest and poet" for commemoration on 8 March in the *Common Worship* version of the Revised Common Lectionary introduced in the Church of England in 1997. Given the Cuddesdon connections of Edward King, Bishop of Lincoln, who is commemorated with a lesser festival in the lectionary on the same day, 8 March assumes something of a patronal function for Ripon College, Cuddesdon. See Mark D. Chapman, "King and Kennedy: Two Visions of Ministry for 8 March", *Expository Times* 110 (1999), pp. 141-3. For Studdert Kennedy, see the bibliography given in Michael W. Brierley, "Introducing the Early British Passibilists", *Journal for the History of Modern Theology* 8 (2001), pp. 218-33 at 227 n. 48. There are a dozen letters relating to Studdert Kennedy's connection with Ripon Clergy College in Ripon Hall archives (M0/3 and RCC 4/245).

[7] The principalship of Tony Dyson and the Hall's merger with Cuddesdon are covered briefly in Robert Jeffery's contribution to this volume, and are not discussed in this chapter.

[8] Letter from Francis Fremantle to Major, 13 February 1919 (RHA RCC 4/527).

liberal theology. This chapter therefore seeks to illuminate that significance by concentrating on the history of the College at Ripon, in particular the rise of Henry Major from tutor to principal (1906-19), and the doctrine to which he subscribed.

First, however, a word about previous histories of the Hall and historiography: Alan Stephenson,[9] who trained at the Hall 1954-56, researched the history of the college while he was vice-principal in the 1960s, and wrote it up for an article in *Theology* in 1964.[10] He also worked on the wider history of English modernism for his Hulsean lectures of 1979-80; Ripon Hall thus features in the published version, *The Rise and Decline of English Modernism*, which was being produced when Stephenson died in 1984, and which remains the authoritative (and only) published volume on the subject.[11] Stephenson's style of history-writing, with its concentration on personalities and incidents more than the history of ideas, did not win over all readers.[12] One reviewer characterised it as "his tendency doggedly to compile".[13] I myself find that the connections between, and anecdotes about, different characters bring to life a comprehensive picture; and that the history of an idea cannot be illuminated without reference to the biographies of those who gave it shape. The chapter which follows similarly aims at allowing the characters of Ripon Hall to shed light on the theological movement which it represented.

Bishop's College, Ripon, and Lightfoot Hall

Among the clutch of theological institutions founded in the Victorian era, the bishop's initiative at Ripon was one of the last, preceding only the bishops' hostels at Farnham (1899), Liverpool (c. 1900) and Newcastle (1901).[14] The precise date

---

[9] Alan Malcolm George Stephenson (1928-1984) was Tutor at Lichfield Theological College (1958-62), Vice-Principal of Ripon Hall (1962-71), and Vicar of Steventon (with Milton from 1973) (1971-84). See the obituaries in the *Times*, 7 July 1984, p. 12, and by Wilfrid Browning in the *Church Times*, 20 July 1984, p. 14.

[10] Alan M. G. Stephenson, "Ripon Hall, 1897-1964", *Theology* 67 (1964), pp. 305-10.

[11] Stephenson, *Rise and Decline of English Modernism*.

[12] It also did not please members of the Modern Churchmen's Union, who read that they had a "somewhat uncertain existence" and that the modernist movement had come to an end (Stephenson, *Rise and Decline of English Modernism*, pp. 9, 13 and 18-19). Cf. reference to the "Stephenson debacle" by Donald R. Witts in his obituary of Peter Baelz, *Modern Churchpeople's Union Newsletter* 17 (2000).

[13] Alberic Stacpoole, review of Stephenson, *Rise and Decline of English Modernism*, *Month* 18 (1985), pp. 278-9 at 278. A third of Stephenson's book consists of appendices.

[14] For an introduction to Victorian theological college history, see Frederick W. B. Bullock, *A History of Training for the Ministry in the Church of England in England and Wales from 1875 to 1974*, London: Home Words Printing and Publishing Co., 1976.

at which the hostel began is a matter of debate. In 1897, the third Bishop of Ripon, William Boyd Carpenter,[15] invited Fred Wright to be resident tutor of a hostel for theological students.[16] Wright was an attractive man, who suffered from depression, and enjoyed motorcycling and mountaineering. G. A. Schneider, who as Vice-Principal of Ridley Hall, Cambridge, had taught Wright, visited him in Ripon in September 1897, and was shown round the proposed hostel.[17] On the basis of this information, Frederick Bullock, the authority on theological college history, used the date of 1897 for the foundation of the theological college at Ripon in his history of Ridley Hall.[18] Alan Stephenson also used 1897 in his history of 1964.[19] He claimed that this date was supported by Boyd Carpenter's diary, and the testimony of Boyd Carpenter's daughter, Margaret Girdlestone.[20] These witnesses, however, are not unambiguous.[21] It seems that the first students did not arrive until

[15] William Boyd Carpenter (1841-1918) was Vicar of Holloway (1870-79), Vicar of Lancaster-Gate (1879-82), Canon of Windsor (1882-84), Bishop of Ripon (1884-1911), and Canon of Westminster (1911-18). See further the obituaries in the *Times*, 28 October 1918, p. 4, the *Guardian*, 31 October 1918, pp. 862-3, and the *Church Times*, 1 November 1918, p. 315; William Boyd Carpenter, *Some Pages of My Life*, London: Williams and Norgate, 1911, and *Further Pages of My Life*, London: Williams and Norgate, 1916; and Major, "In Memoriam: William Boyd Carpenter, DD, DCL, DLitt, KCVO", *Modern Churchman* 8 (1918), pp. 349-56, *The Life and Letters of William Boyd Carpenter*, London: John Murray, 1925, and "William Boyd Carpenter (1841-1918)", *Dictionary of National Biography 1912-1921*, London: Oxford University Press, 1927, p. 94.

[16] William Frederick Wright trained at Ridley Hall, served his title at Holy Trinity, Ripon (1896-98), and was Tutor of Bishop's Hostel, Ripon (1898-1903), and Vice-Principal of Bishop's College, Ripon (1903-04). See the obituaries in the *Guardian*, 7 September 1904, p. 1448 (by Battersby Harford), and the *Times*, 8 September 1904, p. 4, and the notes attached to a letter from R. S. Mills to Alan Stephenson, 5 February 1963 (RHA M27/1).

[17] Letter from Frederick Bullock to Alan Stephenson, 12 January 1963 (RHA M27/1).

[18] Frederick W. B. Bullock, *The History of Ridley Hall, Cambridge*, vol. 1, Cambridge: Cambridge University Press, 1941, p. 366.

[19] Stephenson, "Ripon Hall", p. 305.

[20] Alan M. G. Stephenson, "Three Cyclists", *Modern Churchman* 12 (1969), pp. 152-7 at 152-3.

[21] The only reference I can find in Boyd Carpenter's illegible diary is simply to a visit from Fred Wright on 1 September 1897 to go over some books (London: British Library, Boyd Carpenter papers, add. mss. 46765, f. 67). Margaret Girdlestone, daughter of Boyd Carpenter, states that Wright was "beyond doubt" the resident tutor of Bishop's Hostel "by the end of 1897"; but this letter contains inaccuracies of detail, and was recollecting events some 66 years later (letter from Margaret Girdlestone to Alan Stephenson, 8 March 1963 (RHA M27/1)).

September 1898,[22] as this is the earliest date of student entry given in the first college yearbook (that of 1908-09),[23] and was the date of foundation used by the college.[24] Wright was taking services in Holy Trinity Church, Ripon, where he was curate, until the end of 1897.[25] 1898 is thus the date by which the hostel was definitely underway.[26] While Wright was resident tutor, the bishop gave Charles Henry Robinson, diocesan missioner,[27] some responsibility for "oversight" of the hostel, but Wright, who did not get on with Robinson, is credited with having got the hostel off the ground.[28]

Boyd Carpenter had grown up in an evangelical clergy family, but was never himself a convinced evangelical,[29] and began to broaden out while Vicar of Holloway.[30] At Ripon, a cluster of broad churchmen grew around him: Arthur Waugh, Archdeacon of Ripon, appointed in 1894;[31] William Danks, Archdeacon of

[22] Margaret Girdlestone recollected in 1963 that some students lodged in two nearby houses before the hostel was opened (postcard from Margaret Girdlestone to Alan Stephenson, 4 April 1963 (RHA M27/1)).

[23] RHA X7, p. 58.

[24] 1898 was the date given in college prospectuses, and the college celebrated its golden jubilee in Stephenson is incorrect to claim that the date "1897" is "clearly given" in "documents previous to the Great War" ("Three Cyclists", p. 152).

[25] According to the parish registers, Wright first officiated in the church on 3 January 1897, and last officiated on 9 December, signing himself "assistant curate" (letter from George Parr to Alan Stephenson, 28 July 1965 (RHA M27/1)).

[26] It is also the year in which the Churchmen's Union was founded.

[27] Charles Henry Robinson (1861-1925) was Vice-Chancellor of Truro (1890-93), Ripon Diocesan Missioner (1896-1902), and Editor-Secretary of the S. P. G. (1902-25). He was in due course an uncle of John A. T. Robinson. There is no mention of his connection with the Hostel in the biography by Florence Robinson, *Charles H. Robinson: A Record of Travel and Work*, London: SPG, 1928.

[28] Letter from Frederick Bullock to Alan Stephenson, cited above. Cf. letter from Margaret Girdlestone to Alan Stephenson, 25 March 1963 (RHA M27/1). Bullock misinterpreted Schneider's information when he claimed that Robinson was therefore the college's first principal (*History of Ridley Hall*, p. 366).

[29] The obituary in the *Times*, cited above.

[30] Major, *Life and Letters of William Boyd Carpenter*, pp. 138-40 (i.e. earlier than Stephenson claims in *Rise and Decline of English Modernism*, p. 78). Cf. pp. 75, 99 and 136; Samuel Bickersteth, "Recollections of Bishop Boyd Carpenter", in Major, *Life and Letters of William Boyd Carpenter*, pp. 305-16 at 314; and R. B. Tollinton, "Memories of Bishop Boyd Carpenter", in Major, *Life and Letters of William Boyd Carpenter*, pp. 317-20 at 318-19.

[31] Arthur Thornhill Waugh was Vicar of St Mary's, Brighton (1873-95), and Archdeacon of Ripon (1894-1905). He was a Canon of Ripon from 1891 until his death in 1922.

Richmond, appointed in 1894;[32] and W. H. Fremantle, Dean, appointed in 1895.[33] Boyd Carpenter founded his college "on wide and truth-seeking lines", "in the interest of Truth and Christianity."[34] Major explains that the bishop wanted to avoid the clericalism, party-spirit and obscurantism fostered by other colleges.[35] In an article of 1905, Boyd Carpenter outlined his vision for theological training, stating that ordinands had to take on board the new need of society to seek scientific and ethical foundations for all knowledge, and recognise the truth that lay outside the boundaries of Christendom, these values being none other than the outworkings of Love.[36]

In order to take advantage of proximity to the Victoria University, the bishop, inviting Henry Gee in 1900 to become the first principal,[37] "repackaged" Bishop's Hostel as Bishop's College, open to graduates of the newer as well as the older universities from January 1901.[38] Fred Wright was joined by a second tutor,

---

[32] William Danks (1846-1916) was Vicar of Ilkley (1884-90), Rector of Richmond (1890-97), Archdeacon of Richmond (1894-1908), Canon of Ripon (1896-1908), and Canon of Canterbury (1908-16). See further the obituary in the *Guardian*, 6 April 1916, p. 303; Major, "In Memoriam: William Danks, 1846-1916", *Modern Churchman* 6 (1916), pp. 1-2; and Major, "Memoir", in William Danks, *The Gospel of Consolation: University and Cathedral Sermons*, London: Longmans, Green and Co., 1917, pp. xi-xxxiii.

[33] William Henry Fremantle (1831-1916) was Vicar of St Mary's, Bryanston Square (1866-93), Canon of Canterbury (1882-95), and Dean of Ripon (1895-1915). In the latter post he succeeded his uncle W. R. Fremantle. See further Major, "In Memoriam: William Henry Fremantle", *Modern Churchman* 6 (1917), pp. 453-5, reprinted as "William Henry Fremantle", *Modern Churchman* 46 (1956), pp. 256-8; and William H. Draper (ed.), *Recollections of Dean Fremantle: Chiefly by Himself*, London: Cassell and Co., 1921.

[34] Letter from Boyd Carpenter to H. G. Hart, 9 March 1914, in Major, *Life and Letters of William Boyd Carpenter*, pp. 164-5 at 164.

[35] Major, *Life and Letters of William Boyd Carpenter*, pp. 158-60.

[36] William Boyd Carpenter, "The Education of a Minister of God", *Hibbert Journal* 3 (1905), pp. 433-51; hence the emphasis in Boyd Carpenter's own work and the teaching at the college on comparative religion or (as Major knew it) "the science of religion". Stephenson summarises Boyd Carpenter's article in terms of eight points ("Ripon Hall", pp. 305-6).

[37] Henry Gee (1858-1938) was Tutor (1880-84) and Senior Tutor (1885-1900) of London College of Divinity, Principal of Bishop's College, Ripon (1900-02), Master of University College, Durham (1902-18), Professor of Church History (1910-18), and Dean of Gloucester (1917-38). See the obituary in the *Times*, 24 December 1938, p. 12, and G. Colliss B. Davies, *Men for the Ministry: The History of the London College of Divinity*, London: Hodder and Stoughton, 1963, pp. 52-3.

[38] Leaflet about the College (RHA X6, p. 7). For a typical notice about exhibitions for students, see Boyd Carpenter's letter to the editor, *Guardian*, 15 May 1901, p. 646.

Stanley Legg.[39] The principal lived in a rented house, North Lodge,[40] and the students, who were expected to stay for two years,[41] lived with the tutors in 6 Princess Terrace, the original hostel[42] – a house large enough only for four students, so any excess had to be put up in rented lodgings.[43] Gee was keen to have a building with a capacity of forty students,[44] and the Executive Committee spent much of 1902 investigating possible alternative sites.[45] These, however, were ultimately unaffordable, and so the College in December 1902 bought the next-door property, Royd House, or 5 Princess Terrace.[46] Boyd Carpenter, who was widely known as an orator, gave lectures on preaching in his palace;[47] and Canon Garrod, Principal of the Diocesan (teacher) Training College, gave lectures on the principles of teaching.

Meanwhile, there were concerns elsewhere in the country that the "low church" was under-represented among theological colleges. In February 1899, Thomas Jex-Blake, Dean of Wells,[48] chaired a meeting in London "to consider the

[39] Stanley Charles Edmund Legg (1872-1955) was Tutor of St John's Hall, Highbury (1895-1900), Tutor at Bishop's College, Ripon (1901-03), and Sub-Dean of King's College, London (1903-18).

[40] This house had belonged to Samuel Wise (1812-85), diocesan registrar and secretary to the first three Bishops of Ripon, whose son Francis Dickson Wise (1842-1938) was diocesan registrar 1885-1925, and secretary to the college corporation 1901-19.

[41] Minutes of the College Council Executive Committee, 8 March 1901 (RHA RCC 1/2), p. 4.

[42] 6 Princess Terrace had within a few years become 1 Princess Road (Stephenson ("Ripon Hall", p. 305) made a slight slip by giving the original hostel as "1 Princess Terrace").

[43] Minutes of the College Council Executive Committee, 19 July 1901 (RHA RCC 1/2), pp. 10-1.

[44] Memorandum to the College Council Executive Committee (RHA RCC 1/2, p. 1).

[45] Minutes of the College Council Executive Committee, 7 February, 3 March, 20 March, 27 March and 2 June 1902 (RHA RCC 1/2, pp. 15-19).

[46] Minutes of the College Council Executive Committee, 19 December 1902 (RHA RCC 1/2), p. 26. The Governing Body bought 4 Princess Terrace when it came up for sale in 1907, and it became the house for the new principal in 1912. The three houses which thus constituted the College were still standing in 2003.

[47] Major, *Life and Letters of William Boyd Carpenter*, p. 165. For Boyd Carpenter on preaching, see Boyd Carpenter, *Some Pages of My Life*, pp. 306-26, Major, *Life and Letters of William Boyd Carpenter*, pp. 115-35, and the autobiographical notes by R. S. Mills entitled "The Cathedral" (RHA M27/1).

[48] Thomas William Jex-Blake (1832-1915) was Headmaster of Rugby (1874-87), Rector of Alvechurch (1887-91) and Dean of Wells (1891-1911). See the obituaries in the *Times*, 3 July 1915, p. 11, and the *Guardian*, 8 July 1915, p. 622, and Michael E. Sadler,

great efficacy of Theological Colleges, e.g. at Wells, Ely, Leeds etc., but almost exclusively in one direction viz. distinctly High or advanced High; and the lack of such Colleges, Wycliffe & Ridley excepted, on the basis of Holy Scripture".[49] Jex-Blake was a trustee of Wells Theological College, to which his attitude "was always one of courtesy and friendship",[50] but he was also evidently concerned that colleges of other traditions be founded.[51] Jex-Blake brought supporters from Wells to the meeting,[52] and the prominent evangelicals F. J. Chavasse (Principal of Wycliffe Hall, soon to be appointed Bishop of Liverpool) and W. H. Barlow (Vicar of Islington) were also in attendance; Handley Moule, the first Principal of Ridley Hall and future Bishop of Durham, had sent his apologies. The meeting agreed on "[t]he need of another Clergy School mainly for graduates of Oxford & Cambridge on the same lines as Wycliffe Hall & Ridley Hall",[53] to be situated in Birmingham. This was because Birmingham presented opportunities for pastoral training, and was now developing its own university.[54]

The governors were not uniformly evangelical, however. By May, such important figures for the future of Anglican modernism as Michael Glazebrook,[55]

"Thomas William Jex-Blake (1832-1915)", *Dictionary of National Biography 1912-1921*, London: Oxford University Press, 1927, pp. 298-9.

[49] Minutes of meeting, 8 February 1899 (RHA LH1/1), p. 1.

[50] Edward L. Elwes, *The History of Wells Theological College*, London: SPCK, 1923, p. 75.

[51] Edmund Knox (father of Wilfred and Ronald), who was soon brought in on the project (at the time Bishop of Coventry, and later Bishop of Manchester), states in his memoirs (Edmund A. Knox, *Reminiscences of an Octogenarian: 1847-1934*, London: Hutchinson and Co., 1935, p. 178) that the project was carried out under the auspices of Lady Wimborne, as "part of the great protest which Lady Wimborne had inaugurated against Ritualism".

[52] Thomas Bernard, the Canon Chancellor of Wells, and his son Edward Bernard, Canon of Salisbury.

[53] Minutes of meeting, 8 February 1899 (RHA LH1/1), p. 2.

[54] Minutes of meeting, 20 February 1899 (RHA LH1/1), p. 5. The older theological college at Birmingham, Queen's College, founded in 1828, appears to have been labouring under some difficulty; cf. principal's report to the Governing Body, 6 June 1901 (RHA LH2/1), p. 24. It was suspended from 1907 to 1923.

[55] Michael George Glazebrook (1853-1926) was Headmaster of Clifton College (1891-1905) and Canon of Ely (1905-26). He chaired the Governing Body of Ripon Hall 1919-24. See the obituaries in the *Times*, 3 May 1926, p. 8, and the *Guardian*, 21 May 1926, p. 393; Major, "In Memoriam: Michael George Glazebrook (1853-1926)", *Modern Churchman* 16 (1926), pp. 57-8, reprinted as "Michael George Glazebrook (1853-1926)", *Modern Churchman* 46 (1956), pp. 307-8; and Norman Whatley, "Michael George Glazebrook (1853-1926)", *Dictionary of National Biography 1922-1930*, London: Oxford University Press, 1937, pp. 340-1.

and Hastings Rashdall,[56] had joined the committee which would become the Midland Clergy College's Governing Body. Rashdall had made a case earlier in the year for "more moderate, more thoughtful, and less ultra-ecclesiastical" training, "one theological school (not confined to a particular diocese) at which a liberally minded man could find real intellectual guidance and stimulus".[57] Two sub-committees, formed to find a house and a principal,[58] acted swiftly: on 20 July, Jex-Blake announced the opening in October of a college for Oxbridge graduates marked by devotion to the study of scripture, loyalty to the prayer-book, and practical work, along the lines of Dr Vaughan and Bishop Lightfoot.[59] On 18 October 1899, the Bishop of Worcester, J. J. S. Perowne, opened the new college

[56] Hastings Rashdall (1858-1924) was educated at New College, Oxford. He taught at St David's, Lampeter (1883), University College, Durham (1884-88) and as Fellow of Hertford College (1888-95), before becoming Fellow of New College (1895-1917) and Canon of Hereford (1910-17), and Dean of Carlisle (1917-1924). He was President of the Modern Churchmen's Union 1923-24. For Rashdall, see the bibliography in Mark D. Chapman, "Hastings Rashdall", in F. Wilhelm Bautz and Traugott Bautz (eds), *Biographisch-Bibliographisches Kirchenlexikon*, vol. 6, Herzberg: Bautz, 1994, cols. 1368-73, and also: Major, "The New Dean of Carlisle", *Modern Churchman* 7 (1917), pp. 97-102, "Hastings Rashdall", *Modern Churchman* 13 (1924), pp. 634-42, and "Hastings Rashdall (1858-1924)", *Modern Churchman* 46 (1956), pp. 230-1; R. M. Pope, "Hastings Rashdall: Some Personal Reminiscences", *London Quarterly Review* 151 (1929), pp. 30-5; Margaret Marsh, *Hastings Rashdall*, Lambeth Palace: unpublished S. Th. Diploma thesis, 1986; David G. Nicholls, *Deity and Domination: Images of God and the State in the Nineteenth and Twentieth Centuries*, London and New York: Routledge, 1989, pp. 54-6; Jane Garnett, "Hastings Rashdall and the Renewal of Christian Social Ethics, c. 1890 – 1920", in Jane Garnett and H. Colin G. Matthew (eds), *Revival and Religion since 1700: Essays for John Walsh*, London and Rio Grande, OH: Hambledon Press, 1993, pp. 297-316; Anthony O. Dyson, "Hastings Rashdall", in Margaret Marsh, *Hastings Rashdall: Bibliography of the Published Writings*, Leysters: Modern Churchpeople's Union, 1993, pp. 1-15, and "Hastings Rashdall as Social Theologian: Critical Methodology and the Rhetoric of Brotherhood", in Oswald Bayer and Alan M. Suggate (eds), *Worship and Ethics: Lutherans and Anglicans in Dialogue*, Berlin and New York: Walter de Gruyter, 1996, pp. 59-87; Brian L. Hebblethwaite, "Hastings Rashdall (1858-1924)", in Trevor A. Hart (ed.), *The Dictionary of Historical Theology*, Carlisle: Paternoster Press, and Grand Rapids, MI: William B. Eerdmans Publishing Co., 2000, pp. 455-6; and Dorothy Postle and Margaret Marsh, *Hastings Rashdall: Dean of Carlisle 1917-1924*, Whitley Bay: Dorothy Postle, 2000.

[57] Hastings Rashdall, letter to the editor, *Times*, 31 March 1899, p. 5.

[58] Minutes of the Executive Committee, 31 May 1899 (RHA LH1/1, pp. 9-14).

[59] Thomas W. Jex-Blake, letter to the editor, *Times*, 20 July 1899, p. 7. Cf. the appeal for money in the *Times*, 1 September 1899, p. 6.

in Richmond Hill Road, Edgbaston.[60] The house had accommodation for a principal, his family and servants, and up to five students, who stayed for one year. The principal was John Masterman,[61] and he started with two students, joined by a third at the beginning of 1900.[62]

There was soon tension over the College's aims, in particular its proscription of "unauthorized variations, doctrinal or ceremonial" to the prayer-book.[63] After a quiet day for local clergy held at the College on 1 June 1900, the rector of Birmingham, A. J. Robinson, reported to the governors an eye-witness statement that the Vicar of Edgbaston, Canon Strange, presiding at the quiet day communion, had taken the eastward position, worn a coloured stole, and mixed the wine with water. "The Chairman [Jex-Blake] & Mr. Buxton supported the view of Canon Robinson that this was altogether inconsistent with the *raison d'être* of the [Midland Clergy College]."[64] The principal was called in to the meeting, and after he denied that the mixing had taken place *during* the service, the governors resolved that the principal himself should preside on future quiet days; but by November, Masterman had accepted another post and, as principal, resigned. Against the wishes, significantly, of Rashdall and another liberal governor, Herbert Ryle (Hulsean Professor of Divinity and President of Queens' College, Cambridge), and against the advice by letter of Perowne, the governors accepted Masterman's resignation.[65]

The new principal was John Harford-Battersby,[66] Vice-Principal of Wycliffe

---

[60] Newspaper cutting (RHA LH2/1, p. 1). The diocese of Worcester covered Birmingham until 1905, when under Perowne's successor Charles Gore, Birmingham became a separate see.

[61] John Howard Bertram Masterman (1867-1933) was Vicar of Devonport (1896-99), Principal of the Midlands Clergy College (1899-1900), Warden of Queen's College, Birmingham (1901-07), Vicar (and Sub-Dean from 1908) of St Michael's, Coventry (1907-12), Rector of St Mary-le-Bow, London (1912-22), and the first Bishop of Plymouth (1923-33). C. F. B. Masterman was his brother. See the obituaries in the *Times*, 27 November 1933, p. 8, the *Guardian*, 1 December 1933, p. 843, and the *Church Times*, 1 December 1933, p. 642.

[62] Record of students 1899-1900 (RHA LH2/1, pp. 53-5).

[63] College leaflet (RHA LH2/1, p. 2); cf. minutes of the Executive Committee, 31 May 1899 (RHA LH1/1), p. 10.

[64] Minutes of the Governing Body, 26 June 1900 (RHA LH1/1), p. 35.

[65] Minutes of the Governing Body, 6 November 1900 (RHA LH1/1), pp. 39-42.

[66] The governors' first choice was Sidney Arthur Alexander (1866-1948), Reader of the Temple (1893-1902), but he declined (minutes of the Governing Body sub-committee, 6 and 16 November 1900, (RHA LH1/1), pp. 42-3). Alexander became Canon Missioner of Gloucester (1902-09) and Canon Treasurer of St Paul's (1909-48).

Hall.[67] Harford-Battersby had good evangelical credentials: his father was the founder of the Keswick convention. Yet he also had liberal sympathies: as an Old Testament specialist, he had assimilated a certain amount of biblical criticism. He had studied under the "Cambridge triumvirate" of Westcott, Lightfoot and Hort,[68] and, harbouring for them much affection, had the early intention of renaming the College "Lightfoot Hall". "The Midland Clergy College" did not sound attractive, which the College above all needed to be if it was to survive; whereas "Lightfoot Hall" evoked precisely "the type of teaching we wish to give and the type of men we wish to turn out":[69] that is to say, "the love of truth, the patient scholarship, the use of historical methods of study and criticism, the fearless welcoming of light from every quarter, and the application of the truths thus ascertained to the pressing problems of individual and social life".[70] The name "Lightfoot Hall" was duly adopted by the governors in June 1901.

The Hall, however, always struggled to attract students. Masterman had felt that finding students was the governors' responsibility, and not his own.[71] Two fresh faces appeared for October 1900, replacing the two first students who had been ordained, and four more each in 1901 and 1902.[72] The half-fee scholarships handled by the governors at Oxford and Cambridge were slow to attract candidates,[73] and the College failed to make much local impact.[74] Harford-Battersby mooted the possibility of a merge with Queen's, Birmingham, retaining both sites, in his first report to the governors,[75] but the governors "were not at present prepared to consider" it.[76]

The governors were more willing to run with Harford-Battersby's suggestion, five months later, of a public meeting to celebrate Lightfoot's memory and effect

---

[67] John Harford-Battersby (1857-1937) was Vicar of Pembury (1889-98), Vice-Principal of Ridley Hall, Cambridge (1898-1900), Principal of the Midlands Clergy College (1901-02), Principal of Ripon Clergy College (1902-12 and 1915), and Canon of Ripon (1911-37). See Bullock, *History of Ridley Hall*, pp. 300 and 367, and the recollections of R. S. Mills entitled "The Staff" (RHA M27/1). He changed his name on 6 May 1902 to John Battersby Harford (Bullock, *History of Training for the Ministry*, p. 45).

[68] For whom see Peter B. Hinchliff, *God and History: Aspects of British Theology 1875-1914*, Oxford: Clarendon Press, 1992, pp. 73-98.

[69] Principal's report to the Governing Body, 6 June 1901 (RHA LH2/1), pp. 26-7.

[70] Circular letter from John Battersby Harford, 24 September 1901 (RHA LH2/1, p. 47).

[71] Principal's report to the Governing Body, June 1900 (RHA LH2/1), p. 8.

[72] Record of students 1900-02 (RHA LH2/1, pp. 56-65).

[73] College leaflet (RHA LH2/1, p. 13).

[74] Cf. minutes of the Governing Body, 3 June 1902 (RHA LH1/1), p. 52.

[75] Principal's report to the Governing Body, 6 June 1901 (RHA LH2/1), pp. 24-6.

[76] Minutes of the Governing Body, 6 June 1901 (RHA LH1/1), p. 46.

something of a plug for the Hall,[77] not, as Harford-Battersby suggested, in Birmingham with Frederick Temple, the Archbishop of Canterbury, in attendance, but under the archbishop's auspices at Lambeth Palace.[78] This took place on 18 January 1902, and saw Harford-Battersby unpack his five hallmarks of the Hall's education, but brought no dramatic turn in student numbers.[79]

Financial strain therefore compelled the governors in June 1902 to consider moving from Birmingham, and "putting the College into definite Diocesan connexion".[80] The Hall was not financially viable with the small number of students it accommodated, and the governors felt that associating the Hall more closely with a bishop, as other colleges had done, would provide the support which the Hall could not generate on its own, while the tradition of the Hall would be guaranteed by their own retention of the power to appoint the principal. They resolved to investigate the location of the College at Peterborough (where Barlow was by now Dean), Exeter (where Ryle was by now bishop) "or elsewhere", and meet again in a month's time.[81]

By the next meeting, Ripon had become a possibility.[82] There were no immediate prospects at Peterborough, and Ryle had indicated that the chapter and clergy of Exeter were too high for the Hall to be established successfully there. Bishop's College, Ripon, had, however, a vacancy in the principalship, and its unwritten ethos matched the tradition of Lightfoot Hall as it had been set out by Harford-Battersby (now Battersby Harford).[83] Jex-Blake seems to have been content to terminate his own involvement on the withdrawal of the Hall from Birmingham, for the governors agreed to proceed with discussion on the terms that Battersby Harford would be principal of the new college, Boyd Carpenter would chair the new Governing Body, the Governing Body would retain the power of appointment of the principal, and the new college would continue to cater only for graduates. In August, Boyd Carpenter chaired a joint meeting of the two institutions' governing bodies which accepted these terms, and agreed that the new college would begin in October;[84] and at meetings the following month, it was

[77] Principal's report to the Governing Body, 8 November 1901 (RHA LH2/1), pp. 36-7.

[78] Minutes of the Governing Body, 8 November 1901 (RHA LH1/1), p. 49.

[79] *Report of a Meeting held at Lambeth Palace in Support of the Claims of Lightfoot Hall* (RHA LH2/1, p. 51); cf. Stephenson, *Rise and Decline of English Modernism*, pp. 81-2.

[80] Minutes of the Governing Body, 3 June 1902 (RHA LH1/1), p. 52.

[81] Ibid., p. 53.

[82] Minutes of the Governing Body, 4 July 1902 (RHA LH1/1), p. 55-7.

[83] Cf. Alan M. G. Stephenson, "Theology in the Theological College", *Modern Churchman* 9 (1965), pp. 88-101 at 99.

[84] Minutes of the Governing Body, 19 August 1902 (RHA LH1/1), pp. 58-60.

Figure 5.1. Bishop's College, Ripon

Figure 5.2. Ripon Ordination Group 1908

decided that the new college would be called Ripon Clergy College, and its subscribers, known previously as the Midland Clergy College Corporation, would be called the Ripon Clergy College Corporation.[85] In October 1902, Battersby Harford and four Lightfoot students began at Ripon, bringing the number of students at Ripon for the first time into double figures, and the Midland Clergy College Corporation, which had been responsible for training twelve priests in the Church of England, closed. A final notice to members in February 1903 read,

> Since M. C. C. Corporation first began its work in 1899, Theological Colleges have been formed on the same lines in both the Northern and the Southern Province, by Bishops with whom M. C. C. C. is in full sympathy; and the Governors believe that by merging in one College two separate Foundations, a Clergy School or College may be founded on a stronger and more durable basis than was possible for each singly ... Really "We run our old course in a country new."[86]

Stephenson was right to claim that the chief significance of the amalgamation, historically speaking, was that Rashdall now joined Boyd Carpenter on the Governing Body of Ripon Clergy College.[87]

---

[85] Minutes of the Governing Body sub-committee, 15 September 1902 (RHA LH1/1), pp. 63-4.

[86] Governors' report and accounts, February 1903 (RHA LH1/1, p. 70).

[87] Stephenson, "Ripon Hall", p. 307, and *Rise and Decline of English Modernism*, p. 83, where he claims that Glazebrook also saw his governorship transferred. Glazebrook, however, does not seem to have joined the governors until October 1914 (minutes of the corporation annual general meeting, 12 October 1914 (RHA RCC 1/1, p. 2)). Stephenson himself noted this with a marginal annotation in the minutes of the Governing Body for November 1914 (RHA RCC 1/2, p. 239).

Henry Major at Ripon, 1906-14[88]

Henry Dewsbury Alves Major was born at Plymouth on 28 July 1871, to Henry Daniel Major and Mary Ursula Alves.[89] He was the oldest of four children, though his only sister died at the age of 8, and one of his brothers died in 1893 at the age of 21.[90] In 1878, the family emigrated to Katikati, a remote part of New Zealand which had only recently been settled, and the young Henry's farm-work in this volcanic region stimulated an interest in geology.[91] He did not get on with his father, and was encouraged by the local vicar and bishop to apply to St John's College, Auckland,[92] for further education and theological training under the

---

[88] For Major, see W. Gordon Fallows, "In Memoriam: Henry Dewsbury Alves Major, 1871-1961", *Modern Churchman* 4 (1961), pp. 153-4 (the address at his funeral); James S. Bezzant, "In Memoriam: Henry Dewsbury Alves Major, 1871-1961", *Modern Churchman* 4 (1961), pp. 155-9; Charles E. Raven, "Our Debt to Dr. Major", *Modern Churchman* 4 (1961), pp. 218-21; Alan M. G. Stephenson, "Henry Dewsbury Alves Major (1871-1961)", *Dictionary of National Biography 1961-1970*, Oxford: Oxford University Press, 1981, pp. 715-16; Stephenson, *Rise and Decline of English Modernism*; and, for the fullest treatment, Pearson, *H. D. A. Major and English Modernism 1911-1948*. Material subsequent to Pearson includes David P. Pym, "Henry Major's Modernism: Its Criticism in the Early Writings of Alan Richardson", *Modern Churchman* 33 (1991), pp. 31-8; Clive R. Pearson, "Henry Dewsbury Alves Major: 1871-1961", in *The Dictionary of New Zealand Biography*, vol. 3, Auckland and Wellington, New Zealand: Auckland University Press and Department of Internal Affairs, 1996, p. 325; C. Richard Truss, "Response", in Jonathan R. Clatworthy (ed.), *The New Liberalism: Faith for the Third Millennium*, London: Modern Churchpeople's Union, 1998, pp. 109-15; Adrian Hastings, "'On Modernism': Centenary Lecture, given at Lambeth Palace, 10 November 1998", *Modern Believing* 40/2 (1999), pp. 5-15; and Brierley, "Introducing the Early British Passibilists", pp. 223-7. There were obituaries in the *Times*, 28 January 1961, p. 8 (cf. the additional remarks in the *Times*, 31 January, 10 February and 16 February), the *Guardian*, 28 January 1961, the *Manchester Guardian*, 30 January 1961 (by Ronald Preston), the *Church Times*, 3 February 1961, and the *Churchman*, May 1961, p. 9.

[89] Major's father died in 1902, and his mother died in 1904 while he was in Oxford.

[90] The remaining brother, Arthur C. Major, ran a newspaper in New Zealand before becoming a lawyer.

[91] For the reasons for the migration, and bibliography pertaining to the settlement at Katikati, see Pearson, *H. D. A. Major and English Modernism*, p. 30 nn. 19 and 20, and the volume by Gray listed on p. 302. There is further material in Pearson's useful annotated transcript (being prepared at the time of writing (October 2003) and intended for publication) of the manuscript of Major's early autobiography (Major, *Autobiography (to 1908)*, Bodl., H. D. A. Major papers NB1).

[92] Major, *Autobiography (to 1908)*, pp. 12-16; letter from M. J. Thorp, 1 November 1967, Bodl., H. D. A. Major papers M25/1.

warden, William Beatty.[93] In 1890, therefore, despite his father's opposition,[94] Major moved to Auckland and commenced his studies, completing through New Zealand University a bachelor of arts degree in 1894, and a master's in geology in 1895.[95] That same year, Beatty became Vicar of St Mark's, Remuera, Auckland, and Major was ordained as his curate.[96] During his curacy, Major met his wife, Mary McMillan, who brought him, through marriage, the sizeable private income that would later assist his modernist enterprises.[97]

Major was *locum tenens* Vicar of Waitotara (1899-1900), and then Vicar of Hamilton (1900-02). His parish ministry made him aware of a general indifference towards Christian faith; and at both Remuera and Hamilton he started a gymnasium to demonstrate that the Church could be robust and attractive. But he also became aware at Hamilton that theology in the Anglican Church in New Zealand was slow to assimilate the new knowledge of higher criticism, and so in 1903 he came to expand his theological horizons with undergraduate study at Oxford (1903-05),[98] where his clerical orders were put to local use: he covered two Sundays at Longworth in September 1904 for J. R. Illingworth, of *Lux Mundi* fame;[99] filled in at St Martin's and All Saints', Oxford, in July 1905;[100] provided

[93] William Beatty was Warden of St John's College, Auckland, 1887-94. For Beatty, see Allan K. Davidson, *Selwyn's Legacy: The College of St John the Evangelist, Te Waimate and Auckland, 1843-1992: A History*, Auckland, New Zealand: College of Saint John the Evangelist, 1993, pp. 112-13 and 116.

[94] Major, *Autobiography (to 1908)*, p. 13. Cf. letter from Major to Mary McMillan, 25 January 1898 (RHA M0/2).

[95] Major's thesis for his master's degree, "The Volcanic District of the Whangarei Heads", is preserved in Bodl., H. D. A. Major papers M25/2.

[96] Major was ordained deacon on 22 December 1895, and priest on 20 December 1896, by Bishop Cowie of Auckland in St Mark's Church, Remuera.

[97] Pearson, *H. D. A. Major and English Modernism*, p. 32 n. 23. They married on All Saints' Day 1899, not, as Pearson states, when Major was Vicar of Hamilton.

[98] Cf. letter from Major to Mary Major, 29 July 1902 (RHA M0/2).

[99] Letters from J. R. Illingworth to Major, 2 July and 17 September 1904 (RHA RCC M0/1). Cf. Major, *Autobiography (to 1908)*, pp. 35 and 66.

[100] Letters from A. J. Carlyle to Major, 24 May, 28 May, 28 June and 14 July 1905 (RHA M1/103-6). Cf. letter from Major to John Battersby Harford, 28 December 1905 (RHA P1/442), and letter from A. J. Carlyle to John Battersby Harford, 30 December 1905 (RHA P1/443).

Figure 5.3. Henry Major

assistance at South Hinksey in the autumn;[101] and in December, became an honorary curate to Charles Whittuck at the University Church, Oxford.[102] He was minded, however, to take up work in a theological college.[103] In New Zealand in 1901 he had applied for the wardenship of St John's, Auckland,[104] and the year he arrived in England, he wrote an article for the *Westminster Review*, arguing that laypeople felt distanced from the clergy by what they perceived as a lack of reason in clerical teaching. "We believe it to be due," he suggested, "to the type of training given to the clergy by many of the theological colleges," which turned good laymen into ecclesiastics.[105]

Meanwhile, Ripon Clergy College was undergoing a few changes of staff. The ordination of several members of the amalgamated college had brought a decline in numbers, so that one of the tutors, Stanley Legg, had to be given notice, while the other, Fred Wright, was made vice-principal;[106] but the College suffered a blow in August 1904 when Wright was killed with three other climbers in a fall in the Italian Alps. He was replaced by the Old Testament scholar Lawrence Brown, who started as chaplain and tutor in the autumn of 1904,[107] and by William Coombs,

---

[101] Letters from William Curry to Major, 4 October and 28 November 1905 (RHA M1/189 and M0/1).

[102] See Major, *Autobiography (to 1908)*, p. 66, and the letters from Whittuck to Major in RHA M0/3. Whittuck was Vicar 1905-23.

[103] Major, *Autobiography (to 1908)*, p. 66. Cf. Major's letter to Boyd Carpenter, 6 April 1911 (RHA VP1/4): "I gave up parish-work deliberately in order to do theological college work because I thought the Church stood a very good chance of being ruined by the type of men many of our theological colleges are turning out."

[104] Davidson, *Selwyn's Legacy*, p. 125. References from the lecturer in modern languages and literature, and the Bishop of Wellington, are preserved in Bodl., H. D. A. Major papers M25/1; the post eventually went in September 1902 to Harold Anson. The following year, he served briefly on the College's Governing Body as the Bishop of Wellington's representative (Major, *Autobiography (to 1908)*, p. 45; cf. Davidson, *Selwyn's Legacy*, p. 327). Major was also an examiner on the New Zealand Board of Theological Studies (testimonial from John Haselden, 3 November 1902 (RHA M0/1)). Cf. letter from Major to Mary Major, 18 September 1902 (RHA M0/2).

[105] Major, "Want of Confidence in the Clergy", *Westminster Review* 160 (1903), pp. 462-5 at 464.

[106] Minutes of the Governing Body, 2 May 1903, and of the Governing Body Executive Committee, 12 June 1903 (RHA RCC 1/2), pp. 37-8 and 41.

[107] Sydney Lawrence Brown (died 1947) was Vice-Principal of Bishop's Hostel, Newcastle (1905-10), Warden of St Asaph and Bangor Clergy Education School (1910-15), Rector of Fryerning (1915-27), Vicar of Brentwood (1927-35), Professor of Hebrew and Old Testament at King's College, London (1935-47), and Canon of Worcester (1944-47).

who came in 1905 as senior lecturer and also rector of Copgrove.[108] In 1905, Brown was appointed Vice-Principal of the Bishop's Hostel at Newcastle, and his place was taken in October by H. H. Williams. Williams, however, had a crisis of faith, and left at the end of term.[109] The College was therefore on the lookout again.

Battersby Harford wrote to Willoughby Allen, the sub-rector of Exeter College, Oxford.[110] Allen replied on 23 December 1905,

> My dear Principal,
>   Is marriage a bar? If not I know an admirable man Rev H D A Major 26 Polstead Road Oxford. He is a New Zealander and held a cure of souls there. He came to Oxford three years ago to take a degree and has means sufficient to enable him to live here with a wife and two children. He obtained the Greek Testament Prize in 1904 and a 1st in Theology in 1905. He is a man of wide reading and general attainment about 34 years old. I have never heard him lecture but am told that he is a good preacher and am sure that he would be a good teacher. His one drawback is that he is a little deaf and (in consequence perhaps) a little awkward and gauche in society. But he is most interesting to talk to and gets

[108] William Reginald Coombs (died 1955) was Rector of Copgrove and Senior Tutor of Ripon Clergy College (1905-10), and Vicar of St John with St Barnabas, Leeds (1910-18), Bishop Thornton (1918-20), Holy Trinity, Habergham Eaves (1920-28), Adlington (1928-37), and Warton (1937-47).

[109] For Williams, see Geoffrey Tillotson, "Harold Herbert Williams: 1880-1964", *Proceedings of the British Academy* 51 (1965), pp. 455-66, and Geoffrey Tillotson, "Sir Harold Herbert Williams (1880-1964)", *Dictionary of National Biography 1961-1970*, Oxford: Oxford University Press, 1981, pp. 1079-81. Williams, who had excelled in theology at Christ's College, Cambridge, and held a curacy in Devon 1904-05, went back to Devon after his term at Ripon, as curate of Crediton, and resigned his orders in 1909 "having seemingly come to want more freedom of judgement than was suitable for a cleric" (Tillotson, "Harold Herbert Williams", p. 1080; cf. Williams's letters to John Battersby Harford (RHA P1/1025-30)). In due course he became a critic of modern English literature, distancing himself from his clerical past: when Stephenson tracked him down during his researches of the 1960s, Williams replied, "Dear Sir, I cannot in the least remember holding the position at Ripon Hall to which you refer, and very unlikely it is. Yours sincerely" (letter from Harold Williams to Alan Stephenson, 4 February 1963 (RHA M27/1)).

[110] Willoughby Charles Allen (1867-1953) was Chaplain and Fellow of Exeter College (1894-1908), Principal of Egerton Hall, Manchester (1908-14), Archdeacon of Manchester (1909-16), Archdeacon of Blackburn (1916-20), Rector of Chorley (1916-22), and Rector of Saham Toney (1922-32). He was a New Testament specialist, and wrote the I. C. C. commentary on Matthew. After he became Archdeacon of Manchester, he had a long exchange of views with Major in the pages of the *Modern Churchman*. See Allen's letters to the editor, *Modern Churchman* 2 (1913), pp. 483-4, 533-4 and 584-6, in response to Major, "The Advent Hope", *Modern Churchman* 2 (1912), pp. 406-12, and Major's replies, *Modern Churchman* 2 (1913), pp. 484-5, 534-7 and 586-8.

on admirably with young men as he is sympathetic in manner and has many interests. He is a strong Churchman of moderate views and would teach nothing extreme but is a man of strong personal religion.[111]

Battersby Harford wrote to Major on 26 December, stating that Williams had been "unexpectedly called elsewhere", and giving details of the lectureship which "in your case would probably mean the Vice Principalship, if we found ourselves in accord".[112] The two men met in London two days later. Major wrote to Battersby Harford on 4 January, "I am quite willing to accept the post of Chaplain & Lecturer at Ripon College. I have for several years wanted to do theological College work, & it is largely for that reason that I have taken a degree in theology here – for I regard the future usefulness of the Church as largely dependent upon the influence of its theological Colleges."[113] Major was happy to reside in the College in term-time as required, but Boyd Carpenter did not think that this was compatible with Major's marriage, and so the appointment was made subject to final approval after a term's trial. Hence, at the end of the first term, Battersby Harford reported to the Governing Body that such was Major's work as chaplain that he desired to make him Vice-Principal.[114] Soon afterwards, Boyd Carpenter made Major his librarian.[115] His family, having spent the first term in Oxford, were installed in September in a house in Ripon.[116]

It was during the period from Major's commencement at Ripon in January 1906 to his first edition of the *Modern Churchman* in April 1911 that his theology made the alignment with modernism which was to prove so decisive for the direction of his life and influential for English theology. The mature expression of

---

[111] Letter from Willoughby Allen to John Battersby Harford, 23 December 1905 (RHA P1/431). Major, it seems, had done some sort of care or supervision of a couple of students (letter from Willoughby Allen to Major, 15 June 1905 (RHA RCC M0/1)).

[112] Letter from John Battersby Harford to Major, 26 December 1905 (RHA M0/1).

[113] Letter from Major to John Battersby Harford, 4 January 1905 (sic) (RHA P1/435). Major wrote to Battersby Harford at the end of his first term, "I have thought it was a kind of work in which I might best serve the Church, & I certainly have found my first experience of it very congenial" (letter from Major to John Battersby Harford, 26 March 1906 (RHA P1/446)), and again, at the end of the summer, "I am quite satisfied & count myself greatly blessed in having the opportunity of doing work which I have wished for some years to be able to do" (letter from Major to John Battersby Harford, 26 September 1906 (RHA P1/451)).

[114] Minutes of the Governing Body Executive Committee, 19 March 1906 (RHA RCC 1/2), p. 81. He was made vice-principal from October 1906.

[115] Major, *Autobiography (to 1908)*, pp. 77-9. He remained librarian to the Bishop of Ripon until 1919.

[116] Letter from Major to Mary Major, 1 May 1906 (RHA M0/2).

Major's theology is to be found in his Noble lectures delivered at Harvard in 1925-26, published as *English Modernism*,[117] but his basic doctrinal position was firm by early in the First World War. It is therefore important to understand the nature of his theological position in January 1906, and how it developed and was expressed up to 1915.

Apart from the essentially Tractarian religious influence exerted on the young Major by his mother and his vicar, William Katterns,[118] the theology of Major when in New Zealand was influenced by three main sources. First, it was shaped by his theological tutor, William Beatty, who belonged "to the old-fashioned Broad church school of which Maurice and Kingsley were the typical representatives".[119] Major wrote of Beatty, "he indoctrinated me" – not least, as a devotee of Maurice, in the rejection of hell.[120] Second, Major's view of the bible was affected by his concurrent education in science, and particularly by his professor in natural science, Algernon Thomas, who "compelled [Major] to believe in biological evolution".[121] "Evolution became for me the Divine *method* of creation ... I had learnt to think of the Universe as a process."[122] Third, Major's reading of a Swedenborgian tract seems to have helped him towards the conclusion around which much of his theology was framed, that the value of the scriptures (and anything else) lay primarily in its "spiritual and moral truth".[123] The earliest extant theological writings of Major, and the only ones from his time in New Zealand, are sermons preserved from his days as Vicar of Hamilton, some in manuscript, and some published in the *Waikato Times*.[124] While they are not

[117] Major, *English Modernism: Its Origin, Methods, Aims: Being the William Belden Noble Lectures delivered in Harvard University, 1925-1926*, Cambridge, MA: Harvard University Press, and London: Humphrey Milford, 1927.

[118] For Katterns, see Major, *Autobiography (to 1908)*, pp. 12-3.

[119] *Church Gazette*, July 1928, p. 7, cited in Davidson, *Selwyn's Legacy*, p. 112.

[120] Major, *Autobiography (to 1908)*, p. 30, and Major, "A Modernist's Pilgrimage: Summary of an Address delivered to the Society for the Study of Religions on 17th. January, 1946", *Religions* 55 (1946), pp. 4-11 at 5. Cf. Major, "The Renaissance of F. D. Maurice", *Modern Churchman* 41 (1951), pp. 99-103 at 102-3.

[121] Major, *Autobiography (to 1908)*, pp. 33-4. There is material on Thomas in Clive Pearson's annotated transcript of the autobiography.

[122] Major, "Modernist's Pilgrimage", p. 5 (Major's emphasis).

[123] He was also influenced at this time by Illingworth's *Personality: Human and Divine* (Major, *Autobiography (to 1908)*, pp. 34-5). Clive Pearson examines some of the connections between the theologies of Major and Illingworth in his annotated transcript of Major's autobiography.

[124] Major, *New Zealand Sermons*, Bodl., H. D. A. Major papers NB2.

remarkable, Major demonstrates in them a capacity for biblical criticism,[125] and his acceptance of Broad Church teaching concerning eternal torment.[126]

Anglican New Zealand biblical criticism, however, was not enough for Major.[127] He came across a BD examination paper from the University of Durham, and did not understand its questions.[128] This was one of the reasons for his decision to undertake further learning at Oxford,[129] where under the biblical critics Samuel Driver, successor to Pusey as Regius Professor of Hebrew, and William Sanday, Lady Margaret Professor of Divinity,[130] "Major made the most fundamental revision of the tradition of faith he had received".[131] Major was soon writing about the impact that biblical criticism had on theological studies,[132] and engaging with books on comparative religion, on account of having to teach it at Ripon.[133]

When writing about the lectureship in Ripon, Battersby Harford had commented, "Ours is a non-party College ... The teaching Staff may be described as moderate liberal Evangelical Churchmen, if you take these words in their *best* sense – Lightfoot, Hort, Westcott, Sanday & our friend W. C. Allen may represent

---

[125] See for example Major's sermon on the synoptic apocalypses ("Signs of the Times"), *New Zealand Sermons*, pp. 73-85.

[126] Major, *New Zealand Sermons*, pp. 40-1 and 65.

[127] For the relative conservatism of Anglican theology in New Zealand in the 1890s, see Davidson, *Selwyn's Legacy*, pp. 114-16.

[128] Major, *Autobiography (to 1908)*, p. 54.

[129] Another reason for moving was Major's living accommodation in Hamilton (Major, *Autobiography (to 1908)*, pp. 54-5).

[130] Major wrote memorials to Sanday and Driver in the *Modern Churchman*: "In Memoriam: Samuel Rolles Driver", *Modern Churchman* 3 (1914), pp. 609-12, and "In Memoriam: William Sanday, DD, LL.D., Litt.D., FBA", *Modern Churchman* 10 (1920), pp. 407-13.

[131] Pearson, *H. D. A. Major and English Modernism*, p. 34; cf. Major, *Autobiography (to 1908)*, pp. 57-64.

[132] For example, Major, "St Paul's Presentation of Christ", in F. W. Orde Ward (ed.), *Lux Hominum: Studies of the Living Christ in the World of To-day*, London: Francis Griffiths, 1907, pp. 251-94 at 255-7; and two pamphlets by Major in the library of Ripon College, Cuddesdon, *The Bearing of Modern Biblical Study upon the Interpretation of the Old Testament*, Manuals of the Biblical Study Society, ed. Hewlett Johnson, 1908, and *The New Light and the Old Bible*, 1911.

[133] Major, "Modernist's Pilgrimage", pp. 7-9, and Pearson, *H. D. A. Major and English Modernism*, pp. 47-53. The fruit of this study can be seen in Major, *The Science of Religion and its Bearings upon Christian Claims*, London: Francis Griffiths, 1909, and Major, "The Science of Religion and the Religion of the Future", *Interpreter* 7 (1911), pp. 303-13, reprinted in Major, *The Gospel of Freedom*, London: T. Fisher Unwin, 1912, pp. 169-84.

our line."[134] Major replied, "I daresay you may wish to know exactly where I stand in the matter of 'views' ... I am a member of no Church organisation or party, as I do not believe in them."[135] Relatively little is known about Major's conscious conversion to the modernist cause. After a term at Ripon, Major was keen to meet Rashdall, one of the governors, who was a member of the Churchmen's Union.[136] Major decided to join the Churchmen's Union during convalescence from very serious pneumonia, which afflicted him on return from a trip to the Holy Land, in March-May 1907.[137] In September 1907 he wrote to Battersby Harford,

> I think I ought to tell you that I intend joining the Churchmen's Union. I have never belonged to any society within the Church existing to represent the views of a party, but reflection in the leisure of convalescence has compelled me to see that parties can only be opposed by parties. The Liberal-Church view gets little consideration because Liberal Churchmen are unorganised & isolated.[138]

Major first attended the annual meeting of the Churchmen's Union in 1908, and in May 1909 his vocation for theological teaching and his developing allegiance to modernism converged in a lecture to the Churchmen's Union at St Martin's-in-the-Fields on the need for a liberal theological college.[139] By 1911 he was a member of the Union's council, and he rapidly became a focus for the movement's organisation and strategy.

The result for Major's doctrine of all these influences – Broad Church, evolution, Swedenborgianism, biblical criticism, comparative religion and the

[134] Letter from John Battersby Harford to Major, 26 December 1905 (RHA M0/1, Battersby Harford's emphasis).

[135] Letter from Henry Major to John Battersby Harford, 28 December 1905 (RHA P1/442).

[136] Letter from Major to John Battersby Harford, Easter Monday 1906 (RHA P1/448). For the founding and early history of the Churchmen's Union, see Stephenson, *Rise and Decline of English Modernism*, pp. 55-75.

[137] Stephenson, *Rise and Decline of English Modernism*, p. 87. The trip and illness may explain why the only comment by Major on the affair of R. J. Campbell is the brief allusion in Major, *Gospel of Freedom*, pp. 172-3. For the affair, see the bibliography in Michael W. Brierley, "Naming a Quiet Revolution: The Panentheistic Turn in Modern Theology", in Arthur R. Peacocke and Philip D. Clayton (eds), *"In Whom We Live and Move and Have our Being": Reflections on Panentheism in a Scientific Age*, Grand Rapids, MI: William B. Eerdmans Publishing Co., forthcoming, n. 102; and also Thomas A. Langford, *In Search of Foundations: English Theology 1900-1920*, Nashville, NY: Abingdon Press, 1960, pp. 32-40.

[138] Letter from Major to John Battersby Harford, 30 September 1907 (RHA P1/459).

[139] The *Times*, 24 May 1909, p. 19; cf. Major, "Theological Colleges", *Modern Churchman* 1 (1911), pp. 441-7 and 505-13.

Churchmen's Union – which themselves derived principally from the enlightenment project of science, but also from idealist philosophy and religious experience (as amplified by mysticism),[140] was panentheism. Panentheism was one of the features of English modernism identified by Alan Stephenson.[141] Elsewhere, I have identified a number of linguistic and doctrinal hallmarks of panentheism, the presence of which can indicate how far a given theologian is a panentheist: description of the cosmos as God's body; language of God working "in and through" the cosmos; description of the cosmos as a sacrament; language of "inextricable intertwining"; assertion that God is to some extent dependent on the cosmos; assignment of intrinsic, positive value to the cosmos; the doctrine of passibility; and a degree christology.[142]

A number of these characteristics can be found in Major's writings up to 1915, demonstrating that his doctrine was (not unambiguously) panentheistic. Perhaps the most important is the language of God working "in and through" the cosmos: God is "in" the cosmos (divine immanence), and yet the word "through" implies that there is more to God than merely the cosmos (divine transcendence). Thus Major, in his earliest essay after leaving Oxford, claimed that revelation is "not independent of, but limited, coloured, expressed, by the human consciousness through which it is made".[143] A few years later, he wrote, "The general acceptance of the theory of creation by evolution – as a process still in existence – seemed to compel theologians to recognize God as working in and through His creation".[144] God is "ever creating not from without but from within", "in and through the inspired human consciousness".[145] In his Noble lectures, Major asserted that although God was still prior to, and independent of, creation, "God is in all things,

---

[140] Cf. Major, *English Modernism*, p. 103, and Pearson, *H. D. A. Major and English Modernism*, p. 45. Major was not adverse in his early writings to referring to God as "ideal".

[141] Stephenson, *Rise and Decline of English Modernism*, p. 7. Stephenson (p. 194) remarks that Major used the word panentheism "early in the century": references which I have found are Major's description of a poem by Emily Bronte as "panentheistic" in "The Theology in the Last Lines of Emily Bronte", *Modern Churchman* 1 (1911), pp. 458-62 at 460 (cf. p. 461); and his description of God's relation to creation as "panentheistic" in "Christology of the Twentieth Century", *Modern Churchman* 25 (1936), pp. 675-81 at 681.

[142] Brierley, "Naming a Quiet Revolution".

[143] Major, "St Paul's Presentation of Christ", p. 257.

[144] Major, "Theological Readjustment", *Interpreter* 8 (1912), pp. 171-83, reprinted in *Gospel of Freedom*, pp. 91-109, at 174.

[145] Major, "An Apology for Modern Churchmen", *Modern Churchman* 3 (1913), pp. 11-17 and 76-84 at 81-2.

but not equally, and all things, but not equally, are in God".[146] Major saw that reconfiguration of the traditional doctrine of God had implications for a host of dependent doctrines, such as original sin, the atonement, resurrection, the ascension, and the second coming.[147]

In connection with God creating and revealing Godself through the natural processes and laws of the universe, Major held a panentheistic conception of miracle. This denies any interventionist or irruptionist method of divine action, since God cannot override God. Hence any miraculous event or phenomenon must have a natural explanation, whether or not that explanation is known, either now or in the future. Major, who was confronted by the issue of miracle through the affair of J. M. Thompson,[148] indeed held this doctrine: he argued that a miraculous act could not be against nature, because the extent of what is natural is not known.[149] In his Noble lectures, he asserted that "nothing in Nature can be contrary to Nature", and quoted Augustine's definition of miracles as "'portents which are not contrary to Nature, but are contrary to what we know of Nature'".[150]

The other most prominent feature of panentheism in Major's early work is his degree christology.[151] Panentheists tend to think of Christ as different from other persons by degree rather than kind, because if God is somehow "in" the cosmos generally, then God's work in Christ needs to be related with some continuity to that cosmic work, and not isolated from it; otherwise there is a dichotomy between God in Christ and the rest of the cosmos. Major viewed incarnation, like creation, as a process,[152] and asserted that Christ was the "supreme manifestation" or the

[146] Major, *English Modernism*, p. 103. God "includes the whole Universe within Himself" (Major, *A Modern View of the Incarnation*, privately printed pamphlet for the Anglican Fellowship Conference, 5-7 April 1915 (RHA M25/6), p. 19).

[147] Major, "Theological Readjustment", pp. 178-81.

[148] Major, "The Case of the Rev. J. M. Thompson", *Modern Churchman* 1 (1911), pp. 237-43, and "Miracles", *Modern Churchman* 1 (1911), pp. 244-50; cf. Major, "Modernist's Pilgrimage", p. 7. For the Thompson affair, see A. Goodwin, "Reverend James Matthew Thompson: 1878-1956", *Proceedings of the British Academy* 43 (1957), pp. 271-91; W. Norman Pittenger, "James Matthew Thompson: The Martyr of English Modernism", *Anglican Theological Review* 39 (1957), pp. 291-7; Langford, *In Search of Foundations*, pp. 124-6; and Pearson, *H. D. A. Major and English Modernism*, pp. 61-7.

[149] Major, "The Danger of Appeals to the Miraculous", *Modern Churchman* 1 (1911), pp. 310-18 at 314.

[150] Major, *English Modernism*, p. 130.

[151] Stephenson noted that degree Christology was a feature of English modernism in *Rise and Decline of English Modernism*, p. 8.

[152] Major, "A Modern View of the Incarnation", *Modern Churchman* 3 (1913), pp. 465-74 at 473.

"supreme achievement" of divine immanence,[153] and that the divine nature was manifested in Jesus to a "unique degree".[154] Indeed, in his most extensive discussion of the incarnation, a paper written in 1915 which marks the end of his basic doctrinal development, Major stated that Christ differs from other persons by degree rather than by kind, although differences by degree can amount to a difference by kind;[155] and in his Noble lectures, Major again explicitly affirmed a degree christology.[156]

Passibility is a hallmark of panentheism to which Major subscribes in passing;[157] and the assignment of intrinsic, positive value to the cosmos, though not explicit, is at least implicit in Major's view of evil as privative.[158]

These hallmarks of panentheism, present in Major's early writing, therefore testify to the basic panentheistic orientation of his doctrine. The ambiguity in Major's panentheism derives from his doctrine of revelation, which ran the risk of underplaying divine revelation and immanence in nature.[159] Major held that revelation was "internal"[160] – that God revealed Godself in the growing rational, moral and spiritual faculties of the human soul, which were the highest points of creation[161] – and that the authority of this human consciousness, which was the Holy Spirit, took priority over the authorities of the bible and the Church.[162] This

---

[153] Major, review of B. H. Streeter (ed.), *Foundations*, *Modern Churchman* 2 (1913), pp. 465-76 at 471; Major, "Theological Readjustment", p. 174; and Major, "Modern View of the Incarnation", p. 471.

[154] Major, *Science of Religion*, pp. 24-5; and Major, *Modern View of the Incarnation*, p. 12.

[155] Major, *Modern View of the Incarnation*, p. 27.

[156] Major, *English Modernism*, p. 159. Cf. p. 168; Major, "The Dynamic of the Incarnation", *Modern Churchman* 16 (1926), pp. 566-80 at 567 and 570; and Major, "Christology in the Twentieth Century", pp. 678 and 680.

[157] Major, *Modern View of the Incarnation*, p. 20. For commentary, see Brierley, "Introducing the Early British Passibilists", pp. 226-7.

[158] Major, *Modern View of the Incarnation*, p. 25.

[159] Cf. Major, "Modern Churchmen and Religious Experience", *Modern Churchman* 8 (1918), pp. 193-7 at 194.

[160] Major, *Science of Religion*, p. 34.

[161] Major, "The Knowledge of God", *Magazine of St Andrew's Church, Chipping Barnet*, August 1908 (RHA M25/2); cf. Major, "Apology for Modern Churchmen", pp. 78-81, and Major, "Authority in Religion", *Optimist* 9 (1914), pp. 160-2 at 160.

[162] Major, "The Interpretation of the Bible by the Church and by the Christian Teacher", *Liberal Churchman*, March 1908, pp. 34-57, reprinted in *Gospel of Freedom*, pp. 113-41; cf. *Gospel of Freedom*, pp. vii-ix. The priority of human conscience was confirmed for Major by his reading of Bishop Butler and Samuel Coleridge (Major, "Modernist's Pilgrimage", p. 6). He conceived that human conscience could be wrong, but observed that

could leave the impression, however, that the only place where God was "in" the world was the human mind.[163] Moreover, Major's symbolisation of this revelation as the spirit of divine sonship bestowed by the Father, could also imply that the divine and the human were separate and individual entities, rather than the "one nature" which he envisaged.[164]

It is also possible to detect in Major's early writings a growing militancy. He seems to have deduced from the struggle of evolution that heroism is a virtue, and its opposite, cowardice, is a vice.[165] The fact that he regarded self-sacrifice as one of the "conditions of success" is an insight into his dedication both to Ripon Hall and to modernism.[166] He was certainly regarded by others as "a character of heroic mould".[167] This willingness to suffer for what he perceived to be the truth gives the impression that Major was expecting, if not actually looking for, a fight. "Modern Churchmen do not desire to be prosecuted; but if nothing short of prosecution can demonstrate that they have a right, as honest men, to exist within the National Church, they would be unworthy of their profession, if they were not willing to suffer for it to the uttermost."[168] Major's founding of the monthly *Modern Churchman* in 1911 can also be interpreted in terms of his increasing militancy for the modernist cause within the English Church.[169] He remained editor for forty-six years.

April 1911 was a critical month for Major. At the same time that the first issue of *Modern Churchman* brought his modernism to a new level of self-consciousness and visibility, friction and frustration began to surface at the College, and his path

historically in cases of conflict with the bible or the Church, it had been proved to be right ("Interpretation of the Bible by the Church", pp. 53-4).

[163] Cf. Pearson, *H. D. A. Major and English Modernism*, p. 27.

[164] Major, *Science of Religion*, pp. 25-6.

[165] See the address given by Major at the College reunion in 1908: "The Call of Faith", *Expository Times* 20 (1908), pp. 12-15, reprinted in *Gospel of Freedom*, pp. 187-97. Cf. Pearson, *H. D. A. Major and English Modernism*, p. 37.

[166] Major, "The Broad and the Narrow", *Modern Churchman* 3 (1913), pp. 402-5 at 405.

[167] R. H. Charles, "A Sermon Preached in Ripon Minster on January 22, 1922", in Major, *Life and Letters of William Boyd Carpenter*, pp. 321-32 at 328.

[168] Major, "Signs of the Times", *Modern Churchman* 1 (1911), pp. 110-21 at 112. Cf. Major, "Signs of the Times", *Modern Churchman* 1 (1911), pp. 408-20 at 409: "Controversy may be uncongenial, but it is often one of the most effective means of education."

[169] See Major, "Ourselves and Our Aim", *Modern Churchman* 1 (1911), pp. 7-11. For the significance of the journal for modernism and its part in the galvanisation of Major's own modernism, see Pearson, *H. D. A. Major and English Modernism*, pp. 57-60, and cf. Major, "'How Fields were Won'", *Modern Churchman* 27 (1937), pp. 195-200 at 196.

to more senior responsibility became a long and difficult one as a result. Major had given an address at Ripon in March on "The New Light and the Old Bible", which caused a local stir.[170] It led to a series of exchanges between Major and W. St Clair Tisdall in the columns of the *Ripon Observer*, and a flurry of private correspondence between Major and Battersby Harford during the Easter vacation, which turned into a debate about the College's future direction.[171] Major was mindful that Boyd Carpenter, whose personality brought the College some financial support, was ageing and infirm, and considered that the "College Ideal" with its loyalty to the truth (which ironically had been written originally by Battersby Harford for Lightfoot Hall) cut the College free from evangelical ties.[172] Battersby Harford naturally felt greater loyalty to the liberal-evangelical or evangelical-liberal governors who supported the College because of its theological position, and whose alienation would thus threaten the College's financial security. He therefore believed that the College could not be identified with any single party, and thought that this indeed suited the formation of spiritual pastors, whose critical training should not be "overdone".[173] Battersby Harford, however, agreed that the liberal contingent of the Governing Body should be strengthened,[174] resolving that he himself must join the Churchmen's Union;[175] and when, on the advice of his brother,[176] he suggested to Major that Major's pastoral position required him not to be provocative with his public views,[177] Major heightened the

---

[170] The address, which exists in pamphlet form in the library of Ripon College, Cuddesdon, was given on 7 March and reported in the *Ripon Observer* on 9 March. Cf. Pearson, *H. D. A. Major and English Modernism*, p. 44 n. 55, and the letter from Major to Hastings Rashdall, 16 May 1912 (RHA VP1/47).

[171] RHA P1/470-80. Major's own record of the correspondence is in RHA VP1/3-15.

[172] Letter from Major to John Battersby Harford, 7 April 1911 (RHA P1/471). Cf. letter from Major to John Battersby Harford, 10 April 1911 (RHA P1/475): "I feel that the heresy of Evangelicalism lies in its determination to make the N. T. say what the XXXIX articles say, or its pet leaders say. I cannot but think that this tendency causes great searchings of heart to the modern minded."

[173] Memorandum on the College by John Battersby Harford, 7 April 1911 (RHA P1/473).

[174] Major suggested some names of possible governors to William Boyd Carpenter on 10 April 1911 (RHA VP1/10).

[175] Letter from John Battersby Harford to Major, 12 April 1911 (RHA P1/476).

[176] Page of a letter from G. Harford to John Battersby Harford, undated (RHA P1/474).

[177] Letter from John Battersby Harford to Major, 21 April 1911 (RHA P1/478): "The present situation, as I read it, demands of both of us a very great deal of restraint & sound judgment. There are many things which we may wish to say & which may be quite true and yet which we must either not say or say in such a way as not to hurt & alienate those who might otherwise be friends ... It doesn't seem heroic, I know, to sit still & say nothing, but

stakes by asking curtly if he was being asked to resign the editorship of the *Modern Churchman*,[178] which Battersby Harford denied.[179]

At the same time, Major had been offered a parish back in New Zealand. He wrote to Boyd Carpenter,

> [A]lthough my views of theological colleges and their work have changed but little, I find myself wondering whether Ripon on its present lines is going to do much to change things...Most of our governors appear to be "dead-heads" ... There are many liberal minded Churchmen – cleric and lay – who might be on our Governing Board who are not there ... I am thinking of our future – and to judge by the way we are going I do not think we have very much future unless our position is greatly strengthened. Should we lose you at any time, I feel that our position would immediately become precarious. At least to put it quite plainly mine would ... There is only one thing I think I really care for and that is to bring about such an ideal of Churchmanship that thoughtful, educated, religious men may be drawn to the Church, instead of being repelled as is too often the case ... To be of real use it seems to me [Ripon] must be made stronger ... These things have been in my mind several years ... If one could liberalise the whole of the N. Z. Church it would not liberalise the Church in England; but if one did liberalise to some extent the Church in England, it would affect the Church throughout the whole Empire; that is why I feel the centre to be so important and Ripon is part of the centre.[180]

It is a sign of the precariousness that Major felt that when in 1911 the living of Copgrove (having been vacated by Coombs's move to Holbeck) was offered to Battersby Harford as an additional post, and turned down as the governors thought that the work of the College would suffer,[181] Major, aware that Boyd Carpenter was retiring and that a new bishop of Ripon might not view him so favourably, took it up instead.[182] He wrote five years later, "The reason I took Copgrove was

in many cases I am sure that for the sake of the College we must just do that. We must not compromise the College by expressing our private opinions in public ways."

[178] Letter from Major to John Battersby Harford, 21 April 1911 (RHA P1/479).

[179] Letter from John Battersby Harford to Major, 22 April 1911 (RHA P1/480).

[180] Letter from Major to William Boyd Carpenter, 6 April 1911 (RHA VP1/4). Cf. letter from Major to Mrs. Carpenter, 17 April 1909 (RHA M1); Major, *Gospel of Freedom*, pp. xvii-xviii; and letter from Major to Cecil Welland, 2 October 1915 (RHA M1): "If you want a change in the Spirit of the Church of England you must change the spirit of the clergy and you must do it mainly in the theological colleges."

[181] Minutes of the Governing Body Executive Committee, 11 February 1911 (RHA RCC 1/2), p. 149.

[182] Up to that point, Major had been acting as curate of North Stainley (Stephenson, "Henry Dewsbury Alves Major", p. 716). Major was instituted at Copgrove by the Bishop

Ambassadors of Christ

because it gave me a position by means of which I could maintain my hold on the College against the Bishop".[183]

Battersby Harford, however, who had declined a living in Bristol in 1909,[184] accepted in 1911 a residential canonry at Ripon, and when the governors in 1912 decided that this was not compatible with the principalship, he resigned as principal and became secretary to the Governing Body.[185] By now, Boyd Carpenter had been replaced as Bishop of Ripon by Thomas Drury, who became chair of the governors, with Boyd Carpenter remaining as warden.[186] Major, who in November and December 1911 had published what was effectively his manifesto for a theological college run on liberal lines,[187] privately expressed doubts that the College would survive.[188] Two of the governors in Ripon who distrusted Major for his views,[189] Kilner (the Archdeacon of Craven) and Gresford Jones (the Vicar of

of Knaresborough in November 1911 and retained the living until 1919. For six months in 1917-18 he also looked after the neighbouring, larger village of Burton Leonard. Similarly, when in Oxford, Major accepted the living of Merton when it was offered to him by his old college, Exeter, in the autumn of 1929: he was instituted by the Bishop of Oxford in January 1930, not without opposition (for which see Stephenson, *Rise and Decline of English Modernism*, p. 142), and it was the last of his responsibilities from which he stood down (in June 1960, shortly before his 89th. birthday). Cf. Pearson, *H. D. A. Major and English Modernism*, p. 8 n. 23.

[183] Letter from Major to Hastings Rashdall, undated (end of July 1916) (RHA M2). Cf. letter from Major to Alfred Lilley, 8 December 1911 (RHA M1): "a beneficed clergyman has a stability & power of defence which does not belong to his unbeneficed brother". Cf. also letter from Major to Hastings Rashdall, 30 September 1914, in which he talks of the "protection" of Copgrove against being "deprived by a zealot for orthodoxy" (RHA VP1/189); and the letter from Major to Percy Gardner, early 1912 (RHA VP1/20).

[184] Letter from John Battersby Harford to Major, 21 July 1909 (RHA M1).

[185] Minutes of the Governing Body Executive Committee, 28 March 1912 (RHA RCC 1/2), p. 160.

[186] Thomas Wortley Drury (1847-1926) was Principal of the Church Missionary College, Islington (1882-99), Principal of Ridley Hall (1899-1907), Bishop of Sodor and Man (1907-11), Bishop of Ripon (1912-20), and Master of St Catherine's College, Cambridge (1920-26). See further Bullock, *History of Ridley Hall*, pp. 357-444. Cf. the comments on Drury in the letter from J. L. G. Hill to Alan Stephenson, 8 July 1965 (RHA M27/2).

[187] Major, "Theological Colleges"; cf. Major, "Ministerial Training", *Optimist* 7 (1912), pp. 77-84.

[188] Letter from Henry Major to Percy Gardner, early 1912 (RHA VP1/20).

[189] Cf. reference to "the question of the V[ice] P[rincipal]" minutes of the Governing Body Executive Committee, 28 March 1912 (RHA RCC 1/2), p. 161; letter from Major to Percy Gardner, early 1912 (RHA VP1/20), speaking of Battersby Harford's resignation from the principalship ("& then it is not improbable that I may become Principal, unless the

Bradford), moved for Major's dismissal.[190] It was pointed out, however, that the appointment of the vice-principal lay in the hands of the principal, and the governors voted instead to call this fact to attention.[191] Major got wind of it, and drafted a letter of resignation, which he sent for advice to Rashdall;[192] but Rashdall wrote back and the resignation was not submitted.[193]

Drury chaired the sub-committee charged with producing the short-list for the principalship, and it is no coincidence that the four candidates named for interview were all of evangelical persuasion: Charles Boughton, the Vice-Principal of Wycliffe Hall;[194] G. Foster Carter, the rector of St Aldate's, Oxford; R. L. Collins, the Principal of Bishop Wilson Theological College on the Isle of Man; and J. R. Darbyshire, the Vice-Principal of Ridley Hall (later Bishop of Glasgow and Galloway).[195] Rashdall wrote to Major, "The College, as it has been for the last few years, has been the most hopeful undertaking of the Liberal party in the Church of England, and it would be an ill day for us if it were transformed into a party Evangelical Seminary".[196] Lancelot Raimes and Bernard Hartley, both old Riponians and curates of William Manning (Vicar of Chipping Barnet and secretary of the Churchmen's Union), met with Boyd Carpenter in London and

more Evangelical Governors who dislike my 'views' are able to appoint some one else"); and letter from Hastings Rashdall to Major, 29 April 1912 (RHA VP1/23).

[190] Letter from Arthur Waugh to Major, 2 June 1912 (RHA VP1/96).

[191] Minutes of the Governing Body, 13 April 1912 (RHA RCC 1/2), p. 163.

[192] Letter from Major to John Battersby Harford, 3 May 1912 (not apparently sent) (RHA VP1/31).

[193] Letter from Hastings Rashdall to Major, May 1912 (RHA VP1/26). Cf. letter from Major to John Battersby Harford, 29 June 1914 (RHA RCC4/36).

[194] Charles Henry Knowler Boughton (1883-1943) was Chaplain (1907-09) and Vice-Principal (1909-12) of Wycliffe Hall, Oxford, Principal of Ripon Clergy College (1912-14), Vicar of Calverley (1915-22), Secretary of the British and Foreign Bible Society (1922-28), and Vicar of Knighton (1928-1943).

[195] By the time of the interviews, Foster Carter had been replaced by T. W. Gilbert. Other candidates included W. K. Lowther Clarke, Rector of Cavendish (later editorial secretary of S. P. C. K.); B. K. Cunningham, Principal of Farnham Hostel (later Principal of Westcott House); Lonsdale Ragg, Rector of Tickencote; R. B. Tollinton, Rector of Tendring and son-in-law of Boyd Carpenter, and in due course chair of the Ripon Hall governors, 1924-32 (see further Major, "In Memoriam: Richard Bartram Tollinton", *Modern Churchman* 22 (1932), pp. 423-5, reprinted as "Richard Bartram Tollinton", *Modern Churchman* 46 (1956), pp. 328-9); E. S. Woods, later Bishop of Lichfield; A. W. F. Blunt, later Bishop of Bradford; and Major (minutes of the Governing Body Executive Committee, 25 April 1912 (RHA RCC 1/2), pp. 167-8). Cunningham and Tollinton declined to be considered (see letter from R. B. Tollinton to Major, 1 May 1912 (RHA VP1/28)).

[196] Letter from Hastings Rashdall to Major, 2 May 1912 (RHA VP1/30).

ascertained that he desired Major's principalship,[197] and then sent a circular to past and present Riponians inviting them to petition Drury not to make an appointment that would sever Major's connections with the College.[198] Drury then met Major about his position at the College and the public airing of his views. Major made clear that his conscience would not permit him to curtail his freedom of expression, and went away with the impression that the most he could hope for was a new principal who would not narrow down the "College Ideal", and would keep him as a colleague.[199]

Archdeacon Waugh, at the next sub-committee meeting, when the candidates were interviewed, immediately brought up Major's name, and further questioned if some of the sub-committee members, not being members of the Ripon Clergy College Corporation, had been entitled to vote on the elimination of names. Drury pressed on with the interviews, however, and the sub-committee agreed to put the names of Boughton and Collins before the Governing Body.[200] At this meeting of the governors, Waugh raised again the omission of Major, with the support of Fremantle, Rashdall, and the former principal, Henry Gee. A greater number of governors, however, were in favour of Boughton, who was duly elected.[201] One former student resigned his membership of the College Union in protest at this departure of the College from its "non-party" lines.[202]

Battersby Harford was at least open to critical thought, and the mutual tolerance, if not respect, between himself and Major had outweighed their theological differences.[203] Boughton, however, was firmly conservative, as well as

---

[197] Cf. letter from William Boyd Carpenter to Major, 28 May 1912 (RHA VP1/49).

[198] Letter from Lancelot Raimes to Mary Major, 7 May 1912 (RHA VP1/34).

[199] Letter from Major to Hastings Rashdall, 16 May 1912 (RHA VP1/47).

[200] Minutes of the Governing Body sub-committee, 17 May 1912 (RHA RCC 1/2), p. 173.

[201] Minutes of the Governing Body, 29 May 1912 (RHA RCC 1/2), pp. 176-7. For the letter Major wrote to his wife following the meeting, see RHA VP1/85. Fremantle's letter to Major following the meeting is transcribed in Stephenson, *Rise and Decline of English Modernism*, pp. 95-6. Rashdall wrote, "I cannot adequately express my indignation at the injustice with which you have been treated, or my admiration at the way you have behaved in the matter. Few men would [have] done the same" (letter from Hastings Rashdall to Major, 31 May 1912 (RHA VP1/55)).

[202] Letter from Home McCall to Major, 5 June 1912 (RHA VP1/69). Cf. letter from Home McCall to John Battersby Harford, 17 May 1913 (RHA P1/433).

[203] Cf. Wallace H. Elliott, *Undiscovered Ends: Autobiography*, London: Peter Davies, 1951, p. 64. For insight into the relationship between the two men, see the letter from John Battersby Harford to Major, 14 July 1916 (RHA M2): "We are heart & soul one in loyalty to our College ideal & probably, as you say, one in our essential convictions, the difference being that you, with a wider knowledge of modern knowledge & thought & with an intense

being more strict in discipline,[204] and his retention for himself of all chapel addresses indicated that he was suspicious of Major's teaching. He and Major "were so far apart in thought, and vision, and concept, that it was evident, at least to some of us, that before long something would crack".[205] A more serious crisis indeed arose. In 1913, Boughton privately aired his difficulties concerning Major with Drury, who urged him to continue, on the grounds that Major might be offered another post. But in June 1914, Boughton reported to the governors, "While bearing ungrudging witness to the learning, ability and devotion to his work and to the men of the V. P., I cannot say that I am altogether satisfied". He suggested that Major's lectures were not suited to the men, and that he did not receive from Major the help he desired in the discipline and devotional atmosphere of the College. In the light of fewer students, "[t]his therefore seems a suitable opportunity to ask Mr. Major to retire", and the proposal to remove Major was approved by the local governors present, provided that the absent governors were content that the matter had not been specified on the printed agenda.[206]

> It really is a most awkward situation. It means another trial of strength between the Governors who are conservative & wish for a "safe" policy and the Governors, who feel that the future is with the progressives ... I am afraid the mistake was letting Dr. Drury become Chairman & not moving [the College] two years ago.[207]

intellectual honesty & love of clearcut conclusions, come more quickly to decisions, whereas I am less sure that I know the whole of the facts & therefore hesitate to abandon positions, until I am quite sure that they are untenable." Battersby Harford's reference in this letter to his intention, when resuming the (acting) principalship of the College in 1915, to become more intimate with Major, confirms that their previous period as colleagues had been marked by some tensions.

[204] See the evangelicalisation and "de-modernisation" of the "College Ideal" in the College yearbook for 1914, compared with that for 1913, and the change in tone of the biennial College reunion (RHA RCC X8 and X9). Cf. the reference to the College as "casual" in 1911 by a former student, P. B. Phelps, in a letter to Alan Stephenson, 23 January 1963 (RHA M27/1).

[205] H. T. Horrox, "Ripon Clergy College, 1912-1913: A Memoir" (RHA X27, RH History 1), p. 10. Cf. letter from Lucius Smith (Bishop of Knaresborough) to Major, 20 June 1914 (RHA VP1/100): "I suppose I knew that a crisis was bound to come sooner or later."

[206] Minutes of the Governing Body, 18 June 1914 (RHA RCC 1/2), pp. 223-5.

[207] Letter from John Battersby Harford to Boyd Carpenter, 2 July 1914 (RHA RCC 4/253).

Major had "had no idea that the thunderbolt was coming",[208] and when Boughton asked him for his resignation,[209] sent to Rashdall for advice.[210] Rashdall was outraged at Boughton's lack of consultation,[211] and felt, with Major, that the future of liberal theological training was at stake. He wrote to Battersby Harford,

> If it were merely a question of Major's personal comfort, convenience, and prospects, he would no doubt be only too delighted to get away on any terms. But he feels – and I think rightly – that much is at stake. The great difficulty of the Liberal (even moderate Liberal) section in the Church is that all the places of Clerical education are anti-liberal. Ripon has hitherto been, as it was founded to be, the one exception. And now this is to be turned into an inferior Wycliffe Hall. Whereupon I think one ought to fight to the last gasp ... It is surely contrary to the principles of natural justice to dismiss a man without (1) giving him notice of what was intended and allowing him to be heard. (2) giving notice to the G[overning] B[ody] of the motion to be proposed.[212]

Sympathy for Major was close at hand in "the most remarkable gathering of Anglican Liberals that the century had yet seen"[213] – the first annual conference of the Churchmen's Union – which occurred within a week at Ripon,[214] and where it was decided to attempt to rescind the governors' resolution approving Major's dismissal at the next governors' meeting. Having been offered as an escape clause the livings of Pershore, and Steventon, Major decided not to resign, but to leave Ripon only if compelled. He wrote to Herbert Ryle,

[208] Letter from Major to William Boyd Carpenter, 27 June 1914 (RHA VP1/104).

[209] Letter from Charles Boughton to Major, 25 June 1914 (RHA VP1/102).

[210] Letter from Major to Hastings Rashdall, 27 June 1914 (RHA VP1/105); cf. letter from Major to John Battersby Harford, 29 June 1914 (RHA RCC 4/36).

[211] "I am utterly disgusted ... We must fight to the finish, and if they beat us, have the whole affair published in the most public way imaginable" (letter from Hastings Rashdall to Major, 28 June 1914 (RHA VP1/106)). Cf. letter from Major to Francis Kilner, 21 September 1914, and letter from Arthur Waugh to Major, 28 September 1914 (RHA VP1/177 and VP1/183).

[212] Letter from Hastings Rashdall to John Battersby Harford, 28 June 1914 (RHA RCC 4/47). Cf. letter from Wilfrid Harding to Cavendish Moxon, 11 August 1914: "To me the attempt to change the policy & distinctive teaching of the College was (2 years ago) and is now a profound mistake of far-reaching importance to the Church of England" (RHA RCC 4/318).

[213] The phrase is Stephenson's (*Rise and Decline of English Modernism*, p. 101).

[214] For the conference, see Major, "The Ripon Conference", *Modern Churchman* 4 (1914), pp. 161-73.

I confess my desire to stay and work at Ripon must seem strange, almost improper, after the resolution of the recent meeting, but my desire is based on the conviction that a theological college where a certain type of liberal ordinand can find a congenial and helpful place of training is essential for the welfare of the Church. If Ripon is to become a replica *in parvo* of Wycliffe Hall there is no particular use for it as Wycliffe Hall can do that particular work better. It would then be necessary to found a new theological college on entirely modern lines.[215]

Major thought that the best line of defence was attack.[216] Cavendish Moxon, an old Riponian, whipped up support from old members;[217] Frederic Harrison, one of the current students of the College, organised them into raising again a protest.[218] Every governor, in the weeks running up to the next meeting, was in receipt of Major's defence,[219] a letter signed by eight of the liberal governors,[220] and a letter signed by all the current students.[221] The letter from the liberal governors was quite explicit:

> In view of the previous attempt to get rid of Mr. Major as Vice-Principal and the opposition which was offered to his election as Principal, it is quite impossible to believe that the efficient motive for the present proposal is to be sought in anything but objection to his real or supposed theological opinions, or the opinions of others which have appeared in *The Modern Churchman*, of which he is the Editor.[222]

While the College governors were being canvassed over the summer, prior to their forthcoming meeting, Drury's first attempt at a solution was to get Boughton to withdraw his request to the governors to approve Major's dismissal, thus

---

[215] Letter from Major to Herbert Ryle, 16 July 1914 (RHA VP1/133).

[216] Letter from Lucius Smith to Major, 30 September 1914 (RHA VP1/188); cf. the reply, 1 October 1914 (RHA VP1/190).

[217] Letter to old members (RHA RCC 4/286); cf. letter from Cavendish Moxon to Major, 23 July 1914 (RHA VP1/141). As a result of the circular, Moxon collected over 46 letters which he passed to Waugh: see the letter from Arthur Waugh to Major, 29 September 1914 (RHA VP1/186). For the letters, see RHA RCC 4/297-350. For Moxon, who was later secretary of the Churchmen's Union (1916-19), see Stephenson, *Rise and Decline of English Modernism*, p. 282.

[218] Letter from Frederic Harrison to Major, 20 September 1914 (RHA VP1/176).

[219] Letter from Major to the governors, 29 September 1914 (RHA RCC 4/294).

[220] Letter from eight governors to the governors, undated (RHA RCC 4/278).

[221] Letter from students to the governors, 16 September 1914 (RHA RCC 4/295).

[222] Letter from eight governors to the governors, undated (RHA RCC 4/278). Drury admitted as much in a letter to John Battersby Harford, 10 July 1914 (RHA RCC 4/285).

restoring the status quo.[223] It had dawned on the liberal contingent, however, that a mere rescission of the resolution would not solve the problem, as it would leave in place both Boughton and Major, whose relationship was deteriorating. They therefore planned to go further, by censuring Boughton.[224] Drury, feeling that a rescission would be a vote of no confidence not only in Boughton, but also in the local governors, himself (as their chair) and his churchmanship, decided that if the resolution was overturned he would step down as chair.[225] He therefore prepared for the governors' meeting by obtaining for Boughton the offer of the living of Calverley, near Bradford. International war having broken out in August, Kilner (who was by now Bishop of Richmond) suggested that the College might be closed for the duration,[226] which prompted Rashdall and Waugh to send a last-minute circular to liberal governors stressing the importance of their presence at the forthcoming meeting.[227]

The letters which former students wrote in defence of Major make remarkable reading: virtually every student testifies to the influence Major had on him, and a large number suggest that in dismissing Major the College would be delivering its own death sentence. Lancelot Raimes, an old student, went further: "I feel very strongly that [the governors'] decision will either mar or make the future of the College ... It is not only the future of the College that is at stake, but, I will make bold to say, the future of the *Church.*"[228] More remarkable still is the similarity of comments fifty years later, in the recollections gathered by Alan Stephenson when researching the history of Ripon Hall in the 1960s: student after student describes Major's character in terms of excellent scholarship, fierce sincerity, and disarming charm, kindness and diffidence – qualities which made him very popular.[229] One

[223] Letters from Thomas Drury to William Boyd Carpenter, 23 August and 6 September 1914, and letter from Charles Boughton to Major, 10 September 1914 (RHA RCC 4/259, RCC 4/260, and VP1/170); cf. letter from Major to Charles Boughton, 9 September 1914 (RHA M1).

[224] Letter from Hastings Rashdall to Major, 9 September 1914 (RHA M1).

[225] Letter from Thomas Drury to William Boyd Carpenter, 2 July 1914 (RHA RCC 4/252); incomplete letter from Thomas Drury (RHA RCC 4/281); and letter from Thomas Drury to John Battersby Harford, 8 August 1919 (RHA RCC 4/207).

[226] Cf. letter from Major to Francis Kilner, 21 September 1914 (RHA VP1/177).

[227] Letter from Hastings Rashdall and Arthur Waugh to certain governors, undated (RHA RCC 4/280).

[228] Letter from Lancelot Raimes to Cavendish Moxon, 21 July 1914 (RHA RCC 4/339, Raimes's emphasis).

[229] RHA M27/1 and M27/2. Cf. Elliott, *Undiscovered Ends*, p. 64.

student recorded in his diary, "one cannot help but love him";[230] Cyril Emmet in his diary described Major as "lovable in the extreme".[231]

At a very well-attended meeting of the governors in October 1914, the governors' resolution of June was rescinded, and, moreover, an additional resolution was passed that the June resolution had intended no slur on Major's character or ability as a Christian teacher. A sub-committee led by Boyd Carpenter was appointed to look into the future of the College in the light of numbers, finances, and the war.[232] Soon afterwards, Calverley was accepted by Boughton from the beginning of 1915. Drury resigned as chair, and Boyd Carpenter was reinstated in that rôle in November 1914. The governors, sufficiently sensitive to resist putting Major in sole control, appointed Battersby Harford as acting principal.[233] Major had survived a second assault on his position on account of the theology which he propounded, but the realisation of his vision for an avowedly liberal theological college was not yet guaranteed.

Henry Major and the First World War

The outbreak of war soon made an impact on the College. By the first week of November, the College had lent six beds to Ripon Hospital to help cater for wounded soldiers,[234] and by February 1915, troops had been quartered in the

[230] Extracts from the diary of Thomas Hope Floyd for 1927 (RHA M27/2). Cf. letter from George Waight to Mary Major, 28 January 1961, Bodl., H. D. A Major papers M25/4: "No-one could fail to love him."

[231] Letter from Dorothy Emmet to Alan Stephenson, 25 April 1965 (RHA M27/2). Cf. letter from Josiah Richardson to Major (undated, c. 1911) (RHA M1) ("You are one of the very few men who make me feel I should like to call them friends. Any man, with a heart, must soon learn to love you."), and Gordon Fallows's follow-up to the obituary in the *Times* ("His was a character which inspired affection", *Times*, 16 February 1961).

[232] Minutes of the Governing Body, 12 October 1914 (RHA RCC 1/2), pp. 230-5. Cf. the letter from J. L. G. Hill to Alan Stephenson, 8 July 1965 (RHA M27/2), which remarks that the outbreak of war did the College a service.

[233] Minutes of the Governing Body, 27 November 1914 (RHA RCC 1/2), p. 240. This occasionally led to frustration: Major wrote to Battersby Harford on 14 June 1915, "I wish you would let me have *complete internal control* at Ripon" (RHA RCC 4/88, Major's emphasis); cf. letters from John Battersby Harford to Major, 17 June and 19 June 1915 (RHA M1).

[234] Minutes of the Governing Body Executive Committee, 6 November 1914 (RHA RCC 1/2), p. 237.

College properties.[235] By the end of 1915, there was only one student, and so the governors decided to close the College for the duration of the war, and the College property was let.[236] The student went to Ridley Hall.

Some old Riponians became chaplains to the forces.[237] Others, ignoring the Archbishop of Canterbury's pronouncement that clergy should not be combatants, signed up to fight, with Major's support.[238] One priest combatant was Raimes, who had trained at Ripon Clergy College 1910-11, and contributed an article "Church and Stage" to the *Modern Churchman*.[239] He had held a commission in the 5th. Durham Light Infantry prior to his ordination in 1911, and left his curacy at Chipping Barnet to become a combatant. He was killed on 1 June 1916. In an obituary in the *Modern Churchman*, Major quoted Manning, his training incumbent, who made extraordinary use of the word "splendid":

> For twenty months he was training men at home ... Then, after three weeks at the front, came the news, very brief, very sad, very splendid – "Sniped; shot in the head; died ten minutes later, never regained consciousness".[240]

Raimes was the first of eight Ripon Clergy College men to fall in the First World War. The second, also a priest combatant, was Roger Ingoldby, who trained for a year at the College before being ordained in 1909 to a curacy under Hubert Handley at St Thomas's, Camden Town.[241] He then served a parish in Lincolnshire, and after that, the Archbishop's Mission to Canada, where he was at the outbreak of war. Joining the Alberta Dragoons as a private, he arrived in

[235] Minutes of the Governing Body Executive Committee, 19 February 1915 (RHA RCC 1/2), p. 244.

[236] Minutes of the Governing Body, 20 December 1915 (RHA RCC 1/2), p. 257.

[237] For reflections of old Riponians on chaplaincy in the forces during the war, see the letter from A. W. Fletcher to John Battersby Harford, 9 August 1915 (RHA P1/67); letters from Norman Kent to John Battersby Harford, 23 July 1915 and 10 February 1916 (RHA P1/324-6); letter from A. T. Woodman Dowding to Major, 12 March 1916 (RHA M2); and letter from J. A. S. Griffiths to Major, 18 May 1917 (RHA M2).

[238] See Alan B. Wilkinson, *The Church of England and the First World War* (1978), second edition, London: SPCK, 1996, pp. 39-46; Major, "Combatant Clergymen", *Modern Churchman* 4 (1915), pp. 605-10; and Major's unpublished letter to the editor of the *Times*, 22 February 1915, Bodl., H. D. A. Major papers, Scrapbook 1 (1890-1929), p. 58. For one former student's wrestling with the question of whether or not to fight, see RHA P1/401-2.

[239] Lancelot Raimes, "Church and Stage", *Modern Churchman* 1 (1911), pp. 205-13.

[240] Major, "Captain the Rev. Lancelot Raimes", *Modern Churchman* 6 (1916), pp. 143-4 at 144.

[241] For Handley, see Major, "Hubert Handley (1854-1943)", *Modern Churchman* 33 (1943), pp. 236-41.

France in February 1915, and a few months later was promoted to second lieutenant in the Royal Dublin Fusiliers. It was in this company that, at the age of 30, he went over the top on the first day of the Battle of the Somme, 1 July 1916, and was killed.[242] A hospital visitor reported the testimony of one Private Leeson: "[Leeson] completely broke down when he spoke of Lieut. Ingoldby who he said had saved his life – Leeson was wounded in the right arm and at the same time was buried through a shell exploding. Lieut. Ingoldby though in supreme danger all the time dug for half an hour to rescue Leeson and succeeded in doing so, immediately afterwards being killed himself."[243]

The other Ripon Clergy College men to fall in the First World War were Ernest Gooderham, who, having trained at the College 1911-12 and been ordained to a curacy at Crouch End, went out to France as a priest combatant in the Machine Guns Corps in October 1916, and was killed by a shell in December;[244] Hughie Ellis, who began at the College in the Trinity Term, 1914, left to join the Royal Welsh Fusiliers, and died in France in May 1917; Nettleton Leakey, who trained at Ripon Clergy College 1912-13, was ordained to a curacy at Devonport, and died of sunstroke and meningitis as a chaplain in East Africa in July 1917;[245] Wilfrid Harding, who trained at Ripon Clergy College in 1912 and took a title at Luddenden, was prompted to enlist as a chaplain by an article Major wrote for the *Modern Churchman* in 1914,[246] and was killed at Passchendaele in October 1917, aged 31 and married;[247] Henry Lawson, who spent a term at the College in 1914, was ordained to a title at Stourton, Leeds, and died as a chaplain on the Somme in March 1918 (aged 29 and married); and George Craven, who spent two terms at the College before being ordained to a title at Smethwick in 1914, and died as a chaplain with the 4th. Rifle Brigade in Greece in December 1918 at the age of 27. These eight were commemorated by a screen which was erected in the chapel of the new Ripon Hall.

---

[242] See the obituary in the *Modern Churchman* 6 (1916), pp. 233-4. For the history of that day, see Martin Middlebrook, *The First Day on the Somme: 1 July 1916* (1971), London: Penguin, 2001.

[243] Letter from Fred Ingoldby to John Battersby Harford, 6 August 1916 (RHA M2).

[244] Cf. letter from Dora Gooderham to Battersby Harford, 23 January 1917 (RHA RCC 4/111). In *Crockford's Clerical Directory* he is listed as Briggs-Gooderham.

[245] For his reflections on chaplaincy ministry, see the letter from Nettleton Leakey to John Battersby Harford, 5 January 1917 (RHA RCC 4/107).

[246] Major, "The Present National Crisis", *Modern Churchman* 4 (1914), pp. 244-5. See the letter from Wilfrid Harding to Major, 24 August 1914 (RHA VP1/163); and cf. letter from Wilfrid Harding to Major, 25 August 1915 (RHA M2).

[247] "Killed instantaneously by a shell, while helping stretcher bearers bring in the wounded" (letter from Alice Harding to Major, 29 November 1917 (RHA M3)).

It was not long after the closure of the College that Major, whose latest manifesto on theological training had been delivered at the Churchmen's Union conference at Rugby in September 1915,[248] was thinking about its re-opening. In May 1916, he raised the subject with Boyd Carpenter, and shortly afterwards with Battersby Harford at an ecumenical conference of theological tutors at Queens' College, Cambridge. Major was prepared, if steps were not taken for Ripon Clergy College, to steer a new initiative through the Churchmen's Union. He wrote to Boyd Carpenter,

> For years past I have felt – & my life is the best testimony to the depth of that conviction – that the Church's efficiency depends on her having theological Colleges in which the Ripon ideal of *your* time is secured & developed. If Ripon C. C. is not to be re-opened & prepared to receive men by the time peace is declared then those who realise the need for a theological college training of the Ripon type are bound to take steps to secure it for some of our ordinands so that the Church & Nation may have a succession of clergymen who will be a means of help & guidance to many who are getting none at present.[249]

In the crises of 1912 and 1914, the re-location of the College had been mooted as a way of harmonising its mixed sympathies. The governors most opposed to Major were local to Ripon, and transferring the College elsewhere might encourage their resignations.[250] Rashdall was convinced after the 1914 crisis that "it is quite clear that we cannot capture the College unless we move. The question is 'whither?'"[251] Drury's rôle in events had convinced Rashdall that the location should be determined by the sympathy of the bishop, and for this reason he favoured Southwark. "I am afraid Oxford would be out of the frying-pan into the fire," he wrote,[252] mindful that the bishop of Oxford was Charles Gore. Another

---

[248] Major, "The Training of the Clerical Mind", *Modern Churchman* 5 (1916), pp. 520-8.

[249] Letter from Major to William Boyd Carpenter, 12 July 1916 (RHA RCC 4/268, Major's emphasis). Cf. letter from Major to John Battersby Harford, 12 July 1916, and letter from John Battersby Harford to Major, 14 July 1916 (RHA M2).

[250] Cf. letter from Hastings Rashdall to Major, 31 July 1916 (RHA M2). Rashdall thought that Major could never be principal while the college was still at Ripon (letter from Hastings Rashdall to Major, 3 November 1916 (RHA M2)).

[251] Letter from Hastings Rashdall to Major, 15 January 1915 (RHA M1). William Boyd Carpenter also suggested re-location (letter from W. H. Fremantle to Major, 30 April 1915 (RHA M1)).

[252] Letter to Major, 15 January 1915. Cf. letters from Hastings Rashdall to Major, 17 November 1914 and 26 July 1915 (RHA M2 and M1). "The maxim for a Liberal College must be 'When they persecute you in one city, flee you to the next'" (letter from Hastings Rashdall to Major, 31 July 1916 (RHA M2)).

reason to move was the hostility of high churchmen in the diocese of Ripon. In 1915, the *Guardian* had reported a paper on the incarnation given by Major at Harrogate to the Yorkshire branch of the Churchmen's Union, and the Principal of Leeds Clergy College, R. H. Malden, threatened to censure Major by securing the withdrawal of diocesan grants from ordinands at Ripon Clergy College.[253] It looked for a moment as though Major's trial for heresy would come at this point.[254] The matter was referred to the Bishop of Ripon, and in the meantime the College closed, but the episode had not been a pleasant one for Major.[255] Drury summed up the two reasons for moving the College as follows:

> I have always recognised the fact that the original purpose of the Founders was that the College should run on at least more liberal lines than those of most Theological Colleges, and as the distant members [of the Governing Body] more especially represent that view, the present position is unfavourable to their exercising their proper measure of control. For the same reason it may be to the advantage of the College to move it to a diocese where such an ideal would receive a readier welcome from the clergy than it does in this diocese.[256]

Major desired to move to a university town, and his preference, outlined in a letter to Rashdall at the end of July, 1916, was for Oxford.[257] He realised that any

[253] Letters from R. H. Malden to John Battersby Harford, 14 June and 17 July 1915 (RHA M1). Cf. letters from Arthur Hollis to John Battersby Harford, 8 June 1915; Major to John Battersby Harford, 18 June (extract) and 25 July 1915; E. Highfield to Major, 20 June and 23 June 1915; and John Battersby Harford to John Hardwick, 16 July 1915 (all RHA M1).

[254] Letter from Major to Hastings Rashdall, 26 July 1915 (RHA M1): "My views have cleared in this matter [of the Virgin Birth] during the last four years & I am therefore quite willing to make the statement & be deprived of the Vice-Principalship & if it be tried legally to be deprived of the Rectory of Copgrove also, but my mind is not clear as to whether this is the occasion & whether I am from the point of view of the Liberal cause, the best victim." See also letters from Hastings Rashdall to Major, 27 July and 29 July 1915 (RHA M1), and Pearson, *H. D. A. Major and English Modernism*, pp. 82-5. For discussion about the publication of the paper, see the letters from John Battersby Harford to Major, 6 August and 9 August 1915, and from Major to John Battersby Harford, 8 August and 10 August 1915 (RHA M1).

[255] Letter from Major to Thomas Drury, 23 October 1916 (RHA M2).

[256] Letter from Thomas Drury to Major, 26 October 1916 (RHA M2). See his fuller letter to William Boyd Carpenter, 1 December 1916 (RHA M2).

[257] Letter from Major to Hastings Rashdall, undated (RHA M2). On account of Rashdall's unease about Gore, however, Major responded to the Bishop of Knaresborough's suggestion later in the year that the College would grow "in the richer soil and freer air of Oxford", that "Oxford is regarded as out of the question" (letters from Major to Boyd

preparations for moving the College to Oxford would have to be made secretly, in order to prevent Gore's obstruction. He also, of course, still desired the principalship.

> My own view is quite clear that I can hold only one post in the College and that is *Principal*. The course is full of difficulty and will require careful steering and I do not feel inclined to work under another man who in days of disaster will himself or his friends declare that I am the Jonah. Moreover I have strong views as to methods after 10 years at Ripon and have never had any opportunity of carrying them out ... There is no personal ambition in my saying this. The post is in some ways a very precarious one and is uncongenial to my wife. As you know I was willing to stand aside four years ago and take a subordinate place. The compromise was a failure and a cause of misunderstanding. If anyone can make the College succeed I can. If not I feel it is not likely to succeed as a Liberal College.[258]

Later that year, on Major's proposal, the Churchmen's Union set up a committee to consider the training of ordinands, and the practical means to procure it. The report of the committee, which was approved by the Union Council in May 1917, encouraged theological colleges to associate more closely with universities, which could provide "scientific and open-minded treatment of theological questions".[259] By this time, Boyd Carpenter was exploring possible houses for his clergy college in south London,[260] and one possibility was that Major should re-

Carpenter, 1 September, 1 November and 27 November 1916 (RHA RCC 4/271-3); from Lucius Smith to Major, 24 October 1916 (RHA M2); and from Major to Lucius Smith, 24 October 1916 (RHA M2)).

[258] Letter from Major to Hastings Rashdall, undated (end of July 1916) (RHA M2, Major's emphasis). Cf. letter from John Battersby Harford to William Boyd Carpenter, 31 July 1916 (RHA M2), in which Battersby Harford passed on the concerns of W. W. Jackson, Major's old head of house at Exeter College, that Major was too identified with the "advanced Broad Church" to be principal of a college with a non-party heritage.

[259] See Major, Hastings Rashdall, and Michael G. Glazebrook, "The Training of Ordinands", *Modern Churchman* 6 (1917), pp. 580-6 at 583-4. This was approved with minor alterations and printed as *The Training of the Clergy: A Report Presented to the Council of the Churchmen's Union by the Very Rev. Hastings Rashdall, D. Litt., D. C. L., F. B. A.; Rev. Canon Glazebrook, DD; Rev. H. D. A. Major, BD; and Adopted by that Body on May 15, 1917*, London: John Murray, 1917.

[260] Letter from John Battersby Harford to Major, 3 May 1917 (RHA M2). Cf. letter from John Battersby Harford to Major, 10 January 1918 (RHA RCC 4/378). "During the last year of his life [Boyd Carpenter] was intensely interested in finding a suitable house ... Of all his interests, and they were many, this was the nearest to his heart and occupied his thoughts very greatly during those last months, and in his last moments filled

open the College while also rector of St Olave's, Hart Street,[261] with Charles Raven as his vice-principal and curate;[262] but Major's application as rector was not successful.[263]

The search for a suitable property was made more urgent early in 1918, when the Central Advisory Council on Training for the Ministry (CACTM), which had been set up in 1913, asked the College to prepare to receive service-ordinands at the close of the war:[264] the College governors charged Boyd Carpenter with chairing a sub-committee (which included Major) to find a location.[265] Attention focused in the spring on a house in Streatham, and an appeal for funds was launched in order that an offer could be made.[266] The money, however, did not come in, and the house was let go: liberals were reluctant to support the venture without guarantees and safeguards that the College would maintain a liberal policy.[267] The liberals' idea of a liberal college was more strident than that of Boyd Carpenter, and may have been influenced by the experience of the College's mixed governorship and the threatened position under which Major had worked for over

his mind" (Minnie Tollinton, "Memories of Her Father", in Major, *Life and Letters of William Boyd Carpenter*, pp. 292-304 at 302; cf. Major, *Life and Letters of William Boyd Carpenter*, p. 162, R. B. Tollinton, "Memories of Bishop Boyd Carpenter", pp. 319-20, and Charles, "Sermon Preached in Ripon Minster", p. 329).

[261] Letters from William Boyd Carpenter to Major, 5 May and 23 May 1917 (RHA M2).

[262] For Raven, see Ian T. Ramsey, "Charles Earle Raven: 1885-1964", *Proceedings of the British Academy* 51 (1965), pp. 467-84; Frederick W. Dillistone, *Charles Raven: Naturalist, Historian, Theologian*, London: Hodder and Stoughton, 1975; Gordon S. Wakefield, "Hoskyns and Raven: The Theological Issue", *Theology* 78 (1975), pp. 568-76; W. Owen Chadwick, "Charles Earle Raven (1885-1964)", *Dictionary of National Biography 1961-1970*, Oxford: Oxford University Press, 1981, pp. 868-70; Ian Summerscales, "Charles Raven on Transcendence, Immanence and Christ", *Modern Churchman* 27/1 (1984), pp. 23-9; and Peter J. Bowler, *Reconciling Science and Religion: The Debate in Early-Twentieth-Century Britain*, Chicago and London: University of Chicago Press, 2001, pp. 277-86. For an anecdote with important bearing on Raven's life and work see Don Cupitt, *Kingdom Come in Everyday Speech*, London: SCM Press, 2000, pp. 80-1.

[263] Letter from Pallister Young to Major, 17 July 1917, and letter from William Boyd Carpenter to Major, 19 July 1917 (RHA M3).

[264] Minutes of the Governing Body, 10 January 1918 (RHA RCC 1/3); cf. circular letter from Walter H. Frere, 3 December 1917 (RHA RCC 4/361).

[265] Minutes of the Governing Body, 10 January 1918 (RHA RCC 1/3).

[266] Appeal leaflet (RHA RCC 4/118).

[267] Letters from Major to Richard Stapley, 28 June and 2 July 1918, and letter from Major to William Boyd Carpenter, 2 July 1918 (RHA RCC 4/444 and 4/447-8).

two years.[268] Boyd Carpenter and Major managed to agree on a way forward by packing the Governing Body with liberals.[269]

By now, the idea of relocating the College in a university town was catching on. Boyd Carpenter felt its attraction,[270] and some years later Major explained to former members, "He feared little ecclesiastical backwaters as places for the training of ordinands, and felt that the presence of a University was one of the best permanent antidotes to clericalism, sectarianism and obscurantism".[271] After enquiries at six university centres (London, Cambridge, Oxford, Birmingham, Leeds and Manchester), the Executive Committee decided in November 1918 to look for a house in Oxford.[272] The Churchmen's Union committee on the training of ordinands, which had reported on practicalities in October 1918, encouraged support for the new foundation of Ripon Clergy College, and members of the Churchmen's Union were approached for funds.[273] Boyd Carpenter's death in October 1918 provided Major with a new way of promoting the College: with the agreement of the bishop's family, he described the new college as a memorial to the bishop who had founded it, and appealed for £20,000.[274] His own path to the principalship was still not entirely clear: he was not on the Executive Committee, and had indirectly to get the question of the principalship put on the agenda for the governors' meeting in January 1919.[275]

---

[268] Letters from William Boyd Carpenter to Major, 5 and 10 July 1918, and letters from Major to William Boyd Carpenter, 9 and 13 July 1918 (RHA RCC 4/449-50 and 4/453-4).

[269] Letter from William Boyd Carpenter to Major, 17 July 1918, and letter from Major to William Boyd Carpenter, 19 July 1918 (RHA RCC 4/455 and 457). "By their election Modernist support was secured for [Boyd Carpenter's] foundation and the Modernist character of this theological college guaranteed" (Major, "'How Fields were Won'", p. 199).

[270] Letter from William Boyd Carpenter to Major, 10 October 1918 (RHA RCC 4/480).

[271] Major, "Since 1915" (RHA X28, RH History 1).

[272] Minutes of the Governing Body Executive Committee, 23 November 1918 (RHA RH1/3); cf. minutes of the Governing Body, 23 January 1919 (RHA RH1/3). Glazebrook favoured Oxford (letter from Michael Glazebrook to Major, 2 November 1918 (RHA RCC 4/629)), and Major thought it good for modernism to be based in a setting of antiquity and tradition (letter from Major to Michael Glazebrook, 4 December 1918 (RHA RCC 4/636)).

[273] Cf. Major, "Educate your Masters", *Modern Churchman* 8 (1918), pp. 408-12, and letter of Michael G. Glazebrook, William B. Gordon and Richard Stapley to the editor, *Modern Churchman* 8 (1918), pp. 446-8.

[274] Appeal leaflet entitled "Memorial to the late Bishop Boyd Carpenter" (RHA RCC 4/117). Cf. Charles, "Sermon Preached in Ripon Minster", p. 328.

[275] Letter from Major to William Gordon, 6 December 1918, letters from William Gordon to Major, 7 and 17 December 1918, and letter from William Gordon to Mary Major, 9 December 1918 (RHA RCC 4/510, 512-3 and 517).

At the governors' meeting, the late Boyd Carpenter was replaced as warden by the Bishop of Southwark, Hubert Burge,[276] who had joined the governors in 1916 and given assistance when the house in Streatham (in his diocese) was being considered as a possible site for the College (fortuitously, he was soon appointed Bishop of Oxford).[277] Major was appointed principal after Battersby Harford, Rashdall and Glazebrook had assured the governors that he would respect the convictions of the liberal evangelicals who had nurtured the Midland Clergy College, and after Glazebrook presented another rallying-letter from former students of the College urging that Major be appointed.[278] Major later recalled how Cyril Norwood came out of the governors' meeting at Church House, Westminster, to the room where Major was waiting, to tell him that he had been appointed principal and to bring him in to the governors, and how Herbert Ryle, now Dean of Westminster, at the head of the table, expressed to Major the governors' concern about moving to Oxford where Gore was bishop:

> I said I did not think the permanent location of a college should be determined by the temporary accident that a certain man at that time was Bishop of Oxford, and a policy that was based on apprehensions of the future was not a sound one. I recalled the character who was apprehensive in "Pilgrim's Progress" because he heard lions roaring, but he went forward and found the lions chained.[279]

Major, in orchestrating the governance of the College by liberals and attaining its principalship, had succeeded in turning "the Ripon Clergy College into a full-blown Modernist Institution" and made the existence of a liberal theological college in England secure.[280] Its existence remained so until jeopardised, ironically, by Major's own longevity.

---

[276] Hubert Murray Burge (1862-1925) was Fellow (and Dean from 1895) of University College, Oxford (1890-1900), Headmaster of Repton (1900), Headmaster of Winchester (1901-11), second Bishop of Southwark (1911-19) and successor to Charles Gore as Bishop of Oxford (1919-25). He remained warden of Ripon Hall until his death. See the obituaries in the *Times*, 11 June 1925, p. 16, the *Church Times*, 12 June 1925, p. 703, and the *Guardian*, 19 June 1925, p. 542-3, and also G. R. B. Charnwood (ed.), *Discourses and Letters of Hubert Murray Burge*, London: Chatto and Windus, 1930, and Alfred Cochrane, "Hubert Murray Burge (1862-1925)", *Dictionary of National Biography 1922-1930*, London: Oxford University Press, 1937, pp. 137-8.

[277] He also seems to have been Boyd Carpenter's choice (letter from Michael Glazebrook to Major, 11 November 1918 (RHA RCC 4/631)).

[278] Minutes of the Governing Body, 23 January 1919 (RHA RCC 1/3).

[279] Golden jubilee luncheon speeches (RHA X31, RH History 1), pp. 7-10 at 8-9.

[280] Alan M. G. Stephenson, "English Modernism", *Modern Churchman* 13 (1969), pp. 145-52 at 147.

Liberal Theology, Henry Major and Ripon Hall, Oxford

Major was looking to establish the College either in the heart of the city or in seclusion ("some second Littlemore").[281] Various houses had been explored before St Stephen's House, in Parks Road, was mentioned to Richard Stapley by his land agent on 31 January 1919.[282] Within three weeks an offer had been made on the house, and within another four weeks a prospectus for the new college had been issued.[283] The college, re-named "Ripon Hall", and fitted out with accommodation for the principal, a chaplain, and seventeen students,[284] opened on 9 October 1919 "with a small group of demobilized officers".[285]

One of the characteristic features of the new college was that Major sought the most rigorous academics for his teaching colleagues. If truth was to be sought after at all costs, then the most respected thinkers were required to lead the search. In looking for a new vice-principal, Major first tried Charles Raven,[286] before settling

---

[281] Major did not favour suburbia. "I take it that somehow ours is to be a Second Oxford Movement – Banbury Rd hardly seems the spot" (letter from Major to Michael Glazebrook, 4 December 1918, (RHA RCC 4/636)).

[282] Letter from S. W. Hickson to Richard Stapley, 31 January 1919 (RHA RCC 4/906). St Stephen's House had been founded opposite Wadham College in Parks Road, Oxford, in 1876, had closed for the war, and was re-opening in Norham Gardens, Oxford, under the principalship of G. A. Michell (Bullock, *History of Training for the Ministry*, p. 71).

[283] Letter from Edmund Brooks & Son to Major, 21 February 1919 (RHA RCC 4/544). The first £4,000 of the Ripon Clergy College appeal money was used to buy the freehold.

[284] Hubert Handley, *A Visit to Ripon Hall*, London: Williams and Norgate, 1925, p. 5. The vice-principals generally held university posts, and so were not resident. Major, during vacations, lived with his family in a cottage in Bagley Wood, having bought it in 1919 and named it "Copgrove Cottage". He exchanged it in 1923 for a house at Eastleach in the Cotswolds, and from Eastleach moved into Merton Vicarage in 1930. In all three houses students were often and generously entertained.

[285] Principal's report to the governors, 10 July 1946 (RHA uncatalogued papers). The official opening had been due to take place on 7 October, but was postponed because of the railway strike until 24 October, when W. W. Jackson, formerly rector of Exeter College, Oxford, unveiled a copy of Riviere's portrait of Boyd Carpenter (*Oxford Chronicle*, 31 October 1919, university pages II-III; Major, "Ripon Hall, Oxford", *Modern Churchman* 9 (1919), pp. 347-8). For Jackson's speech at the unveiling see "The Founder of Ripon Hall", *Modern Churchman* 9 (1919), pp. 385-7. The portrait currently hangs in the dining room of Ripon College, Cuddesdon. For a brief description of life at Ripon Hall in the mid-1920s, see Handley, *Visit to Ripon Hall*; cf. the account of "York House" and "Dr. Henry" in the novel by J. Michaelhouse (Joseph McCulloch), *Charming Manners*, London: J. M. Dent and Sons, 1932, pp. 55-65.

[286] Letters from Charles Raven to Major, 29 January, 26 May and 25 June 1919 (RHA RCC 4/533, 602 and 611).

for Cyril Emmet;[287] and when Emmet died suddenly of pneumonia on a visit to the States in July 1923, Major approached R. H. Lightfoot, L. W. Grensted and V. J. K. Brook, as well as Mervyn Haigh,[288] before appointing, from the beginning of 1925,[289] James Bezzant.[290] Bezzant was in due course succeeded by Leslie B. Cross.[291] The list of chaplains who staffed the Hall in the 1920s and

[287] Cyril William Emmet (1875-1923) was Vicar of West Hendred (1906-20), and from 1920, Fellow and then Dean of University College, Oxford. He was Vice-Principal of Ripon Hall (1920-23), appointed to the Archbishops' Doctrine Commission in 1922, and the father of the philosopher Dorothy Emmet. See the obituaries in the *Times*, 24 July 1923, p. 8, and 25 July 1923, p. 16, and the *Guardian*, 27 July 1923, p. 694. See also Major, "In Memoriam: Cyril William Emmet", *Modern Churchman* 13 (1923), pp. 217-19, and Reginald W. Macan, "A Fellow-Worker with the Truth", *Modern Churchman* 14 (1925), pp. 626-31; and, for Emmet's theology, Ernest W. Barnes, "The Abiding Significance of Jesus: Cyril Emmet and His Faith", *Modern Churchman* 13 (1923), pp. 501-6, and Lily Dougall, *God's Way With Man: An Exploration of the Method of the Divine Working suggested by the Facts of History and Science*, ed. B. H. Streeter, London: Student Christian Movement, 1924, pp. 119-24.

[288] Minutes of the Governing Body, 9 October 1923, and minutes of the Governing Body Executive Committee, 4 March 1924 (RHA RCC 1/3); and letter from Victor Brook to Major, 2 May 1924 (RHA M4).

[289] In 1924, A. T. Woodman Dowding was appointed after advertising, but he moved on to a living after serving for one term, the long vacation term 1924 (minutes of the Governing Body Executive Committee, 26 August 1924 (RHA RCC 1/3)).

[290] James Stanley Bezzant (1897-1967) trained at Ripon Hall (1921-23), and was Vice-Principal of Ripon Hall (1925-33), Chancellor of Liverpool Cathedral (1933-52), and Dean of St John's College, Cambridge (1952-64). See the obituaries in the *Times*, 28 March 1967, p. 10, and the *Church Times*, 31 March 1967, p. 15; David L. Edwards, "Canon J. S. Bezzant", *Modern Churchman* 10 (1967), pp. 306-7; and Donald M. MacKinnon, "Canon J. S. Bezzant", *Modern Churchman* 10 (1967), p. 308.

[291] Leslie Basil Cross (1895-1974) was, until 1947, Chaplain (from 1923), Fellow (from 1927) and Senior Tutor (from 1945) of Jesus College, Oxford, and Vice-Principal of Ripon Hall (1933-53). See the brief obituary in the *Times*, 19 April 1974, p. 18.

1930s is equally impressive: John Hardwick,[292] F. Leslie Cross,[293] Geoffrey Allen,[294] Alan Richardson,[295] and Hedley Sparks.[296]

The motto of the new college was "Nisi Dominus", being the first words in Latin of Psalm 127.1b, the text wittily inscribed on Ripon town hall.[297] The joke soon arose that Ripon Hall stood for "everything except the Lord", not least when modernist theology in general, and Major's theology in particular, came to public attention on account of the annual Churchmen's Union conference for 1921. The conference, held at Girton College, Cambridge, was on "Christ and the Creeds", and became infamous for igniting christological controversy.[298] In the

---

[292] John Charlton Hardwick (1885-1953) trained at Ripon Clergy College in 1911, was Chaplain 1921-23, and was Vicar of Partington (1923-53). See further Major, "In Memoriam: John Charlton Hardwick, 1885-1953", *Modern Churchman* 43 (1953), pp. 13-6.

[293] Frank Leslie Cross (1900-68) was Tutor (1925-28) and Chaplain (1926-27) of Ripon Hall, Librarian of Pusey House (1927-44), and Lady Margaret Professor of Divinity at Oxford (1944-68). See further Thomas M. Parker, "Frank Leslie Cross: 1900-1968", *Proceedings of the British Academy* 55 (1969), pp. 363-75.

[294] Geoffrey Francis Allen (1902-82) trained at Ripon Hall (1924-27), and after a brief curacy in Liverpool, returned there as Chaplain (1928-30). He was Fellow and Chaplain of Lincoln College, Oxford (1930-35), a CMS missionary in China (1935-44), Archdeacon of Birmingham (1944-47), Bishop in Egypt (1947-52), Principal of Ripon Hall (1952-59), and Bishop of Derby (1959-69). See the obituaries in the *Times*, 12 November 1982, p. 14, and the *Church Times*, 12 November 1982, p. 11.

[295] Alan Richardson was Professor of Theology at Nottingham (1953-64), and was Chaplain of Ripon Hall 1931-33. Stephenson (*Rise and Decline of English Modernism*, p. 109) suggests that he trained at Ripon Hall in the 1920s, but in fact he trained at Ridley Hall. For Richardson, see Ronald H. Preston, "Alan Richardson (1905-1975)", *Dictionary of National Biography 1971-1980*, Oxford: Oxford University Press, 1986, pp. 772-3.

[296] Hedley Sparks, Professor of Theology at Birmingham (1946-52), and Oriel Professor of the Interpretation of Holy Scripture at Oxford (1952-76), trained at Ripon Hall 1930-33, and was Chaplain 1933-36, and chair of governors 1959-71. For Sparks, see Sebastian P. Brock, "Hedley Frederick Davis Sparks: 1908-1996", *Proceedings of the British Academy* 101 (1998), pp. 513-36.

[297] "Except the Lord keep the city, the wakeman waketh but in vain" – witty because the "wakeman" was a traditional civic dignitary of Ripon.

[298] For Girton and its aftermath, see John F. W. Boden-Worsley, "Memories of Modernists and Others", *Theology* 41 (1940), pp. 9-15, 74-80 and 151-9 at 151-9; Alan M. G. Stephenson, "Girton 1921", *Modern Churchman* 11 (1967), pp. 11-25; Stephenson, *Rise and Decline of English Modernism*, pp. 99-149; Keith W. Clements, *Lovers of Discord: Twentieth-Century Theological Controversies in England*, London: SPCK, 1988, pp. 93-106; and Pearson, *H. D. A. Major and English Modernism*, pp. 90-166. All three members of the college staff gave papers at the conference. Students attended the annual (Modern)

correspondence which followed, Major published a letter in the *Church Times* in defence of his paper at the conference,[299] which prompted a priest in the diocese of Southwark, C. E. Douglas, to petition Burge, Bishop of Oxford, with a formal charge of heresy against Major.[300] Burge asked Major for a defence, which Major produced by December,[301] and then, in January 1922, on the testimony of Professors Headlam, Watson and Lock of Oxford, Burge dismissed the charges. In response, Douglas appealed unsuccessfully to the Archbishop of Canterbury.[302] These events, notwithstanding the probability of Major's vindication, must have weighed heavily upon the Hall: if the verdict had gone against him, Major would have had little choice but to resign. As it was, four students to whom places had been granted at the Hall withdrew their acceptances.[303] Major, however, emerged from the episode with renewed confidence.[304]

If the members of the Hall were aware of the surrounding theological noise, they were also aware of the noise of the city centre. As early as 1924, options had been explored both for extension and a quieter site,[305] and in 1926 the governors

Churchmen's Union conferences, stewarding lectures and preparing the chapel for daily worship: see "Ripon Hall under Dr. Major, 1935-45" (RHA X29, RH History 1), pp. 8-9.

[299] Major, letter to the editor, *Church Times*, 9 September 1921, p. 224. For the original paper, see Major, "Jesus, the Son of God", *Modern Churchman* 11 (1921), pp. 270-8. See also Major's introduction to the published papers: Major, "The Modern Churchmen's Conference of 1921", *Modern Churchman* 11 (1921), pp. 193-200.

[300] The letter is printed in Stephenson, *Rise and Decline of English Modernism*, pp. 131-2.

[301] Major, *A Resurrection of Relics: A Modern Churchman's Defence in a Recent Charge of Heresy*, Oxford: Basil Blackwell, 1922.

[302] See Hubert M. Burge, *The Doctrine of the Resurrection of the Body: Documents Relating to the Question of Heresy raised against the Rev. H. D. A. Major, Ripon Hall, Oxford*, London: A. R. Mowbray and Co., 1922; and C. E. Douglas, *The Appeal to His Grace the Archbishop of Canterbury concerning the Refusal of the Lord Bishop of Oxford to Hear an Accusation brought against the Rev. H. D. A. Major of Professing Disbelief in the Truth of the Creeds*, London: Faith Press, 1922.

[303] Minutes of the Governing Body Executive Committee, 4 May 1922 (RHA RCC 1/3). Those who did come to the Hall, like their predecessors, held Major in high esteem: old Riponians commemorated twenty-one years of Major's association with the college in 1927 by presenting him with a portrait, which currently hangs in the dining room of Ripon College, Cuddesdon (*Times*, 27 April 1927).

[304] This was demonstrated by his Assize sermon preached in Oxford in January 1922: see Major, "The Shaking of the Heavens", *Challenge*, 20 January 1922, p. 159, and Pearson, *H. D. A. Major and English Modernism*, pp. 132-3.

[305] RHA RCC 4/670-7 and 679. Cf. the reference to "somewhat noisy quarters" in the annual report of the governors for 1930 (RHA RCC 1/3), and RHA RCC 4/948.

made unsuccessful offers on a house in St Giles, Oxford.[306] So it was not a blow to the Hall when it transpired in 1929 that the site in Parks Road was likely to come under offer from an expanding Bodleian Library.[307] At a meeting of the Governing Body's executive meeting in July 1932, Major reported that several avenues which he had explored in Oxford had turned out to be dead-ends, but that "Berkeley House on Foxcombe Hill" was "in many ways very suitable".[308]

The house and grounds at Foxcombe were beautiful, and made an extraordinary setting for a theological college.[309] H. G. Woods, president of Trinity College, Oxford, later master of the Temple and a member of the Churchmen's Union, had put up the original red brick house in the 1890s. The eighth and last earl of Berkeley, who acquired the estate in 1897, had by 1904 built the additions of the tower, the great hall, the billiards room, the library, the kitchens and the laboratory, and created an Italian garden. Berkeley called the house Foxcombe, and lived there until 1916 when he inherited Berkeley Castle in Gloucestershire.[310] Reginald Macan, master of University College, who lived locally, was instrumental in securing the interest of Ripon Hall.[311] Looking out from Boars Hill, the "Parnassus" of Oxford,[312] over the unsurpassed views of the Oxford spires clustered in the basin of the Thames, one can imagine Major's sense of sitting-in-judgement, not only on the intellectual life of the university, but also on the theological inheritance of the city itself. After renovation and alterations,[313] and the promulgation of a university statute to allow undergraduates to keep term at a place otherwise outside the university's bounds for residence,[314] the new Ripon Hall was opened on 28 July 1933 by T. B. Strong, who had succeeded Burge both

---

[306] This house is in fact now used for the university's theology faculty.

[307] Minutes of the Governing Body Executive Committee, 30 October 1929 (RHA RCC 1/3).

[308] Minutes of the Governing Body Executive Committee, 20 July 1932 (RHA RCC 1/3).

[309] For a description of college life on Boar's Hill during Major's principalship, see the anonymous memoir "Ripon Hall under Dr. Major, 1935-45".

[310] Alan M. G. Stephenson, "Ripon Hall: Architectural and Historical Notes" (RHA, RH History 1).

[311] Stephenson, *Rise and Decline of English Modernism*, p. 144.

[312] Stephenson, "Theology in the Theological College", p. 100.

[313] An appeal for funds was launched in November 1932 (*Oxford Mail*, 24 November 1932). The renovations, which included turning the billiards room into a chapel, resulted in room for a principal, a tutor, a chaplain and over thirty students.

[314] RHA RCC 4/772-3 and 775-6. Cf. *Oxford University Gazette*, 1 March 1933.

Figure 5.4. Ripon Hall, Parks Road, Oxford

Figure 5.5. Ripon Hall, Boar's Hill

as Bishop of Oxford and as warden of the Hall.[315] The opening was closely followed by an inspection.[316]

Shortly after midday on 29 January 1935, faulty wiring in the room of a student, Norman Woodhall, began a fire, which, fanned by strong wind, got into the roof of the west wing. Fire brigades from both Abingdon and Oxford took over an hour to bring the blaze under control, using water from the pond, and the west wing of the college was gutted.[317] Students and staff managed to save about half the furniture, but possessions of three students and the housekeeper were destroyed. A replacement wing with accommodation increased by a third storey, which acquired the name "Phoenix Wing" and was opened on 8 October by the vice-chancellor,[318] ensured that the fire did the college an eventual service.

The Second World War caused a huge disruption to college life.[319] When London was evacuated in late 1939, a Roman Catholic girls' school was billeted for three weeks in the college, and after the schoolgirls moved out, Queen's College, Birmingham came for a term to share the premises and worship (but not the teaching).[320] The number of available ordinands radically decreased on account of the war, and an attempt to fill the rooms by admitting into residence senior undergraduates and research students at Oxford did not bear fruit. The college was therefore adapted in 1940 into a convalescence unit for those with nerve injuries from the Wingfield-Morris Orthopaedic Hospital, and the students were farmed out to stay with residents of Boar's Hill.[321] "Principal's rare use of a telephone, or an

[315] The fullest account of proceedings appeared in the *Church of England Newspaper*. For Strong, see Harold Anson, *T. B. Strong: Bishop, Musician, Dean, Vice-Chancellor*, London: SPCK, 1949, and Claude M. Blagden, "Thomas Banks Strong (1861-1944)", *Dictionary of National Biography 1941-1950*, London: Oxford University Press, 1959, pp. 849-50.

[316] Previous inspections of the Hall had been carried out by the Bishop of Edinburgh and the Dean of Lincoln in 1921, and by the Dean of Salisbury in 1926.

[317] The fullest account of the fire appeared in that day's *Oxford Mail*, p. 5.

[318] *Oxford Mail*, 9 October 1935.

[319] It also took the lives of four old Riponians, two lay and two ordained: Basil Fanshawe, who had been a student at the college 1934-6, was killed in March 1940, serving with the Royal Air Force; Thomas Harris, who trained at the Hall in 1934 and was ordained the same year, died as a chaplain in the Royal Navy in December 1941 at the age of 29; Mervyn Lamb, who had been a student at the college 1937-40, joined the Oxfordshire and Buckinghamshire Light Infantry, and died in Tunisia in April 1943 at the age of 28; and Arthur Parry-Williams, who entered Ripon Hall in 1931 and was ordained in 1937, died as a chaplain with the Field Artillery in December 1943.

[320] "Ripon Hall under Dr. Major, 1935-45", pp. 11-12.

[321] The Hall was not derequisitioned by the Ministry of Health until the end of June 1947.

interview, followed by a suave letter assuming continued part occupation of the premises, secured retention of the Chapel and Library and a dignified retreat to the South Lodge for the remainder of hostilities."[322] South Lodge had been the tutor's residence, and when the principal moved in it was expanded by two cells, one for the tutor and one for the librarian.[323] The war brought Major an honorary canonry of Birmingham, into which he was installed in August 1941. It also brought the chief blow of his life: the loss of his younger son Michael on his last training flight with the Rhodesian Air Squadron, in a plane crash at Upper Heyford, not many miles from Merton, where Major was vicar.

Stephenson was right to say that the Second World War "caused [Major] to hold on longer than he should have done".[324] Before the war, the number of students annually reached the limit of accommodation. In the college photographs from after the war, however, Major looks an ancient figure against a small number of students. He was a man of total dedication ("Ripon Hall was Major's life"),[325] but the struggle and wait of 1911-19 to obtain the principalship of the college undoubtedly caused his commitment to the college and his hold on the position of principal to be all the more tenacious; and there came a time when this began to have a negative effect on the college. He had long suffered from deafness, which became an increasing disability,[326] and also suffered from glaucoma.[327] He eventually retired, at the age of 77, at the college's golden jubilee in September 1948.[328]

---

[322] "Ripon Hall under Dr. Major, 1935-45", p. 13.

[323] Major was swift in 1944 to start proceedings for purchasing Foxcombe Rise, the property next to South Lodge, as a house for his successor, the sale of which was completed in 1946.

[324] Stephenson, "Ripon Hall", p. 310.

[325] Bezzant, "In Memoriam", p. 157. Cf. Pearson, *H. D. A. Major and English Modernism*, p. 269. His commitment can be gauged from the facts that he declined any salary while he was on leave in New Zealand for three terms in 1929, and that he dropped his salary from £350 to £250 when the move to Boars Hill exerted pressure on the Hall's finances, and dropped it by a further £100 during the Second World War.

[326] Major attributed this "rheumatism in the ears" to the strong winds through which he had had to ride when carrying out pastoral care as Vicar of Waitotara (1899-1900) (Major, *Autobiography (to 1908)*, p. 44).

[327] Major attributed this to excessive reading by poor light in Parks Road ("Ripon Hall under Dr. Major, 1935-45", p. 13 n. 60).

[328] In the same year, Cyril Norwood, who had been chair of governors since 1940, also stood down. For Norwood, who was president of the Modern Churchmen's Union 1937-47, see Major, "Sir Cyril Norwood (1875-1956)", *Modern Churchman* 46 (1956), pp. 234-7, and G. C. Turner, "Sir Cyril Norwood (1875-1956)", *Dictionary of National Biography 1951-1960*, London: Oxford University Press, 1971, pp. 773-5. The college marked Major's

Major's retention of the principalship was matched by a certain ossification of his theology. In the 1930s and 1940s, Major's failure to adapt theologically alienated the younger generation of modernists who had not known the "security" of theology before the First World War, who had received their training in the 1920s, and who were now beginning to think for themselves. Major refused to accommodate the insights of form criticism, clinging to the historical reliability of the gospel of Mark,[329] and he would not allow sociological or psychological studies to colour his faith in reason or the human conscience, thus exposing the relative conservatism of both his theology and his politics.[330]

> [Major] is of course entirely unaware how much that particular type of modernism is dated in other people's eyes, and how much it is questioned, not only by people of liberal outlook in other circles in the Church, but even with the membership of the Modern Churchman's [sic] Union.[331]

Modernism itself at this time was being eclipsed by Barthianism, was destined to be eclipsed further by biblical theology, and would to some extent be discredited by the extremism of Ernest Barnes, Bishop of Birmingham.[332] "[W]hat is certain is

---

contribution with a bronze bust, which was unveiled by the warden on 26 May 1950 (*Guardian*, 2 June 1950), and is now in the library of Ripon College, Cuddesdon.

[329] On this subject, Major had gained his DD in 1924 (Stephenson, *Rise and Decline of English Modernism*, pp. 138-9). His thesis was published as *Reminiscences of Jesus by an Eye-Witness*, London: John Murray, 1925. He later produced a commentary along the same lines: "Incidents in the Life of Jesus", in Major, T. W. Manson and C. J. Wright, *The Message and Mission of Jesus: An Exposition of the Gospels in the Light of Modern Research*, London: Ivor Nicholson and Watson, 1937, pp. 3-297.

[330] For the details, see Pearson, *H. D. A. Major and English Modernism*, pp. 197-232, and Pym, "Henry Major's Modernism". Cf. Hastings, "'On Modernism'", p. 10 ("Major dominated the Union to an extent that damaged its openness and its reputation, making it an expression of rather establishmentarian Liberal Protestantism"), and Pearson, p. 241 ("[t]here was a real sense in which [Major] never really came to terms with certain twentieth century fashions and technological developments"). At the time of writing (October 2003), Pearson is preparing an article, "Revisiting 'Lucky Old Major'", in response to the pieces by Hastings and Pym, intended for publication in *Modern Believing*, which further illuminates this area.

[331] Letter from Geoffrey Allen to John Boys Smith, 23 May 1953 (RHA P5). Boys Smith replied, "It is tragic that one of such wide experience and practical sense should fail to apply to himself the obvious principle that in younger days he would have applied without hesitation to others" (letter from John Boys Smith to Geoffrey Allen, 28 May 1953 (RHA P5); cf. Pearson, *H. D. A. Major and English Modernism*, pp. 271-2).

[332] For these theological forces in relation to modernism, see Stephenson, *Rise and Decline of English Modernism*, pp. 150-3 and 163-77.

that the liberals of the early 1920s were overtaken by a huge alteration in the political and theological worlds, that Temple moved with the times, but that the MCU, firmly led by Major, was unable to realise what was happening and simply lost significance in consequence."[333]

The problems faced by modernism, and the negative effect of Major's long principalship, can be seen in what happened to Major's successor, Douglas Richardson,[334] and in how Richardson's successor, Geoffrey Allen, restored the fortunes of the Hall.

Major's first choice for a successor was the vice-principal, Leslie B. Cross, but Cross was clear that he did not want the job. His second choice was Geoffrey Allen, whom he approached in 1945, but Allen had only become Archdeacon of Birmingham the year before, and felt it was too soon to move.[335] Douglas Richardson, favoured by Barnes and Inge,[336] but not by Cross or the warden,[337] Hunkin,[338] was Major's third choice, and Major pressed the governors to appoint him; but his principalship was not a success for a number of reasons.

First, Richardson was in his modernism a disciple of Major, whose theology was becoming increasingly isolated as outlined above, and of Barnes, whose controversial and ultra-Protestant *The Rise of Christianity* had been published only the year before Richardson's arrival. His theological stance coincided with an influx of students who were on the catholic side of the ecclesiastical spectrum. One

[333] Hastings, "'On Modernism'", p. 11.

[334] Robert Douglas Richardson (1893-1989) trained at Ripon Hall, was Vicar of Four Oaks (1929-34) and Harborne (1934-47), Principal of Ripon Hall (1948-52), and Rector of Boyton with Sherrington (1952-67). See the obituaries in the *Daily Telegraph*, 4 April 1989, p. 19, the *Times*, 6 April 1989, p. 16 (by Norman Pittenger), and the *Independent*, 7 April 1989, p. 31.

[335] Principal's report to the governors, 10 July 1946 (RHA uncatalogued papers); letter from Geoffrey Allen to Major, 11 July (probably 1945) (RHA uncatalogued papers).

[336] Letter from William Inge to Major, undated, and letter from Ernest Barnes to Major, 25 June 1946 (RHA uncatalogued papers).

[337] Letter from James Bezzant to Major, 31 January 1951 (RHA M23).

[338] Joseph Wellington Hunkin (1887-1950) was Vice-Principal of Wycliffe Hall (1914-19), Chaplain to the Forces (1915-19), Dean of Gonville and Caius College, Cambridge (1919-27), Rector of Rugby and Archdeacon of Coventry (1927-35), and Bishop of Truro (1935-50). He was warden of the college from 1944, when Strong had died, until his own death in 1950. See further the obituary in the *Times*, 30 October 1950; Major, "In Memoriam: Joseph Wellington Hunkin, MC (Bar), OBE, DD", *Modern Churchman* 40 (1950), pp. 364-6; and Alan L. Dunstan and John S. Peart-Binns, *Cornish Bishop*, London: Epworth Press, 1977.

member of the college went so far as to recall, over fifty years later, "The crisis which engulfed Ripon Hall in 1949 was a crisis of belief".[339]

Second, this led to strained relations with CACTM, which inspected the college in May-June 1949. Richardson's modernism was sufficiently embarrassing for it apparently to be arranged that he did not lecture when the inspectors visited.[340] Even so, the inspectors' report contained quite marked criticisms: the inspectors, who included Michael Ramsey, complained among other things of a "doctrinaire Modernism", and were "very disturbed" at the college's tradition of omitting the apostles' creed at morning and evening prayer.[341] There were subsequently allegations that CACTM selectors were making unfavourable comments about the college to ordinands at selection conferences.[342]

Third, Richardson did not hit it off pastorally with the students. He had spent his ministry hitherto in parishes, was not experienced in theological training, and lacked Major's paternalism.[343] Students who had spent the war serving in the forces found Richardson a little too fussy,[344] and loss of the students' confidence was for Richardson a great concern. Richardson also did not get on with the vice-principal, Leslie Cross, who seems to have brought Richardson's pastoral difficulty with the students to the wider attention of Major and Hunkin.[345]

---

[339] "The men who returned to Ripon Hall after the second world war were for the most part Central Anglicans with a broad outlook and therefore liberal, but they were ... essentially orthodox. They were not in sympathy with hardline extreme Protestant Modernism" (letter to myself from a member of the college at the time, 14 July 2003, in my possession). Cf. letter from James Bezzant to Major and Mary Major, 31 May 1950 (RHA M23), and Richardson's memorandum for the governors' meeting, 16 November 1950 (RHA RCC 1/81), pp. 4-5.

[340] Letter to myself from a member of the college, 14 July 2003, in my possession.

[341] Inspection report (RHA RCC 4/1047); cf. the governors' response (RHA RCC 4/1054).

[342] Minutes of the Governing Body, 28 September 1949 (RHA RCC 1/3). Selection conferences were a new method for accepting ordinands, introduced in 1944 (Bullock, *History of Training for the Ministry*, p. 108).

[343] Letter from James Bezzant to Major, 26 September 1951 (RHA M23); cf. letter from James Bezzant to Arthur Adams, 9 March 1961 (RHA M24), and Pearson, *H. D. A. Major and English Modernism*, pp. 267-8 n. 2.

[344] Letter from Alan Dunstan to myself, 12 June 2003, in my possession. Cf. the difference between Major's "house rules" and those of Richardson, in their respective versions of the college document "Between Ourselves" (RHA RCC 6/13).

[345] Letter from Major to Joseph Hunkin, 19 May 1950 (RHA RCC 6/7), letter from James Bezzant to Major and Mary Major, 31 May 1950 (RHA M23), and letter from James Bezzant to Major, 6 June 1950 (RHA M23). Cf. Richardson's memorandum for the governors' meeting, 16 November 1950 (RHA RCC 1/81), pp. 4-6.

Fourth, and a reason which should not be underestimated, Major found it very difficult to let go of the college. His initial suggestion that Richardson serve a year in apprenticeship nevertheless occurred for a term;[346] and, after his departure from the college, he remained its treasurer, and was on the Governing Body's Executive Committee until 1951.

> Ripon Hall was, one may say, [Major's] life, and he continued long after he should have retired, and thereafter made the position of his successor impossible by his continued interferences, even in very small matters, with the responsibilities of his successor ... I watched, with increasing sadness and annoyance, things moving to their predestined near disaster, for which the immense influence of Dr. Major was mainly responsible and from which Geoffrey Allen rescued the Hall. The debt to him is as great, if in another sense, as that which Ripon Hall owes to Dr. Major.[347]

> [Richardson's] failure, such as it was, was largely due to his increasing resentment at Major's interferences after M's retirement from the Principalship – made all the more difficult for him just *because* of his great devotion to Major. The whole business was an unavoidable tragedy.[348]

Fifth, Richardson was not financially experienced, and the college's finances required deft and thrifty handling.

Of these reasons, Stephenson emphasised the first and fourth.[349] Richardson himself alluded to the first, second and fifth.[350] It was the revelation of a large

---

[346] Principal's report to the governors, 10 July 1946 (RHA uncatalogued papers); annual report of the governors 1947 (RCC 1/69).

[347] Letter from James Bezzant to Alan Stephenson, 27 May 1963 (RHA M27/2); cf. letter from James Bezzant to Major, 31 January 1951 (RHA M23), in which Bezzant suggested that Major was "clouding" his service to the college "by continuing to try to direct and influence the Hall's affairs", and that the welfare of the college "requires that the former Principal's retirement shall become absolute". Cf. also Bezzant's letter to Major, 19 September 1950 (RHA RCC 6/7); his comments in Major's obituary in the *Church Times*; his letter to Arthur Adams, 9 March 1961 (RHA M24); and Bezzant, "In Memoriam", p. 158. One instance of this interference was the negotiations surrounding the possible lease of Ripon Hall for a new university college: see the memorandum by Douglas Richardson (RHA RCC 4/987).

[348] Letter from James Bezzant to Alan Stephenson, 21 June 1963 (RHA M27/2, Bezzant's emphasis).

[349] Stephenson, "Ripon Hall", p. 310. Major, in a letter to Geoffrey Allen, 11 February 1953 (RHA M23), listed precisely the remainder.

[350] R. Douglas Richardson, letter to the editor, *Theology* 67 (1964), pp. 460-1. Cf. letter from Douglas Richardson to Major, 7 March 1951 (RHA M23): "The lack of confidence in

deficit in the college budget in early August 1950 which actually prompted Richardson to write to Major (who was still treasurer), wondering if he should "go".[351] He was taken aback when Major replied on 12 August explaining why Richardson should resign, not least because he did not have the confidence of his "V. P. and W." and some students.[352] By "W", Major meant the tutor, Denys Whiteley, but Richardson interpreted it as "Warden", and therefore obtained assurances from Hunkin that he had Hunkin's confidence.

When the MCU annual conference met within days at Girton, misunderstandings and tensions were therefore already running high. Hunkin and Cross conversed about possible successors to Richardson, and after the conference Hunkin approached Geoffrey Allen.[353] Major suggested to governors that they advise Richardson to resign. A sub-committee appointed in September by the Executive Committee of the Governing Body, mindful of the bad atmosphere at the college, passed on to the Governing Body a resolution that the principal should be replaced,[354] and the governors' meeting on 16 November 1950 duly expressed an opinion, which they conveyed to Richardson, that he should move on by the end of the academic year; they also established a "commission" to look into the state of the Hall.[355] The impression left on Richardson, unsurprisingly, was that he was being conspired against. He wrote to his successor, Geoffrey Allen, on 24 July 1953, "a small group ... organised the Hall in opposition to me behind my back and the Governors (despite much individual sympathy) did nothing to help me although aware of my almost totally restricted liberty. I tried to bear with this as a Christian until you should come."[356]

The "commission" consisted of the Bishops of Winchester, Birmingham and Salisbury, and the chair of governors, Boys Smith,[357] and reported "that at a private

me, in so far as it exists, springs primarily from lack of confidence in the Modernism for which you and I have both stood. Your refusal to grasp this all-serious fact ... cannot but have the most serious consequences for both Modernism and the Hall."

[351] Letter from Douglas Richardson to Major, 10 August 1950 (RHA RCC 6/7); cf. letter from James Bezzant to Major, 9 February 1951 (RHA M23), and Lancelot Forster, "Notes" (RHA RH History 1), p. 2.

[352] Letter from Major to Douglas Richardson, 12 August 1950 (RHA RCC 6/7).

[353] Letter from Leslie B. Cross to Joseph Hunkin, undated (RHA RCC 6/7), and letter from Joseph Hunkin to Leslie B. Cross, 23 August 1950 (RHA RCC 6/7); cf. letter from Leslie B. Cross to Major, 30 March 1951 (RHA M23).

[354] Report of the sub-committee of the Governing Body Executive Committee, 22 September 1950 (RHA RCC 1/81).

[355] Minutes of the Governing Body, 16 November 1950 (RHA RCC 1/3).

[356] Letter from Douglas Richardson to Geoffrey Allen, 24 July 1953 (RHA P5).

[357] John Sandwith Boys Smith (1901-91) was Chaplain (1927-34), Tutor (1934-39) and Junior Bursar (1939-40) of St John's College, Cambridge, and Ely Professor of Divinity,

discussion of the subject by the bishops, the archbishop also being present, large support had been forthcoming for the Hall as the comprehensive and oecumenical college of the Church of England".[358] Soon afterwards, in the autumn of 1951, the governors invited Allen to succeed Richardson when Allen became available at Easter 1952, and asked Richardson to continue until then. Allen eventually came for Michaelmas 1952, and Ian Ramsey acted as Principal in the interim term (the long vacation term was cancelled).[359] The governors had encouraged Leslie Cross to allow Allen a clean slate, so Cross resigned in 1953,[360] and was replaced in 1954 by the chaplain, Robert Leaney,[361] who was vice-principal until 1956, when he was succeeded by John Goodwin.[362]

Allen began with ten students in residence, of whom only five were ordinands. It was clear that the college's close association with modernism was contributing to the problem of numbers,[363] and so he and Boys Smith, the chair of governors, were conscious of the need for a "new start", and for the college to broaden out.[364] Allen, himself a man of broad sympathies,[365] wrote in an article on Ripon Hall for parish magazines,

> if modernism means the particular views which were held by a school of Roman Catholic or Anglican Theologians in the past, then we are not necessarily committed to their exact opinions. If modernism means that each generation must study anew for itself the Christian tradition, together with the most enlightened

Cambridge (1940-43), before returning to St John's College as Senior Bursar (1944-59) and Master (1959-69). He was Vice-Chancellor of Cambridge University 1963-65, and chair of governors of Ripon Hall 1948-58. See further the obituary in the *Daily Telegraph*, 7 November 1991, p. 23.

[358] Minutes of the Governing Body, 4 July 1951 (RHA RCC 1/3). In due course (1953), the Archbishop of Canterbury became the new visitor of the college, in succession to Hunkin, and remained so after his retirement in 1961 until his death in 1972.

[359] Ripon Hall observed long vacation terms until 1969.

[360] Letter from Leslie B. Cross to Major, 25 February 1952, and note from Leslie B. Cross postmarked 3 March 1952 (RHA M23).

[361] Alfred Robert Clare Leaney (1909-95) trained at Ripon Hall (1932-33), was Vicar of Mountfield (1936-44), Rector of Eastwood (1946-48) and Wishaw (1948-52), Chaplain (1952-54) and Vice-Principal (1954-56) of Ripon Hall, and Lecturer (1956-64), Reader (1964-69) and Professor of Theology (1969-74) at the University of Nottingham. See the obituary in the *Times*, 6 May 1995, p. 23.

[362] John Fletcher Beckles Goodwin (born 1920) was Vice-Principal of Ripon Hall (1957-62), and Vicar of Merton (1962-70), Heanor (1970-74), and Hazelwood and Turnditch (1974-85).

[363] Letter from Geoffrey Allen to John Boys Smith, 23 December 1952 (RHA P5).

[364] Letter from John Boys Smith to Geoffrey Allen, 16 January 1953 (RHA P5).

[365] Cf. Stephenson, *Rise and Decline of English Modernism*, pp. 179-81.

views in other fields of learning, and that it must bring the insights of the Christian faith to bear on the issues of the contemporary world, then in this sense we certainly hope that both Ripon Hall and other colleges will train a ministry whose attention is firmly directed toward the tasks and issues of the modern world.[366]

Both for the sake of Ripon Hall itself, and for the sake of the revival of a Liberal spirit in the Church, I feel that we must break through the old party divisions, and win the sympathy of these Liberal Catholics and Liberal Evangelicals. I have already many encouraging signs that that is possible. With that policy we are beginning to re-build our connections both locally and with many of the other dioceses; and I hope in due time it will bear fruit in increasing numbers and increasing support for the Hall.[367]

Numbers under Allen picked up again, as did finances with the help of an appeal, but on more than one occasion he had to spell out to Major that it was he, Allen, who now had responsibility for the Hall.[368] Allen's more open policy worked, and CACTM inspectors Douglas Feaver and Eric Heaton, after an inspection in 1956, reported that "Ripon Hall is an excellent theological college in the main stream of Anglican tradition".[369]

Allen remained principal until 1959, when he was succeeded by Gordon Fallows, the Archdeacon of Lancaster, and chair of governors.[370] Major, who had

[366] Geoffrey Allen, "Preparation for Service: Ripon Hall, Oxford" (RHA RH History 1); cf. the college prospectus (as revised by Allen) for 1952 (RHA X4), and Geoffrey Allen, "The Coming Revival of Liberalism", *Church of England Newspaper*, 31 July 1953, p. 7, reprinted in *Modern Churchman* 43 (1953), pp. 269-74.

[367] Letter from Geoffrey Allen to Major, 8 June 1953 (RHA M23).

[368] Letter from Geoffrey Allen to John Boys Smith, 27 March 1953 (RHA P5), letter from John Boys Smith to Geoffrey Allen, 31 March 1953 (RHA RCC 5/5), and letter from Geoffrey Allen to Major, 23 May 1953 (RHA P5). Even in 1959, before Allen's departure had been announced, Major, at the age of 87, was working on a possible successor (letter from Major to Geoffrey Allen, 17 April 1959, and letter from Major to Ian Ramsey, 20 April 1959 (RHA M24)).

[369] C. A. C. T. M. report of inspection (RHA RCC 5/2). Subsequent inspections were made in 1962 and 1971. Cf. the *Church Times's* observation, on the occasion of the college's diamond jubilee, that the tone of the college had changed under the Allen regime (7 March 1958, p. 24; cf. Leslie B. Cross, letter to the editor, *Church Times*, 14 March 1958, p. 12) – an observation which brought the paper's long suspicion of the college to an end.

[370] William Gordon Fallows (1913-79) trained at Ripon Hall (1935-36), was Vicar of Styvechale (1939-45) and Preston (1945-59), Archdeacon of Lancaster (1955-59), Principal of Ripon Hall (1959-68), Bishop of Pontefract (1968-71) and Bishop of Sheffield (1971-79). He was chair of governors 1958-59 and 1971-75. See the obituaries in the *Times*, 18

stepped down as editor of the *Modern Churchman* in 1956,[371] retired from the living at Merton in June 1960.[372] He continued to live at the vicarage, and died there after a fall, on 26 January 1961.[373]

Major had given his life to Ripon Hall.[374] It was his staple diet: the place from which he derived, as well as the place where he expended, his extraordinary energy and strength. Ripon Hall was Major's "great love",[375] his "first pride and joy".[376] "[Y]ou came and made Ripon Hall. For succeeding generations Ripon Hall was you."[377]

The Significance of Ripon Hall

This chapter has sought to show how Henry Major came to be the Principal of Ripon Hall, and how the Hall survived him. The making, near breaking, and re-making of the Hall reflect a similar pattern in the fortunes of the Modern Churchmen's Union, though on a different time-scale. The similarity is not

August 1979, p. 10, and the *Church Times*, 24 August 1979, p. 2, and Harry C. Snape, "William Gordon Fallows", *Modern Churchman* 22 (1979), pp. 188-9. During Fallows's principalship, the college was extended: after plans were prepared in 1961, building work on a new accommodation wing, library and lecture room began in 1963, and the completed building, later named the Rashdall Building, was opened by the former Prime Minister and then Chancellor of Oxford University, Harold Macmillan, on 23 July 1964, and won an award for its architectural design from the Civic Trust in 1965 (*Daily Telegraph*, 24 January 1966). Another significant event during the principalship of Fallows was the decision to admit from 1966 women who were studying or researching theology. Ripon Hall thereby became England's first mixed residential theological college (*Oxford Mail*, 16 December 1965).

[371] See the tribute by the Archbishop of Canterbury: Geoffrey F. Fisher, "Dr. Major and the *Modern Churchman*", *Modern Churchman* 1 (1957), pp. 11-12.

[372] The sermon which Fallows preached at evensong in Merton on Major's last Sunday, "A Modern Aquila and Priscilla", is preserved in Bodl., H. D. A. Major papers M25/4. For an account of the village farewell party earlier in the afternoon, see the diary of Major Hewitt in the same location.

[373] He was buried in Merton churchyard. Mary Major, who returned to New Zealand, died on 15 May 1965.

[374] Cf. John K. Nettlefold, *Unusual Partners*, Cheltenham: Burrow's Press, p. 76.

[375] James Bezzant in Major's obituary in the *Church Times*.

[376] Gordon Fallows in his follow-up to Major's obituary in the *Times*, 16 February 1961.

[377] Letter from G. L. H. Harvey to Major, 13 July 1946 (RHA uncatalogued papers). Cf. letter from T. B. Tunstall to Alan Stephenson, 2 August 1965 (RHA M27/2): "[Major] *was* the Hall."

surprising, since both the Hall and the MCU were so closely tied to the theological phenomenon of English modernism. What this essay has also sought to show, however, is that the theological doctrine which played such a pivotal rôle in the ebb and flow of the college's fortunes was essentially panentheistic in nature. If English modernism has suffered relative neglect, historically speaking, if the place of English modernism in the wider account of English Christianity in the twentieth century has not been fully recognised or appreciated,[378] it is because the panentheism underlying modernism and the significance of this panentheism have not been understood.

This means that in order for their significance to be assessed, the events of English modernism need to be interpreted against a panentheistic backdrop. For example, the controversy over the Girton conference of 1921 needs to be seen as, at root, a debate about the doctrine of God.[379] The Church of England Doctrine Report of 1938 needs to be regarded as the blessing of modernist and thus panentheistic views.[380] And the significance for theological history of Ripon Hall lies in connection with the panentheism which was taught underneath its roof.

Something therefore needs to be said first about the panentheism which modernism conveyed, and second about the influence of modernist teaching at Ripon Hall.

Major was not the only British panentheist of the early twentieth century. Yet English modernism was the chief carrier of panentheism from the Broad Church and idealist movements of the nineteenth century through to the radicalism of the second half of the twentieth century. It was the bridge from nineteenth-century panentheism to the radicalism of the 1960s, across the "great blight" of Barthianism (as Major and Raven called it) in the 1930s and 1940s, on which those two stood as somewhat lonely figures.

The relationship between modernism and the "new radicalism" of the 1960s was, of course, complex.[381] Those whose modernism, like Major's, had become entrenched, were concerned that *Honest to God* and *The Myth of God Incarnate*

---

[378] Cf. Pearson, *H. D. A. Major and English Modernism*, pp. 6 and 9-10.

[379] Cf. ibid., pp. 105-6.

[380] Cf. J. Donald Neil, *God in Everything: A Layman's Guide to the New Thinking*, Sussex: Book Guild, 1984, pp. 58-9. For the doctrine report, see Stephenson, *Rise and Decline of English Modernism*, pp. 136-8 and 153-61, and Pearson, *H. D. A. Major and English Modernism*, pp. 155-66 and 252-7. For the argument that modernist contentions are now largely assumed, see Paul B. L. Badham, "The Revival of Liberal Modernism", in Mark D. Chapman (ed.), *The Future of Liberal Theology*, Aldershot: Ashgate, 2002, pp. 77-87. This is a condensed version of Paul B. L. Badham, *The Contemporary Challenge of Modernist Theology*, Cardiff: University of Wales Press, 1998.

[381] For a detailed description, see Stephenson, *Rise and Decline of English Modernism*, pp. 190-203.

went beyond the bounds of acceptable doctrine (a good number of those who had enjoyed the heyday of modernism in the 1920s were now rapidly ageing). Some were disgruntled that the "new radicals" were getting all the attention for promulgating doctrines which the modernists themselves had long taken for granted. In other words, those who had laboured and suffered long to push out the boundaries of what was doctrinally acceptable in the Church, in order to allow the uninhibited movement of those within, felt threatened when others attempted either to patrol the same boundaries, or to push them out further still. Stephenson detected this tension between the old-style modernism and the "new radicalism" in the choice of Tony Dyson to succeed Gordon Fallows as principal of the college in 1968, when the latter moved, like his predecessor, to an episcopal post. Vice-Principal Stephenson, who was, like Fallows, more of a "traditional modernist", was passed over in favour of the chaplain, Dyson,[382] who was more of a "new radical".[383]

But panentheism underlay the radical theology of John Robinson and others in the 1960s,[384] just as it underlay modernism. Some modernists who saw this continuity of their doctrine with new theology responded to the new theology more sympathetically. This was the case, as Stephenson notes, with a number of old Riponians: George Woods and Howard Root contributed to *Soundings*; James Bezzant contributed to *Objections to Christian Belief*; and Douglas Rhymes, a

---

[382] Anthony Oakley Dyson (1935-98) trained at Ripon Hall (1959-61), and returned there as Chaplain (1963-68) after a curacy in Putney. He was Principal of Ripon Hall (1969-74), Canon of Windsor (1974-77), Lecturer at Kent University (1977-80), and Professor of Social and Pastoral Theology at Manchester University (1980-1998). He was also editor of the *Modern Churchman* (1982-93). See the obituaries in the *Times*, 7 October 1998, p. 23; the *Church Times*, 16 October 1998, p. 6 (by Ronald Preston); *Crucible* (January-March 1999), pp. 46-8 (by Ronald Preston); and *Modern Churchpeople's Union Newsletter* 12 (1998) (by Peter Selby). See also Elaine Graham, "Travelling Hopefully: Theology and History in the Work of A. O. Dyson", *Modern Believing* 40/2 (1999), pp. 20-8.

[383] Stephenson before long went into parish ministry, continuing researches in the history of the Lambeth conferences, and was succeeded by Alan Leonard Dunstan (born 1928), who trained at Ripon Hall (1950-52), was Vicar of Gravesend (1957-63), Chaplain (1963-66) and Vice-Principal (1966-70) of Wycliffe Hall, Oxford, Chaplain of Keble College, Oxford (1970-71), Vice-Principal (1971-74) and Acting Principal (1974-75) of Ripon Hall, Vice-Principal of Ripon College Cuddesdon (1975-78), and Canon of Gloucester (1978-93).

[384] John A. T. Robinson first used the term "panentheism" in "God Dwelling Incognito", *New Christian*, 7 October 1965, pp. 12-13 at 12, reprinted in John A. T. Robinson, *But That I Can't Believe!*, London: Collins, 1967, pp. 64-70, and then widely in *Exploration into God*, London: SCM Press, 1967, which developed the doctrinal suggestions of his controversial best-seller *Honest to God*, London: SCM Press, 1963.

South Bank theologian, became a situation ethicist.[385] In addition, the earliest theologian to translate American process theology for the English scene, Norman Pittenger,[386] was deeply influenced by modernism, having spent the summers of 1933 and 1936 at Ripon Hall.[387] He described Major's *English Modernism* as "one of the two or three books which most influenced me in my youth";[388] and he got Major to read over the proof of his first book.[389] Pittenger was in fact one of the most vocal members of the MCU in urging the organisation to embrace the theology of the 1960s as modernism's legitimate heir.[390]

In recent years, panentheism has come into its own as the doctrine of God which is most able to respond to the concerns of feminist, lesbian and gay, ecological and "economic" liberation theologies, as well as the demands of inter-faith dialogue and the demands of dialogue between science and religion. It is also the doctrine of God which most accurately corresponds to the varieties of religious experience.[391] The development of panentheism to meet these needs owes no small debt to the modernist panentheists who adhered to the doctrine from the First World War to the 1960s.

Second, then, there is the influence of Ripon Hall and of Major as its vice-principal and principal. Letters in the Ripon Hall archives bear testimony to Major's theological liberation of young ordinands and theologians – "ambassadors

---

[385] Stephenson, *Rise and Decline of English Modernism*, pp. 189-92. Stephenson (pp. 185-7) also notes the modernist connections of John Wren Lewis, who influenced *Honest to God*. Oliver Fielding Clarke, who wrote the riposte to *Honest to God*, was an old Riponian, but not a typical one: see the *Observer*, 11 August 1963, and the letter from Oliver Fielding Clarke to Alan Stephenson, undated (RHA M27/2).

[386] For example, W. Norman Pittenger, *God in Process*, London: SCM Press, 1967, and *Process-Thought and Christian Faith*, Digswell Place: James Nisbet and Co., 1968.

[387] "There I attended lectures and profited from the teaching of Dr. Henry D. A. Major" (W. Norman Pittenger, *An Unimportant Life: Memories of Persons, Places, and Work*, General Theological Seminary, New York: Pittenger papers, unpublished autobiography, 1985, p. 41; cf. p. 64). Cf. W. Norman Pittenger, "Current Theology Around the World: England", *Religion in Life* 37 (1968), pp. 170-9 at 172. When Pittenger retired to England in 1966, he was made a governor of the Hall.

[388] Letter from Norman Pittenger to Gordon Fallows, 15 April 1964, Bodl., H. D. A. Major papers M25/4.

[389] W. Norman Pittenger, *The Approach to Christianity*, London: Centenary Press, 1939; letter from Norman Pittenger to Major, 13 April 1938 (RHA M17).

[390] W. Norman Pittenger, "The Work of the Union Today: An American View", *Modern Churchmen's Union Newsletter* 3 (1965).

[391] Brierley, "Naming a Quiet Revolution".

in bonds".[392] "Generations of students remember him with undying gratitude as the greatest single influence in their lives."[393]

> [Mr. Major's] influence over his theological students was extraordinary; it is hard to speak of it without exaggeration. It was a personal influence, all for things high and sacred. In this respect Mr. Major has long seemed to me, weighing my words, to be a man of genius ... Those who have had the pleasure of meeting his present students have found already his mark upon them.[394]

An important example of Major's theological influence is the fact that Geoffrey Studdert Kennedy, the best-known British (and himself an influential) advocate of passibility (itself a feature of panentheism), first derived his doctrine from Major's lectures at Ripon on the philosophy of religion.[395]

There is also the theological influence of other modernist staff at Ripon Hall (for example, the notable liberal theologian Peter Baelz),[396] who made the Hall a veritable factory of modernist, and hence panentheist, Anglican clergy. A number of ordinands spread the Ripon Hall influence in becoming theological teachers themselves.[397] These included (among many others) Norman Sykes, Hedley Sparks, George Woods, Robert Leaney, Bernard Reardon, Ian Ramsey, Ronald Preston, Howard Root, Stuart Hall, John Bowker, Tony Dyson, John Rogerson,

[392] Cf. Major, "Signs of the Times", *Modern Churchman* 3 (1913), pp. 109-18 at 113-15.

[393] Gordon Fallows in his follow-up to Major's obituary in the *Times*, 16 February 1961.

[394] Hubert Handley, letter to the editor, *Guardian*, 13 January 1922, p. 19.

[395] J. Kenneth Mozley, "Home Life and Early Years of His Ministry", in *G. A. Studdert Kennedy: By His Friends*, London: Hodder and Stoughton, 1929, pp. 13-83 at 53; A. T. Woodman Dowding, review of *G. A. Studdert Kennedy*, *Modern Churchman* 19 (1930), pp. 667-8 at 667; and William E. Purcell, *Woodbine Willie: An Anglican Incident: Being Some Account of the Life and Times of Geoffrey Anketell Studdert Kennedy, Poet, Prophet, Seeker after Truth, 1883-1929*, London: Hodder and Stoughton, 1962, p. 48.

[396] Peter Richard Baelz (1923-2000) was Assistant Chaplain of Ripon Hall (1952-53), Rector of Wishaw (1953-56), Vicar of Bournville (1956-60), Dean of Jesus College, Cambridge (1960-72), Regius Professor of Moral and Pastoral Theology at Oxford (1972-79), and Dean of Durham (1980-88).

[397] In addition to the following list which concerns the time from which Ripon Hall became "modernist", Spencer Elliott, Professor of Systematic Theology at St John's College, Winnipeg (1948-56), and Professor of Liturgics and Practical Theology at Emmanuel College, Saskatoon (1956-60), trained at Ripon Clergy College 1904-06.

David Davies, and Stephen Sykes.[398] Not all of these styled themselves modernist or liberal, but something of liberal, panentheist influence rubbed off on them.

Ripon Hall also needs to be seen in conjunction with the MCU. The two acted as counterparts, exercising similar influence in different spheres. Despite the eclipse of modernism as a movement, not least on account of Major's dominance and his failure to adapt, together Ripon Hall and the MCU nurtured the essential part of modernism – the panentheistic strand within English theology – through to greater maturity in the second half of the twentieth century. They bore the responsibility of being panentheism's most conspicuous guardians, and Major is to be credited with having appointed them for the task, even if ultimately he did not assist them in it.

Major's attainment of the principalship of Ripon Hall, on which this chapter has concentrated, is an important episode in English theological history, not just because Ripon Hall and the MCU enabled the transition of panentheistic doctrine from one period of theological history to another; but in particular because of the potency of panentheism for theology today and in the future. There is truth in the prophecy of Boyd Carpenter in the heady days of Major's struggle for the principalship, that "Ripon will one day be as proud to think of H. D. A. M.'s connection with it as King's College, London are about F. D. Maurice";[399] and there is also truth in the prophecy of Bishop Barnes of Birmingham at the unveiling of Major's bust in 1950:

---

[398] *Norman Sykes*, Professor of History at the University of London (1933-43), and Dixie Professor of Ecclesiastical History at Cambridge (1944-58), trained at Ripon Hall 1921-23; *George Woods*, Professor of Divinity at the University of London (1964-66), trained at Ripon Hall 1931-32 (and was Tutor 1936-38); *Robert Leaney*, Professor of Theology at Nottingham (1969-74), trained at Ripon Hall 1932-33 (and was Chaplain 1952-54 and Vice-Principal 1954-56); *Bernard Reardon*, Head of Religious Studies at Newcastle (1963-78), trained at Ripon Hall 1935-37; *Ian Ramsey*, Nolloth Professor of the Philosophy of the Christian Religion at Oxford (1951-66), trained at Ripon Hall 1939-40 (and was Treasurer 1951-66); *Ronald Preston*, Professor of Social and Pastoral Theology at Manchester (1970-80), trained at Ripon Hall 1938-40; *Howard Root*, Professor of Theology at Southampton (1966-81), trained at Ripon Hall 1950-52; *Stuart Hall*, Professor of Ecclesiastical History at King's College, London (1978-90), trained at Ripon Hall 1953-54; *John Bowker*, Professor of Religious Studies at Lancaster (1974-86), trained at Ripon Hall 1959-61; *Tony Dyson*, Professor of Social and Pastoral Theology at Manchester (1980-98), trained at Ripon Hall 1959-61 (and was Chaplain 1963-68 and Principal 1969-74); *John Rogerson*, Professor of Biblical Studies at Sheffield (1979-96), trained at Ripon Hall 1961-63; *David Davies*, Professor of Theology at Lampeter from 1986, trained at Ripon Hall 1962; *Stephen Sykes*, Van Mildert Professor of Divinity at Durham (1974-85), and Regius Professor of Divinity at Cambridge (1985-90), trained at Ripon Hall 1963-64.

[399] Letter from Lancelot Raimes to Mary Major, 7 May 1912 (RHA VP1/34).

When the history of the English Church during the 20th. century comes to be written, [Major] will stand out in a way which will surprise many who have known of his work during the present century and have regarded him as dangerous, unorthodox and self-confident. They will realise that he has given to English Christianity – which is a far greater thing than the Church of England – something which will enable the Christian spirit to take its place again in the thoughts and feelings of our people.[400]

---

[400] *Oxford Mail*, 27 May 1950.

Chapter 6

The Triumph of Wit:
The Runcie Years

Mark D. Chapman

Cuddesdon after the Second World War

After the Second World War Cuddesdon re-established itself under its new Principal, Kenneth Riches, who had been working in the Diocese of St Edmundsbury and Ipswich as director of service ordinands. Perhaps rather ominously, he had received the invitation from Kenneth Kirk, Bishop of Oxford, to take on the post on D. Day, 1944.[1] He was inducted as vicar on 3 February 1945, and after a few years his regime had grown distinctly more liberal than that of his earnest predecessor, Eric Graham. Graham was a relatively austere high churchman, much loved by many students, but not particularly at home as parson of a small Oxfordshire village. A man possessed of great pastoral gifts, Riches succeeded in rebuilding relations between village and college after the War: these had sunk to particularly low levels at the end of Graham's time, principally because of the conversion of two members of the college staff to the Roman Catholic Church. Riches' lighter touch, coupled with his love of gardening and his ability to organise a successful fruit and vegetable show, were much appreciated in the village and earned the college its reputation as something of a country club. One of his first acts on becoming vicar was to remove the hedges around the vicarage, giving a greater sense of unity between principal, college and village. He also re-introduced bell-ringing, and started a sports club as well as a youth club. A member of staff, Ted Shields, organised a successful gymkhana for a number of years, and his wife ran a women's Fellowship. The college attracted high calibre students and many well-known names visited. For instance, in 1950 Michael Ramsey preached, and Harry Williams led the Good Friday three-hour devotion.

---

[1] Lent Letter 1945, CCA LL5.

Riches went on to become Bishop of Dorchester and Archdeacon of Oxford, and was succeeded in August 1952 by Edward Knapp-Fisher, who was chaplain at St John's College, Cambridge, having previously been chaplain at Cuddesdon from 1946-49. He was an altogether different personality from his predecessor. An ascetic bachelor, he lived with his mother, and in some ways he sought to unmodernise the College. His relatively severe regime and spirituality tested the vocations of many students to the limit and there was at times a high drop out rate. He would often take the students on very long walks. Nevertheless, he retained the produce show and proved very popular in the village. At one point he was engaged to a local woman (which might have shocked some of the students), although this was soon broken off. Many were surprised when after some years as Bishop of Pretoria he announced his engagement to Joan Bradley, who had been an undergraduate in Oxford and used to visit the village in the 1950s. They married on 17 June 1965, shortly after Knapp-Fisher had published a book *Belief and Prayer*[2] which he dedicated to the parish and college of Cuddesdon.

In 1954 the College celebrated its centenary with a huge rally of former members. The main festival eucharist celebrated by the Archbishop of York on 22 June had 384 communicants. A recording of the Centenary Service reflects something of the dying days of Prayer Book worship with clipped tones and an adaptation of the General Thanksgiving, and with a dirge-like *Te Deum* and public-school style rendition of *Praise My Soul, The King of Heaven*. And it should also be said that Geoffrey Fisher's dreary sermon on the joy of Christ does not represent a high point of Anglican preaching.[3] Michael Ramsey's sermon on the Transfiguration,[4] preached at the College Festival in 1958, on the other hand, represents the opposite extreme. The official history of the early years of the college was produced by Owen Chadwick, and was to be the first major work of what was to be a glittering academic career. In the 1960s his brother Henry served on the Governing Body, and together they proved to be two of the most influential figures behind the scenes in the development of Cuddesdon in Runcie's time.

Knapp-Fisher's educational philosophy was clearly expressed in his final Lent Letter written shortly before he left in 1960.[5] The original ideals of the College continued to be felt in what he called "withdrawal and fellowship", even when these must have seemed increasingly anachronistic to those churchmen more interested in "relevance" to the world. On the subject of withdrawal he wrote:

> At Cuddesdon we are withdrawn by God, for all too brief a time. From the life we have known in order that while the foundations for regular prayer are laid we may be spared the distractions and temptations inseparable from our more usual

---

[2] London: Darton, Longman and Todd, 1964.
[3] Recording at CCA Z9/3.
[4] Recording at CCA Z9/4. See below, appendix one.
[5] Lent Letter 1960, CCA LL17.

involvements. To assert that we do not need some such measure of withdrawal is the claim of misplaced self-confidence; to acknowledge our need of it is not ostrichism but the humble admission of our utter dependence on God.

A theological college was thus established not primarily as a place of academic study but as somewhere to learn how to pray.

Knapp-Fisher also spoke of the vital importance of fellowship and of the real struggles which emerged from the efforts to live together in community. Cuddesdon certainly did not promise the easy life but was instead a "microcosm of the life of the Church Militant":

> Here again we have to be on our guard against the shallow sentimentalism which some of the associations and overtones of this overworked word ["fellowship"] may easily provoke. ... Here, under God, we learn to live with – yes, and learn to love – those who are very different from ourselves. In a community like this birds of a feather have only limited opportunities of flocking together; for the pattern of life combines with the size of our community to prevent our keeping company only with those who share our own tastes, prejudices and predilections. Here, perhaps for the first time in our lives, we are no longer able entirely to escape the real challenge of love for God and for His children in their manifold diversity. Here we are confronted by the meaning of membership, and in meeting the claims and the strains of our life together we are prepared to meet the pastoral demands of our ministry.

Even though Cuddesdon in the 1950s was hardly representative of English society, with the vast majority of men coming from private schools and Oxford and Cambridge Universities and an almost complete absence of women, there was nevertheless a sense that life together broke down some of barriers that separated one person from another.

For Knapp-Fisher, then, withdrawal and fellowship were basic, "not only to preparation for the Christian ministry but to the whole business of living the Christian life in this world. These are (we may almost say, though strictly we can only ever say it of God himself) *essential*. Everything else we attempt is contingent." Even though the 1950s had seen many changes in the college, especially in relation to the urban component of training with most students spending a period in an urban location, it is true to say that in Knapp-Fisher's mind a theological college was primarily a place to learn to pray and not a place to learn social analysis or even much theology. Indeed, his philosophy was not much different from Liddon's one hundred years before.

In May 1960, shortly after this Lent Letter, Knapp-Fisher announced his resignation to the parish: "Owing to the situation in South Africa, I have been compelled to accede to the urgent request of the Archbishop of Cape Town and the other South African bishops that I should go out to Pretoria with as little delay as possible."[6] He left on 7 June to be consecrated bishop of Pretoria on 19 June, and was enthroned in the cathedral on 23 June. In his farewell letter to the parish Knapp-Fisher looked back affectionately on his time in Cuddesdon as the "happiest period" of his life.[7] However, even before his departure the search had begun for a new Principal.

The Appointment of Runcie

The Cuddesdon Governing Body had been re-organised in the mid-1950s and incorporated by Royal Charter. It was a small and elite group under the chairmanship of the Bishop of Oxford, with two members nominated in turn by the two archbishops. Owen Chadwick, Dean of Selwyn College, Cambridge and the leading academic representative, was entrusted by Harry Carpenter, Bishop of Oxford, with the task of finding a fitting successor to Knapp-Fisher.[8] They were particularly keen on finding somebody who might be able gently to move the college forwards. On 23 February 1960 Chadwick wrote tersely to Tony Tremlett,[9] who had recently been appointed Vicar of St Stephen's, Rochester Row, but who had served under Runcie as Chaplain of Trinity Hall in Cambridge. Tremlett proved to be one of the great ecclesiastical fixers of his generation, having earlier been crucial in arranging Runcie's meeting with Lindy, who was the daughter of the law fellow, Cecil Turner.[10] Chadwick was aware of Tremlett's abilities in the art of manipulation: "You are a lover of Cuddesdon and know all the clergymen in the Church of England. Tell me the names of two people besides Reggie Cant[11] whom you would like to see Principal."[12]

Tremlett wrote back the following day with the name of Dick Wimbush, Principal of Edinburgh Theological College,[13] but he also made the bolder

[6] *All Saints' News*, May 1960.

[7] *All Saints' News*, June 1960.

[8] As well as Chadwick, the members were Carlyle Witton-Davies (1913-93), Archdeacon of Oxford from 1956-82); the Very Revd Alan C. Don, DD (1885-1966, Dean of Westminster from 1946-59); the historian, Sir J. W. Wheeler-Bennett (1902-75) of Garsington Manor, and the Principal.

[9] Anthony Paul Tremlett (1914-92) was chaplain of Trinity Hall from 1950-8, vicar of St Stephen's, Rochester Row from 1958-64 and Suffragan Bishop of Dover from 1964 until his retirement in 1980.

[10] Jonathan Mantle, *Archbishop: The Life and Times of Robert Runcie*, London: Sinclair Stevenson, 1991, pp. 41-3.

[11] Reggie Cant was Chancellor of York from 1957-81. He had earlier been vicar of Little St Mary's, Cambridge.

[12] Chadwick to Tremlett, 23 February 1960, CCA P8/18.

[13] Richard Wimbush (1909-94) trained at Cuddesdon in 1934 and was chaplain from 1934-7. He was Principal of Edinburgh Theological College from 1948-63 and Bishop of

suggestion of his erstwhile Dean, Robert Runcie,[14] even though he was a Westcott man:

> I know that there is a feeling among old Cuddesdon men that Westcott does not understand Cuddesdon, its regime and discipline, etc. But as far as I can gather there has always been an element at Westcott which has wanted to emulate Cuddesdon in this respect. If you were looking for people and could include, so to speak, the right wing of Westcott, a name that stands out is Bob Runcie. He would be most acceptable intellectually and has the additional advantage of being married. I am sure Cuddesdon needs a first-class theological brain as its new principal, and also someone who could attract a first-class staff.
>
> All these three, Cant, Wimbush and Runcie, have senses of humour, which is what I think the place has lacked of late. The principal does need to be a strong personality, and I should have thought that if the Governing Body considered Runcie they would be considering the very best that could be obtained. He would be loyal to the Cuddesdon tradition, and at this point in its history I think intellectual ability matters more than niceness.
>
> I should think Dick Wimbush might be rather out of touch with the rising young academic theologians for collecting the best staff. Does this also apply to Reggie Cant? Although his college would resent losing Runcie, is not this an occasion when that sort of consideration should be ruled absolutely out of court?[15]

Other approaches had already been made in Oxford and it would seem that Runcie was certainly not the Bishop's first choice. Carpenter wrote to Chadwick on 25 February noting that Kenneth Woollcombe, Chaplain of St John's College, Oxford (and eventually his successor as Bishop of Oxford), had been asked to consider the position "with the full support of the Archdeacon [of Oxford] and Knapp Fisher [sic], but it is unlikely that he will accept because he is just committed to work in the USA for five years. Reggie Cant had occurred to me as an outstanding candidate if Woollcombe declines. I shall certainly make bold to approach him, with the hope he will accept." There were other more personal reasons why the bishop was particularly keen on ensuring the right choice of man as principal: "It is now settled that I am to live in Cuddesdon myself and this is a reason for getting the right man at Cuddesdon, though there are many more important reasons too!"[16]

After further thought Tremlett wrote again to Chadwick on 26 February. This time he was more insistent about Runcie as a man of "personality", and thought he might well accept if approached. He also noted Cuddesdon's rather non-intellectual

Argyll and the Isles from 1963-77. He was elected Primus of the Scottish Episcopal Church in 1974.

[14] Runcie had been elected dean in May 1956.
[15] Tremlett to Chadwick, 24 February 1960, CCA P8/19.
[16] Carpenter to Chadwick, 25 February 1960, CCA P8/21.

reputation, which might be alleviated by Runcie's first-class mind: "Since I wrote to you I have thought more about Cuddesdon and I think Bob Runcie would be my first choice. I fancy he might jump at it if offered it." He gave several reasons:

> (1) Lindy would have a home of her own – the beautiful Cuddesdon country and village life and at the same time she'd mother all the young men with whom she'd be priceless. (2) Bob is not going to write books and be a proper Dean of Trinity Hall. He would therefore go sooner or later to something else. He won't get on the Faculty (will he?) – and to be a failed academic is the worst thing anyone can be. The administration, teaching and pastoral work among undergraduates is all right for a bit – but if you're a first class brain is really rather a dead end. (3) though no-one loves Trinity Hall more than I do – Deans can be obtained when needed and I am sure Cuddesdon is more important to the Church as a whole than a College at Cambridge. As we all know Cuddesdon isn't at present very highly thought of intellectually I gather – and the new Principal *must* therefore be someone absolutely A1 academically and also possessed of *personality*. Reggie Cant and Dick Wimbush who are dears, saintly and first class brains – lack personality I think compared with Bob. But there you are. These reflections may be useful but I thought I'd let you have them for what they are worth. Funnily enough I believe Bob would accept it – pushed by Lindy!!!![17]

Chadwick wrote back to Tremlett on 27 February noting that he had already mentioned Wimbush to the Bishop of Oxford, but that he had not mentioned Runcie since he thought that he would not even consider the post:

> I quite agree that Bob would be superb. The possibility had crossed my mind but I had ruled it out on the grounds (a) that Lindy would dislike it very much, (b) that I know he has just refused another quite big offer[18] and (c) I hate the idea of Trinity Hall losing him though I know that this should not stand in the way. I am sure you are right that he ought to be borne in mind.[19]

Margaret Duggan notes that Chadwick also had an anxiety about Runcie's ability to survive in an institution composed completely of Christian believers: "His gifts with the heathen were so remarkable that I was not sure whether it could be right that he should go to a place where he would train none but the committed."[20]

On 2 March Chadwick went to see Runcie to test him out on whether he might accept the post if offered. The following day Runcie wrote to his brother-in-law,

---

[17] Tremlett to Chadwick, 26 February 1960, CCA P8/22.

[18] This probably refers to the chaplaincy of St John's College, Oxford, where the President, W. C. Costin wanted him to replace Woollcombe on his departure to the USA.

[19] Chadwick to Tremlett, 27 February 1960, CCA P8/20.

[20] Cited in Margaret Duggan, *Runcie. The Making of an Archbishop*, London: Hodder and Stoughton, 1983, p. 115.

Angus Inglis, in a letter which reveals something of the Governing Body's intentions in their new Principal:

> Owen Chadwick came to see me yesterday about the possibility of my becoming Principal of Cuddesdon. Obviously it is a big job to be done for the C. of E. but I'm not sure it's my line or that Lindy would enjoy it. But they do want someone who will humanise the place and strengthen the ties with Oxford. It would mean a drop in income but we would get a glorious vicarage and a garden kept up for us. I would certainly prefer to spend a few more years here, and I don't think I would consider any other theological college (including Westcott!), but Cuddesdon is rather different with its parish and church, and a great tradition. Of course it now looks as if we are going to be offered a house in Cambridge which complicates things.
>
> I will keep you informed and welcome any observations. Mind you, I have *not* been offered the job, it's simply that Owen, who is a governor, and the Bishop of Oxford would like to nominate me if I wanted it.[21]

On the same day Runcie replied to Chadwick displaying his typical modesty and a surprising lack of self-confidence:

> I've been thinking a good deal about Cuddesdon since your visit. Tony has produced a strong case – did I believe all his flatteries! – and I have talked to Lindy about it. Surprisingly enough she seems quite keen on the idea from a possibly mistaken notion that we should have more of a home together and she might see more of me! Anyway she sat up in bed reading the Founding of Cuddesdon and felt she might have been some help to S. who was such a trial to Liddon.
>
> I'm convinced that it is a big job worth doing for the C of E but I'm not at all sure that I'm capable of pulling it off. Much will depend on getting a first rate staff and strengthening the ties with Oxford – congenial but expensive projects. I'm very doubtful whether I have sufficient spiritual gifts for the "soul culture" and, of course, I'm very busy and happy here even if I haven't got a permanent niche.
>
> However, I'm inclined to let my name go forward because I shall not be surprised if the Governors settle the matter quickly for me by preferring stronger candidates. If not, I will be happy to consider it in detail and see what is involved.[22]

Armed with this favourable response Chadwick wrote to Harry Carpenter on 5 March:

> There is one name you ought urgently to consider for Cuddesdon and that is R. A. K. Runcie the present Dean of Trinity Hall. I did not suggest it in my first letter because I did not even think he would consider it, but I have now had a talk

---

[21] Runcie to Inglis, 3 March 1960, cited in Duggan, *Runcie*, p. 114.
[22] Runcie to Chadwick, 3 March 1960, CCA P8/22.

with him and it appears that contrary to my expectations he may like the job if he were offered it. He was of course an extremely good Vice-principal of Westcott House and is considerably more "High Church" than Westcott House itself, and I think would fit excellently in with our tradition.

He got a first in Greek in Oxford and is partially self-taught in theology owing to his war service. He is a most attractive man and has a charming wife and one small baby. If I can write any more about him do let me know.[23]

It seems that after Woollcombe had declined the post, an offer was made to Reggie Cant who had similarly refused. Following this, Carpenter wrote to Chadwick on 29 March 1960 about the possibility of Runcie although he still had some reservations about his lack of parochial experience (which in the event were quite unnecessary given his success in the village):

I am much inclined to think seriously of Runcie, after what you have told me. E. K.-F. knows a little of him and also thinks he might be the man. Could you add anything to what you said in your letter to me? He has had very little pastoral experience in a *parish*. Would he do well with the villagers at Cuddesdon, who have had so much from E. K.-F.? I should be inclined to ask him to come over and see me to discuss the matter before making him any offer. I think I am sufficiently senior now to behave in this way, even to a Fellow of a Cambridge College. Would you let me know anything further you could say?[24]

By this stage, Runcie was thinking very seriously about the possibility of accepting the post. He wrote to Inglis on 3 April:

My affairs have been a little disturbed by "possibilities" recently. Costin wrote to me about St John's. There were some advantages, a bit more money and possibly academic security; but in the end I didn't go to see them. A move to a similar sort of job in Oxford would not have been too popular here, and in the end of the day my ambitions are not – because I haven't the gifts – book writing and professorial chairs. Anyway it might not have been a blow to my pride! Owen Chadwick was *slightly* against it because he said I was established at the Hall, and it would take a few years to get established in the same way at another college.

Meanwhile Cuddesdon is now v. much on the map. I am seeing Harry Oxon on Thursday so that I ought then to have some details. So far I've heard nothing, although such is security that I'm constantly being asked whether I've accepted! I wish things didn't move so slowly because it makes other work difficult when the future is unsettled.[25]

[23] Chadwick to Carpenter, 5 March 1960, CCA P8/24.
[24] Carpenter to Chadwick, 29 March 1960, CCA P8/25.
[25] Cited in Duggan, *Runcie*, p. 115.

The meeting with Carpenter took place on 7 April when Runcie was presumably informally offered the post. The formal letter was apparently received when the Runcies were staying with Tremlett at St Stephen's, Rochester Row, where Runcie was preaching the Holy Week addresses. By Easter Sunday the decision had been made and Runcie accepted. He was, it seems, third choice as principal, after Woollcombe and Cant. The *Church Times* noted that "For many years there has been a tradition at Westcott House that the Vice-Principal or Chaplain should be a Cuddesdon man. Now it is considered that justice has been done by the appointment of a Westcott House man as Principal of Cuddesdon."[26]

Even though he was still employed by Trinity Hall until the end of September and was even acting Junior Proctor (a situation he felt made him into a "pluralist on an eighteenth-century scale"),[27] Runcie formally assumed office on 1 August and was inducted into the benefice on 16 September. His income of £1200 (which included £400 from the benefice) was far from modest for a clergyman of the day. He was also given the services of a cleaner.[28] Even before his induction, he and his family were already settling into parish life: Lindy opened the fete on 7 August and the vicar-designate held a bingo competition at the vicarage afterwards.

Building up the Teaching Staff

The main agenda behind Runcie's appointment seems to have been to improve the intellectual and academic credibility of the institution as well as to move on from the somewhat Spartan regime of Knapp-Fisher, in whom, according to Peter Cornwell, there was a "broodingness ... it was very sepulchral, and people were beginning to get a bit restless. It was a time when we were becoming aware that the Church of England in that post-war period had become a little bit sleek and complacent. A lot of people went to church, but there was a slight feeling that beneath this placid surface things weren't quite right – there wasn't enough questioning."[29] It was such questioning that Runcie tried to encourage, but it was always to be firmly rooted in the traditional spiritual disciplines of the College: Runcie was always at heart a conservative liberal. At his first Governing Body meeting on 17 October he expressed caution about adopting a more critical

[26] Cited in Mantle, *Archbishop*, p. 49.

[27] Runcie to Inglis, 2 July 1960, cited in Duggan, *Runcie*, p. 117.

[28] Governing Body Minutes, 14 June 1960. All Governing Body Minutes are found in the minutes book at CCA GB1/1. When the Lichfield scale was introduced in 1960 the Principal was paid £1000 (although he continued to receive an income as vicar), the vice-principal £700, the chaplain, £550 and tutors £475 (Governing Body Minutes, 17 October 1960).

[29] Cited in Humphrey Carpenter, *Robert Runcie: The Reluctant Archbishop*, London: Hodder and Stoughton, 1996, p. 147.

approach to theology and new-fangled educational methods, especially as the college was full: "Despite a good deal of talk about new 'bold and imaginative' methods of theological training there seemed to be an appreciable number of people who preferred methods ancient and timorous, and we were already over-full for 1961, with heavy competition for the few remaining places for 1962."[30]

Also in October 1960 Owen Chadwick expressed his intention of resigning from the Governing Body. His final act was to suggest to Runcie that he attend the WCC meeting at New Delhi the following November: "I remember how Riches used to be unpopular in Cuddesdon because he was never there, but charging about the world, but I take it there is a moderation in all things."[31] Chadwick was replaced by Geoffrey Styler[32] of Corpus Christi College, Cambridge on the nomination of Michael Ramsey, then Archbishop of York. In the event Runcie went to India in Michaelmas Term 1962 to give the Teape Lectures at St Stephen's College, Delhi.

Runcie's first Lent Letter of 1961[33] marked a significant departure from recent precedent and began with sharp humour:

> While twenty-seven victims struggle with the Doctrine II paper in G. O. E. the invigilating Principal, who would much prefer to be discussing for an examiner the assertion that "all good children go to Heaven", must introduce himself to the readers of this annual letter; and where should he start? An autobiography would be immodest, a manifesto impertinent, and a protestation of inadequacy otiose.

He noted that he had been greatly welcomed, and went on to emphasise the strength of the part-time teaching staff, which included Henry Chadwick, David Jenkins, Chaplain of Queen's who lectured on Doctrine, and Professor Hedley Sparks who taught the liturgical use of the Psalms. Before Runcie arrived the Rector of Garsington A. J. W. Pritchard was coming to teach ethics, the Archdeacon of Oxford was teaching Hebrew and Wilfrid Browning New Testament.[34] Runcie also invited Donald Allchin, librarian of Pusey House, to take regular seminars on ecclesiology and ecumenism, and Kenneth Thompson, Rector of Great Haseley, taught doctrine.[35] Allchin continued to lecture on ecumenism throughout the decade and by 1969 his seminars were being shared with students from Heythrop College. Another scholar who taught regularly was Geoffrey

---

[30] Governing Body Minutes, 17 October 1960.

[31] Chadwick to Runcie, 19 October 1960, CCA GB3/1.

[32] Geoffrey Styler had been Vice-Principal of Westcott House before becoming Dean of Corpus from 1948 until his retirement in 1980.

[33] Lent Letter 1961, CCA LL18.

[34] AGM Minutes, 15 May 1960, CCA AGM1/1. Browning taught at Cuddesdon through most of the 1960s.

[35] Lent Letter 1963, CCA LL 20.

Rowell, whose lecture on F. D. Maurice was attended by the Inspection Team in 1969. Other assistance was offered by Miss K. M. Fison (voice), Mrs L. Scott-Joynt (NT Greek), Lady Helen Oppenheimer (ethics), Dr. G. Willis, Rector of Wing (history of liturgy), and Hugh Wybrew of St Stephen's House (liturgy). In addition, tutorials were given by the Oxford tutors, F. W. Dillistone, Alec Graham and Leslie Houlden.[36] All in all, during Runcie's time there was an extremely strong team of visiting lecturers from Oxford.

Runcie also invited large numbers of scholars to lecture at the college on an occasional basis; on 24 May 1961, for instance, Derek Tasker lectured on Youth Work. Runcie's words of introduction were often masterpieces of "warmth, naturalness, self-deprecating humour and a highly developed sense of the way the world is".[37] Throughout Runcie's time as principal many scholars came from Oxford to give one-off lectures, or sometimes courses. These included Eric Heaton, as well as Garry Bennett,[38] whom Runcie had got to know at Westcott,[39] and who became one of Runcie's speechwriters during his archiepiscopate, but who committed suicide in 1988 after his bitter Crockford's Preface in which he attacked his one-time mentor. In 1962 the "Bishop of Guildford delivered six Pastoralia lectures on two hot summer days and nobody was bored for a moment".[40] Runcie's commitment to ecumenism was shown by his asking the Methodist, John Snaith to lecture on the Old Testament in 1963, which he felt would be useful preparation for the forthcoming Anglican-Methodist talks. At the same time the Principal of St Edmund Hall, the distinguished Patristics scholar, J. N. D. Kelly was giving a course on the Athanasian Creed.[41] In 1968, perhaps to satisfy the 1969 Inspectors, there were many visiting lecturers, which included Owen Chadwick on secularisation, as well as the Bishops of Woolwich, Colombo and Malawi (the latter two in England for the Lambeth Conference).[42]

Runcie himself, despite his lack of formal qualifications, lectured on doctrine, prayer and liturgy.[43] His lectures were fondly remembered by many, primarily because of his questioning mind. Peter Cornwell noted that "Edward Knapp-Fisher's lectures on prayer were *ex cathedra*. But when Robert spoke about it, you felt that he still had his L-plates on – we're-all-in-the-same-boat-sort-of-thing."[44] Similarly Richard Harries, who was a student from 1961 to 1963, recalls Runcie's

[36] Inspection Report, 1969, CCA GB3/12.

[37] Richard Harries, "A Developing Style" in David Edwards (ed.), *Robert Runcie: A Portrait by His Friends*, London: Fount, 1990, pp. 18-19, here p. 18.

[38] Governing Body Minutes, 23 March 1962.

[39] See Mantle, *Archbishop*, pp. 38-9.

[40] Lent Letter 1963, CCA LL20.

[41] Governing Body Minutes, 18 October 63.

[42] Inspection Report, 1969, CCA GB3/12.

[43] Governing Body Minutes, 14 March 1961.

[44] Cited in Carpenter, *Robert Runcie*, p. 153.

lectures as a balance between questioning and tradition: difficulties were acknowledged and "were to be lived with on the basis of a gospel faith".[45] Runcie was never a man for simple solutions.

Soon after he took up his post, Runcie was able to make his first new full-time appointments. Lionel Wickham, who went on to a distinguished academic career at Southampton and Cambridge, became tutor in philosophical theology in 1961 after John Brooks had gone to be a parish priest in Zambia. John Ruston, who was curate of the village as well as tutor, also moved to Southern Africa in July 1962 to help Knapp-Fisher with a new scheme for training black clergy. He ended his career as Bishop of St Helena. Ruston was replaced by Peter Cornwell as chaplain and curate, who later reflected on the changes Runcie had made to the previous regime when he had been at the College as a student. Perhaps most interesting was his observation that Cuddesdon had "become a cheerful place where people laughed".[46] In 1963, after a distinguished undergraduate career in Cambridge, Mark Santer was appointed tutor to replace Lionel Wickham, who on marriage had become a vicar in the Wakefield diocese. Santer also became curate so that Peter Cornwell would be able to take on more work for the college.[47] In 1964 Anthony Bird, who had been appointed chaplain in 1960, becoming vice-principal the following year, left the College staff to study medicine at Birmingham.[48] Peter Cornwell was promoted to vice-principal,[49] and Jeremy Saville was appointed chaplain. In 1966 Cornwell left to become vicar of Silksworth and was replaced from 1 January 1967 by Kenneth Jennings who had been vice-principal of Bishop's College, Calcutta and who taught doctrine and New Testament.[50]

In the Lent Letter of 1968 it was announced that Mark Santer was leaving Cuddesdon to be Dean of Clare College, Cambridge.[51] He was replaced as tutor and curate by Michael Scott-Joynt, who taught Old Testament and the Synoptic Gospels as well as A-level divinity at Holton Park Grammar School.[52] After Saville had become Rector of Holt in Norfolk, David Selwyn was appointed chaplain from October 1968.[53] However, he withdrew before taking up the post, becoming a lecturer at Lampeter. James Lawton Thompson, who had been a chartered accountant for five years before ordination and who taught doctrine and ethics, was

---

[45] Richard Harries, "The Pastoral Pragmatist: Runcie as Communicator" in Stephen Platten (ed.), *Runcie on Reflection*, Norwich: Canterbury Press, 2002, pp. 99-114, here p. 101.

[46] Cited in Carpenter, *Robert Runcie*, p. 151.

[47] Governing Body Minutes, 18 October 63.

[48] Governing Body Minutes, 13 July 1964

[49] Governing Body Minutes, 25 March 65.

[50] Governing Body Minutes, 6 September 66.

[51] Lent Letter 1968, CCA LL24.

[52] Inspection Report, 1969, CCA GB3/12.

[53] Governing Body Minutes, 25 March 68.

appointed in his place from September 1968.[54] Runcie's teaching team, if usually very young, was always of a very high calibre: he had the gift for spotting rising talent. The 1969 inspection report noted that there "appeared to be a first rate teaching team, open with one another and with the students, and giving the impression of competence, confidence and courtesy".[55]

Continuity and Change in the Curriculum

The early 1960s was a time when many people were calling for a new theological college attached to one of the modern Universities. The debates on this in the Theological Colleges and Training Commission often led to conflict between Billy Greer, Bishop of Manchester and a former Principal of Westcott House, and Kenneth Riches, by this time Bishop of Lincoln, who had been Principal of Cuddesdon.[56] Runcie had clear views about where he stood in the debate: "it is a pity some of the promoters of the new college have wrapped up their project in rhetoric which is contemptuous of existing methods".[57] While he recognised the need for high calibre teaching staff, university links and for conversation with other disciplines, he was also keen to emphasise the point that Cuddesdon was primarily a place for pre-ordination training, and not a research institution. It was vital to maintain its connections with the past. Any change had to be incorporated into the historical ethos of the college. Consequently, continuing in Knapp-Fisher's path, he observed: "In most cases, if habits of devotion are not acquired at theological college they will never be acquired, and without them, no ministry, however energetic, has much value".[58]

Nevertheless, there was regular discussion about the need to improve training for theology graduates, so that the college would not be offering courses which were simply a replication of the Cambridge Tripos or the Oxford Honour School.[59] Furthermore, and perhaps more importantly given the gradual decline in the numbers of theology graduates, by 1964 there were plans afoot to try to combine reading for a theology degree with a period of residence in Cuddesdon. 1968 was the first year in which men took the Oxford University Diploma in Theology, a one-year rapid introduction to theology, with a further year in residence at Cuddesdon.[60] A few years later in the early 1970s, the College began to matriculate students directly for the BA in theology followed by a year's pastoral training at

---

[54] Governing Body Minutes, 1 October 68.
[55] Inspection Report, 1969, CCA GB3/12.
[56] See Mantle, *Archbishop*, p. 47.
[57] Lent Letter 1961, CCA LL18.
[58] Ibid.
[59] Governing Body Minutes, 23 March 1962.
[60] Governing Body Minutes, 1 October 1968.

Cuddesdon. Students were thus able to combine the initial study of theology with ministerial training. This was later to develop into the standard pattern of training in the 1980s and 1990s when most students were reading theology for the first time.[61]

In Runcie's time the student body was still very traditional: in October 1964, for instance, of the 58 students, 50 were graduates under 40; only 3 were over 40. There was only one non-graduate under 40, and four over 40. Of these graduates 36 had degrees in theology, mainly from Oxford and Cambridge, 10 had degrees in science, 10 in arts and 1 in Town and Country planning.[62] As well as those who spent one or two years in training, some very high calibre students who were very well qualified in theology came for a shorter period, but contributed much to the community of learning. Runcie wrote to Geoffrey Styler, Dean of Corpus Christi College, Cambridge, and one of the Governors, on 7 September 1966: "Bob Morgan and Michael Bourke ... are both very good men, and we are keen to have such lively theologians in the community".[63] The student body was very different thirty years later: from 1991-2003 there were never more than about twelve theology graduates out of a significantly larger student body. At the same time there were large numbers who had no degrees, and even some who had left school with no qualifications.

In his Lent Letter for 1962 Runcie was insistent on the importance of balancing scholarship and tradition with the need for change and for some awareness of the effects of social context on theology and spirituality. Again his masterful use of wit expressed his perhaps reluctant acceptance of the need to move forward. It was a technique designed to persuade even the most diehard of the traditional Cuddesdon product into accepting the need for reform:

> Theological colleges remain under heavy fire, and some of the more petulant articles in the Church press might suggest that if only the vested interests of Principals could be swept aside and the pious huddles in semi-monastic country retreats brought into closer relationship with the scholarship of modern universities a new era would dawn. Now while I am puzzled to relate our struggle to keep solvent and in good repair with "vested interests", and hard put to recognize this sheep-like description of the modern motorized ordinand, I am not wholly out of sympathy with the more constructive and better informed demands for experiment. I would, for example, regret the complete abandonment of such projects as a new and enlarged College of the American style on the campus of a modern university. Furthermore the sacred words "Prayer", "Theology", and "Pastoralia", are not self-explanatory and we need to put this trinity under regular and searching scrutiny. There are text-books of Catholic spirituality quite foreign to normal methods of expression and our more biblical and liturgical piety. There

---

[61] Governing Body Minutes, 2 October 1964.
[62] College Returns at CCA P8/1.
[63] Runcie to Styler, 7 September 1966, CCA GB3/1 7.

is a way of teaching Dogmatics which lacks any perspective of the world in which a man's ministry will be exercised, and a kind of static pastoralia untranslatable into Welfare State conditions. But when all this has been said we need to watch carefully the tendency of so many reforming movements to become externalized and consequently lack any deep spiritual foundation. To state that it remains our overall intention to produce thoughtful and disciplined priests with a power to care and communicate and suffer for the Lord's sake is not to deny that within an unchanging objective lie vast shifts of method and emphasis. So much for my tender conscience.[64]

In the same letter he noted that Max Warren had suggested the college's help in conducting social surveys. In his report to the Governing Body on 13 June 1963, Runcie noted that the college would be undertaking a survey in Portsmouth under the auspices of the Department of Social Science at Southampton.[65] Michael Broady, "the sort of enthusiast who can put some fizz into statistics"[66] had organised the survey which aimed to discover the attitude of the laity to the church's character and mission. Undoubtedly the survey helped give many students a far more realistic understanding of the role of the church than they might have expected from their privileged backgrounds.[67]

By 1963 the Littlemore Psychiatric Hospital course had begun under Andrew Mepham and became a regular feature of the college programme through the decade.[68] In 1965 Martin Rogers, chaplain of Littlemore, became part-time "Director of Clinical Pastoral Training", a position he held until 1973.[69] The 1969 Inspection Report noted that he was "obviously a Master of his subject". It went on to praise his course which occupied one whole day per week over two terms:

While the Church spends much time teaching theological students the doctrines of the faith, it has spent little time teaching its clergy how to act creatively in a society which is constantly changing, and how to help people under stress.

The aims of the course reveal something of the major changes to the curriculum that had developed quietly during Runcie's time as Principal. The aims were as follows:

1. How to identify needs when they exist.
2. What resources are available to help with those needs.
3. How to get the people involved to handle the problems effectively.

---

[64] Lent Letter 1962, CCA LL19.
[65] Governing Body Minutes, 13 June 1963.
[66] Lent Letter 1964, CCA LL21.
[67] See also Duggan, *Runcie*, p. 131.
[68] Governing Body Minutes, 21 March 63.
[69] Governing Body Minutes, 25 March 65.

4. A knowledge of how people work, and interact in groups.

5. A knowledge of how he (the clergyman) reacts in a group and under stress, and the skills necessary to do so creatively.

6. How to handle authority and decision-making.[70]

This side of the curriculum sometimes met with resistance. Runcie noted in his Lent Letter for 1969 that it was an

> uphill struggle for [Rogers] to gain recognition for his work. The whole subject is bedevilled with psychological jargon and Americanese – in jokes about which clergy and academics have been known to take refuge from their insecurities! But the purpose of this side of the training is to balance academic learning with skills necessary to help people with their problems.[71]

A similar course has survived as an integral part of the training until the present time (and often meets with a similar hostility from some of the students who are less than willing to engage with their own insecurities). Other aspects of the curriculum which encouraged students to come to a greater self-awareness had also begun to emerge by the end of Runcie's time. Personal tutors were allotted to students for the term and were encouraged to discuss spirituality and prayer. The Leavers' course organised by the principal discussed "questions of sex, prayer and spiritual direction".[72]

From Knapp-Fisher's time the college visited an industrial deanery for a week to gain experience of urban mission.[73] By the late 1960s, however, it was felt that something else needed to be offered to ensure that students had some greater awareness of the problems of the modern world: efforts were thus made to help students understand the social services and short courses were given on local government. Jeffrey Rowthorn, Rector of Garsington, had been particularly helpful in building up the pastoral training programme, and was to become Pastoral Director to Graduate Students at Union Theological Seminary in New York.[74] In 1969 a link was made with the relatively new housing estate of Berinsfield near Dorchester where students paid regular visits. The 1969 Inspectors commented rather patronisingly that "It is hoped to co-ordinate and concentrate on pastoral

---

[70] Inspection Report, 1969, CCA GB3/12.

[71] Lent Letter 1969, CCA LL25.

[72] Inspection Report, 1969, CCA GB3/12.

[73] In 1962, for instance, the people of Croydon were the lucky recipients of students from Cuddesdon (Lent Letter 1963, CCA LL20). Hull and Derby were also visited in Runcie's early years.

[74] Lent Letter 1969, CCA LL25. One of the Governors, Sir John Wheeler-Bennett of Garsington Manor, wrote to Runcie on 20 August 1969 emphasising the important pastoral work that the students were undertaking in the neighbouring villages, including Garsington, which he felt had been rather overlooked by the inspectors (CCA GB3/15).

training in this area in the future. ... There are no social workers, doctors or 'professional types' living in Berinsfield, and an appointment of a Priest in Charge who will act as Field Officer Tutor for the College has just been made after consultation between the Bishop, the Local Authority and the Principal of the College."[75] The link has continued until the present day. Students were also sent out on placement to the Churchill and Nuffield Hospitals twice a week, and some helped with the teaching of Religious Education at Lord Williams' School, Thame.[76]

The Wider Theological Scene

In his Lent Letter for 1963, reflecting on his experience of India, Runcie pointed to increasing globalisation and the effects this was having on theology: "There is emerging a single world culture which has its expression in the rapidly growing cities in all parts of the world." The answers to the problems that emerged were not obvious. Indeed, he went on:

> The essential question in training for ministry is not "How can we organize theological training so that ordinands are en route to becoming priests who have the answers?" but rather "How can we organize theological training so that ordinands are en route to becoming priests who can face the questions?". If we could succeed in that it might be that God was free to provide us with some of the answers, and as a theologian said to me recently "Such answers would certainly be savingly relevant".[77]

As so often for Runcie, questions were more important than answers.

The year which followed Runcie's visit to India was a particularly volatile time in the Church of England: it was marked by the controversy which emerged from the publication of *Honest to God*, which Runcie had read in draft.[78] He took Robinson seriously, encouraging debate among his staff and students. Cuddesdon was certainly not a place of withdrawal from the lively debates and sometimes radical questioning which were occupying the theological world. 1963 also saw the Paul Report on *The Deployment and Payment of the Clergy*[79] which made some far-reaching and long overdue proposals for the equalisation of stipends and the

[75] Inspection Report, 1969, CCA GB3/12.

[76] Governing Body Minutes, 6 March 1967.

[77] Lent Letter 1963, CCA LL20.

[78] Duggan, *Runcie*, p. 128.

[79] Leslie Paul, *The Deployment and Payment of the Clergy*, London: CIO for Central Advisory Council for the Ministry, 1964.

rationalisation of the provision of clergy. Runcie reflected on this report at length in his 1964 Lent Letter.[80] As usual he began in an upbeat way:

> Custom dictates that this letter brings you news of the College, and while not unscathed by "Honest to God", "Objections to Christian Belief",[81] the Paul Report, and much else, it may be reassuring to some of our readers that the old firm is still very much in business. Indeed in some ways we have never been closer to the circumstances which saw our foundation.

He also noted that the CACTM inspection last summer had found a "sane and healthy community, fulfilling an important role on the deployment of theological education in this country".

However, he then went on to quote from Samuel Wilberforce, a perhaps unlikely ally in promoting the cause for change: "What the Church of England needs is increased liberty to adapt itself to the present needs of the people." Consequently he welcomed the perceived need to adjust ministry to contemporary needs as well as the calls for more specialised forms of ministry:

> I am inclined to believe that we need to produce less men earmarked for the exacting work of a parish priest, but supported and surrounded by other kinds of ministry. Which should be called "supplementary" would remain an academic question. The shortage of clergy is not so serious as their misuse.

In his Lent Letter of 1965,[82] which was written on Edward King's day, Runcie returned to his familiar theme of the central importance of tradition and of reverence for the past which had to be maintained alongside the modern reforms and the need for critical investigation:

> I question whether we are required to cut adrift from the past which has meant so much at Cuddesdon in order to declare a gospel which is relevant today; and according to your taste you will feel either that Cuddesdon is getting into my bones, or that middle-aged complacency is the occupational disease of Principals.

Runcie was deeply critical of Basil Moss's *Clergy Training To-day*[83] which had criticised the traditionalism of the training and what he called the "counter-

---

[80] Lent Letter 1964, CCA LL21.

[81] These were a course of four lectures given in the Divinity Faculty of Cambridge. They were published as a short book with an introduction by Alec Vidler: *Objections to Christian Belief*, London: Constable, 1963. The four lectures were: "Moral objections" by D. M. MacKinnon; "Psychological objections" by H. A. Williams; "Historical objections" by A. R. Vidler; and "Intellectual objections" by J. S. Bezzant.

[82] Lent Letter 1965, CCA LL22.

[83] *Clergy Training To-day*, London: SPCK, 1964.

reformation spirituality" of a college like Cuddesdon. Against the triumph of modern educational technique, Runcie stressed the importance of the consecrated heart and the role of the college to "teach the clergy to be teachers of prayer". "Behind all the exciting talk of 'religionless Christianity'," he went on, "there lurks an uncomfortable feeling that we are producing worshippers and fully paid up church members whose commitment to any rule of faith or any practice of penitence is exceedingly shallow." Runcie showed cautious approval of the developments in theological education so long as they did not detract from the central importance of teaching the clergy how to pray. As so often through his career he saw the need for change, even when he found many of the changes personally difficult (an attitude he was to display many years later over the ordination of women).

Married Students

During Runcie's years, there was some loosening up of the approach towards married students, although the college remained relatively unreformed even at the end of his time. Whereas in Knapp-Fisher's time the few wives and fiancées had been allowed into the college buildings only after the Parish Communion, by 19 September 1962 it was noted to the Governing Body with approval that "three married men lived in the village and were allowed home after Compline. This arrangement appeared to work very well."[84] It did not seem to occur to Runcie and the Governors that this was an unusual way of conducting married life. Whether married students were instructed to keep the greater silence after Compline is not recorded.

By October 1964 numbers of married students had risen to ten, and another was engaged: of these eight lived in or around the village.[85] With his now customary wit, Runcie expressed a further anxiety in his Lent Letter of 1965 when he reported the "somewhat devastating news" of the opening of the Wheatley Teacher Training College for 400 girls.[86] Despite this temptation, however, numbers of married students remained relatively static during Runcie's time. In October 1966, for instance, out of 58 students, 50 were graduates and 11 were married. Of these 9 men slept out of college in local accommodation. At the time there was only one house owned by the college; the rest of the married accommodation was rented.[87] On 6 March 1967 Runcie reported to the Governing Body that there were 12 married men, 10 of whom were living in Cuddesdon or the

---

[84] Governing Body Minutes, 19 September 1962.

[85] College Returns, CCA P8/1.

[86] Lent Letter 1965, CCA LL22.

[87] College Returns, CCA P8/4.

local area with their wives.[88] A national survey was made in 1968 by W. S. F. Pickering of Newcastle University which focused on married students in training, but which also revealed the over-capacity in places. On average there were 41 students in each of the 29 colleges. Among Anglicans 66% were single and 34% married. At Cuddesdon only about 20% were married. Of the 1194 students in ministerial training, 791 were single and 403 married. The survey noted that there was capacity for 1475 students.[89]

Also important for the change in atmosphere towards women and marriage was the fact that Lindy Runcie had managed to pair off a number of the younger tutors, including the vice-principal, Anthony Bird, who married Lindy's German *au pair* and Peter Cornwell, whose wife was a friend of Lindy's who had come to help look after James soon after the birth of their second child, Rebecca, in August 1962. This undoubtedly helped change the atmosphere from the fiercely celibate attitude with its repression of sexual desire even among married ordinands which had prevailed in the 1950s, to one where babies were to be seen within the hallowed confines of college property itself.[90] Nevertheless the College was still very male-dominated and Runcie's own example of married life did not perhaps inspire the students to develop a close, or at least a normal, home life: he seldom ate at home during term-time. Perhaps because of this, Lindy maintained a distance from the college, although she did develop close relationships with the students who stayed at the vicarage.[91] One former student, who was at the college from 1964-66 and who was married by Runcie in All Saints' Church thought that he was under pressure to "regularise" women. Even so, during these years students' wives were allowed into college on Tuesday afternoons to bathe when the men were firmly ensconced in church for sermon practice.[92]

When Mark Santer arrived with his Dutch wife, Henriette, to replace Lionel Wickham, they were appalled at the regime.[93] Santer later spoke about his first impressions of Cuddesdon:

> Robert maintained the old regime; he humanised it, but there were aspects of it which Henriette found very hard – the effects on people newly married of the husband having to have all meals in college. And the wives being very much on the fringe of things. ... there she was in a place where all sorts of interesting people were coming, whom she'd have loved to meet, and she was never allowed to meet them or hear them, to come to any lectures. This denial and exclusion of a

[88] Governing Body Minutes, 6 March 1967.

[89] 13 July 1968. Copy at CCA P8/7.

[90] Duggan, *Runcie*, p. 131.

[91] Duggan, *Runcie*, p. 119; Mantle, *Archbishop*, pp. 64-5.

[92] John Brown to Mark Chapman, 8 June 2002.

[93] Duggan, *Runcie*, p. 131. Things later improved: Henriette became a senior psychologist at the Littlemore Hospital and lectured in the College on the concept of responsibility, Lent Letter 1968, CCA LL24.

contribution that an articulate lay Christian could make, she found very hard indeed. I would say it took years before our marriage recovered from those initial patterns.[94]

Similarly, while a student, David Stancliffe, now Bishop of Salisbury, was forbidden from attending his parents' silver wedding celebration simply because it was occurring on a Friday night. He commented on Runcie in Carpenter's biography:

> There's a fascinating mixture between the lover of the bright lights, and the re-assertion of the true heart of Tractarian spirituality. He clearly does hover between those two worlds. He would love to live a disciplined life of prayer, and yet it doesn't somehow quite come naturally. ... I think he's one of the most insecure people I know. But that's probably one of the things that endears him greatly to others.[95]

Such an attitude towards marriage and relationships cannot of course be blamed solely on Runcie. It also reflects an attitude towards wives and women in general which still prevailed in the Oxbridge and public-school atmosphere in which most of the students had been nurtured. In 1965, for instance, of the thirty-three new students, twenty-one had been to public schools and seventeen to Oxford or Cambridge. Most others had been to grammar schools.[96] It was hardly possible for a theological college principal to reshape the prevailing attitudes of the English establishment (even if he had wanted to). One former student noted that

> in the sixties everyone used to wear the same thing ... When I went for interview at Cuddesdon, Robert wrote to offer me a place *on condition* that I would remove my beard; he said he was open to a defence of the beard, but in the end I went clean-shaven! I still have the correspondence and marvel at his (specious) arguments for disposing of the beard. But this all seemed to epitomise the pull of "of what people might think".[97]

The fact that the staff kept getting married meant that there was an urgent requirement for accommodation. It was decided that cedar wood bungalows should be built on the College Field,[98] for which the Central Board of Finance gave a grant of £8,000.[99] There had also been proposals to build bungalows for a housekeeper

---

[94] Cited in Carpenter, *Robert Runcie*, p. 157.

[95] Cited in Carpenter, *Robert Runcie*, pp. 151-2.

[96] Record of New Students, CCA S1/2.

[97] John Brown to Mark Chapman, 8 June 2002.

[98] Governing Body Minutes, 21 March 63.

[99] Governing Body Minutes, 18 October 63.

and gardener,[100] although these were stalled after the purchase from Mr Cox of two houses in the High Street (which had earlier been a public house) for £5,100.[101] In 1969 planning permission was given for two bungalows for married students to be built in the garden of Old Vicarage. Runcie reported that the new tenant following the departure of Mark Carpenter-Garnier was happy with this.[102] It was also noted that this tenant, who would be moving to the house following his retirement was "a distinguished person" (and who was later revealed as Michael Ramsey).[103]

By 1969 the numbers of married students had increased. Of the 59 students, 32 were single, 8 were engaged, and 19 were married, although only 11 were living out with their wives. The inspectors noted the poor quality of the accommodation that was on offer. Although the College had made available the two Colt Bungalows and three flats, the cottages that were rented were "clearly sub-standard, having no bathrooms or inside sanitation. Arrangements are made for wives – and children – to use the College bathrooms between 6.30 and 7 pm when the men are in Chapel."[104] It was also noted that the bishop's wife let the wives use one of the bathrooms at the Bishop's House. One of the few recommendations of the 1969 Inspectors' Report was to bring these five dwellings up to scratch, since it was felt that the number of married students was unlikely to fall. While Runcie felt that the Inspectors had failed to understand the housing situation completely, he did not feel that there was any need for an official protest.[105] The only other major recommendation from the Report was to make improvements to the library especially in the Reformation and medieval holdings. A further suggestion was made to "remove the heavy Victorian shelving" and replace it with "modern shelving" as in the annexe. Fortunately this was not put into effect and Street's original shelves still survive.[106]

The domestic side of college life changed slowly. It soon became clear that the increasing complexity of the financial arrangements for training required the appointment of a qualified bursar. This was picked up in the 1963 inspection report.[107] Mr F. G. (John) Selby was appointed as resident bursar in 1964. Until 1958 he had been Commissioner of Income Tax and Head of the Inland Revenue in Nigeria, when he had returned to England to train for the priesthood at Cuddesdon.

---

[100] Governing Body Minutes, 23 March 62.

[101] Governing Body Minutes, 3 January 64. The purchase of the houses and the erection of the bungalows were authorised at a special Governing Body meeting on 25 January 1964. The Colt bungalows were completed by 30 July 1965 at a cost of £8,600.

[102] Governing Body Minutes, 14 March 1969.

[103] Governing Body Minutes, 1 October 68.

[104] Inspection Report, 1969, CCA GB3/12.

[105] Runcie to Governors, 11 Aug 1969, CCA GB3/13.

[106] Inspection Report, 1969, CCA GB3/12.

[107] Alan Don to Runcie, 30 Aug 1963, CCA GB3/5.

He was also to be part-time chaplain to the Bishop of Oxford.[108] He lived in one of the recently purchased houses in the High Street at a salary of £250 plus full board.[109] When Runcie left, Selby became curate in the village and Michael Scott-Joynt became a full-time member of staff. A married couple who acted as cook and handyman were appointed in 1965, named (somewhat ironically) Mr and Mrs J. H. Westcott.[110]

Worship and Building

With numbers hovering around the 60 mark, chapel accommodation was proving too cramped. The pre-war proposal to build a new chapel was too expensive, so some more modest suggestions were made. Although the church was used for some morning meditations, and the bishop allowed the use of his chapel for Compline, there was a feeling that something needed to be done about the nucleus of college life.[111] In his 1964 Lent Letter, Runcie mentioned a proposal from the distinguished artist, John Piper to "give us a Chapel which is not ashamed of its Victorian origin, but affords a little more elbow room for the expression of the liturgy". The east end and lower part of the chapel below the moulding were to be painted Venetian (later known as Cuddesdon)[112] red, thereby recreating the colour effect of the original wall paintings without their distractions. The Riddell posts and reredos were to be removed and the original altar was to be restored.[113] There was also to be provision of a cloth of gold curtain to run the length of the East end below the window. The overhead arc lights were to be replaced by hoops above the heads of the congregation, with bare bulbs. The Governing Body gave the go-ahead to cost the plans,[114] and work began in the summer at a cost of about £800.[115] Runcie wrote that the new chapel created a "depth which sends you to your knees, and a basilican resonance which tests our plainsong".[116] John Piper refused to accept a fee for the redecoration but asked for a small stained glass window in the west end

---

[108] Governing Body Minutes, 13 July 1964.

[109] Governing Body Minutes, 2 October 1964.

[110] Governing Body Minutes, 1 October 1965.

[111] Lent Letter 1964, CCA LL21.

[112] Lent Letter 1965, CCA LL22.

[113] The fine though mangled reredos, which had found its way to a church in Banbury, was later replaced in the late 1970s.

[114] Governing Body Minutes, 17 March 1964.

[115] AGM Minutes, 20 July 1964, CCA AGM1/1.

[116] Lent Letter 1965, CCA LL22.

Figure 6.1. Cuddesdon Chapel with the John Piper Decorations

Figure 6.2. Robert Runcie teaching

of the chapel to be charged to the college. This was installed by Patrick Reyntiens and had to be fitted in during their work on the construction of Liverpool Metropolitan Cathedral.[117]

On 3 October 1967 Runcie reported that the College had begun to use the new services: matins and evensong continued as before but Series II was in use for the chapel eucharists.[118] By 1969 the Inspection Report noted a pattern of worship which has continued remarkably unchanged until the present. During the eucharist "free intercession is encouraged and this is moving and relevant". It also noted that students produced "theme services" on occasion and that a small liturgical commission met under the chaplain. "Great emphasis is laid upon the importance of meditation and silence. This has been a feature of this College since its foundation, having been stressed by Henry Parry Liddon." The new Joint Liturgical Group offices were in use in the chapel.[119] Runcie reported to the AGM on 24 July 1969 that "It was found that this was much appreciated, and as a community Cuddesdon had been greatly refreshed by the use of the new Offices". Students took all the weekday offices and read the lessons. They also had many opportunities for leading services in local parishes throughout the year.[120]

The Parish Communion, at which the students were expected to be present, continued to be the high point of the week's activities. A fascinating example of an attempt to be relevant was a parish communion of 29 August 1965 broadcast on the BBC where a "popular" music mass ("The St Andrew setting" by Malcolm Williamson) accompanied what was still a fairly traditional Prayer Book service.[121] All the hymns were music hall type settings of traditional hymns or new hymns by Gordon Hartless, Lancelot Hankey and Michael Brierley. The current Bishop of Ely, Anthony Russell, then a student, featured (somewhat implausibly) on the drums, and the choir was directed by Nigel McCulloch, now Bishop of Manchester. Splendid clarinet obligato was provided by Ben de la Mare. Afterwards Runcie remarked in the Parish Magazine that he had received over 100 letters, most of which were positive, although one thought the music hideous, and another asked why the vicar had forgotten to mention "where coshes, studded belts, etc. should be placed on entering the church, and if purple hearts were on sale in the vestry".[122] This is probably rather a harsh assessment: a recording of the service now sounds embarrassing and patronising, but hardly threatening. The appeal of Malcolm Williamson to the average hooligan was probably negligible. Runcie's sermon says much about his obvious dislike of the music (which was indeed fairly

---

[117] Lent Letter 1965, CCA LL22. See also Duggan, *Runcie*, p. 139.
[118] Governing Body Minutes, 3 October 1967.
[119] Inspection Report, 1969, CCA GB3/12.
[120] AGM Minutes, 24 July 1969, CCA AGM1/1.
[121] Recording at CCA Z9/5.
[122] *All Saints' News*, Oct 1965.

hideous), but also his belief that one needed to make sacrifices of taste for the sake of the Gospel.

Shortly after this service changes were made to the Parish Communion service itself as well as the services in the chapel in response to the liturgical movement then sweeping through Western Christendom. Runcie wrote a long editorial in the November 1965 edition of the Parish Magazine calling for greater simplicity and clarity, as well as more congregational participation. The first half of the service was to be led from a lectern in the body of the church, the priest not going to the altar until the offertory. He was also to face the people, the rationale being that "By seeing the actions which he does in their name, the people will be more able to participate in them. They will feel less like spectators, and more like a family round a table."[123] The eminently clubbable Runcie thus succeeded in informalising the worship, without apparently encountering much opposition.

Teaching accommodation was also in need of upgrading and after Eric Graham's death a fund was set up to refit the Gore lecture room as the Graham Room.[124] What was produced was the latest in 1960s teaching technology, with built-in loudspeakers and sound insulation. The room, which cost £6,018,[125] was much appreciated and was noted by the 1969 Inspectors to be a "tremendous boon to the College".[126] The Dining Room was redecorated using Cuddesdon Red in 1968,[127] and was fitted with a fine modern crucifix designed and made by Sister Angela of the Franciscans in Australia, which had been procured by the principal through the sister sculptress at Freeland.[128]

The Decline in Ordinands: Runcie and the Future of Theological Education

In his later years at Cuddesdon, Runcie was to be increasingly involved in the reshaping of theological education following the sudden but devastating decrease in the numbers of ordinands. On 1 October 1965 he noted to the Governing Body that "colleges might have to surrender some independence over admission for the sake of securing a better planned educational programme through University,

---

[123] *All Saints' News*, November 1965.

[124] Governing Body Minutes, 1 October 1965. Alan Don left a significant bequest to the College which helped pay for the redecoration (Governing Body Minutes, 26 July 1966). Many of the library books stored in the room were sent to the new Anglican Centre in Rome (Governing Body Minutes, 3 October 1967). Owen Chadwick's sermon from the 1966 Festival "A Strange Land" was also made available to old students to help raise the money (Governing Body Minutes, 6 September 66). This is reproduced below, see appendix two.

[125] AGM Minutes, 26 July 1967, CCA AGM1/1.

[126] Inspection Report, 1969, CCA GB3/12.

[127] Governing Body Minutes, 25 March 68.

[128] Governing Body Minutes, 6 September 66.

Theological College and P[ost] O[rdination] T[raining]". He felt that Cuddesdon's consistent numbers and high calibre students put it "in the strongest position to make some of these experiments".[129] On 15 March 1966 he reported to the Governing Body that numbers of ordinands as a whole were falling by at least 30%.[130]

On 4 March 1966 Runcie wrote an article for the *Church Times* on "Training for the Ministry – 1. Intellectual: Presenting the Age-Old Faith in Modern Terms" which is worth citing at length as an expression of Runcie's mature views on theological education and of his cautious yet progressive approach to change:

> Theological colleges have been painfully discovering the need for a much more rigorous mental training than they held out to students in the past. ... those who live in them are healthily engaged with just those fundamental questions of belief, behaviour, spirituality and ministry which few others in the Church can face for the clutter of secondary issues. ...
>
> There are, of course, the frightened conservatives with their tenacious insistence on some ancient system, and on the other hand, the cocksure pioneer with his sweeping denunciation of the rest of the Church. The stiff and woolly are to be found in the colleges as elsewhere in the Church; but you have to be up-to-date with your impressions if you are going to generalise about the ordinands of the mid-sixties, and my impression is that there is now more attention given to fundamental theological questions than ever before.
>
> The intellectual task of the theological college might be summarised thus – to think through a theological problem, relating it to the documents of the Christian faith and to the coherent totality of Christian doctrine and thus aiming at some relevant formulation in modern terms. The procedure in our study of ethics is first to awaken an awareness of the moral problems of men and women today and the situations which give rise to them; then to consider the tools which the Christian tradition has made available for handling ethical problems; and finally to use the tools in such a way that a piece of teaching or counselling or direction can be given which has been not only assimilated as "the truth" but as the truth for the teacher or counsellor, as part of the basis of his own personal life.
>
> Viewed externally, these may seem obvious steps, but they mark something of a revolution in method. They spring from a growing recognition that solemnly intoning "The Bible says" or "The Church teaches" is no substitute for hard thinking.
>
> When a college with a resident staff of three is asked to deal with fifty men, some with degrees in theology, some in arts or science and some with no degrees at all, with an age-span from twenty-one to fifty-five, often joining at different times of the year for a variety of programmes extending one, two, or three years, it is being asked to do an impossible job.

---

[129] Governing Body Minutes, 1 October 1965.
[130] Governing Body Minutes, 15 March 1966.

It is time that the colleges, for their own good and that of the Church and society they exist to serve submitted themselves to a thorough, professional and independent reappraisal of their function and purpose.[131]

It should be noted that these are not the words of a complacent conservative, but of a man desperately trying to work towards a viable system of theological education which might be able to re-invigorate the Gospel in a time of rapid decline. Despite all the changes to the church of the past thirty-five years, his challenge has still to be taken up; such is the power of vested interest.

Something similar was offered to the former members of the college in the 1966 Lent Letter, though with large a dose of humour. "A TV producer told me the other day that his problem was not that clergy did not know how to produce their voices or were poor technicians, but so often they had nothing precise to say." He went on to enunciate the function of the college in helping the clergy gain something to say:

The intellectual discipline of a theological college involves a threefold process of assimilation. There is assimilation with digestion or rejection of the traditional deposit of the faith. There is personal assimilation whereby a man comes to recognize the faith not only as truth but as truth for him, the basis of his own personal life – an all-round task, intellectual, moral and spiritual which will be assisted by other aspects of the College life. Finally there is assimilation for communication – for faith is to be the truth for him, but the truth for others, and must be understood in such a way that it can also be conveyed.

And through all this it was crucial not to confuse "openness with vagueness".[132]

Runcie began to make efforts to work more closely with the other theological colleges in the Oxford area and with Oxford University;[133] he reported on joint seminars with Heythrop College, at the time situated in north Oxfordshire.[134] The resignation of Dr Alan C. Don from the Governing Body was announced 15 March 1966, and he was to die soon afterwards.[135] Runcie wrote to Michael Ramsey, whose turn it was to appoint a successor, on 30 August 1966 with various suggestions. He was particularly keen on building up stronger links with Oxford University. The names considered included Sir John Maud, the Master of University College; the Principal of Culham College; the Dean of Canterbury; Henry Chadwick; Helen Oppenheimer; Ronald Gordon; Michael Stancliffe; and John Lucas of Merton College.[136] Maud was approached by Runcie on 7 Sept

---

[131] *Church Times*, 4 March 1966.
[132] Lent Letter 1966, CCA LL23.
[133] AGM Minutes, 30 July 1965, CCA AGM1/1.
[134] Lent Letter 1966, CCA LL23.
[135] Governing Body Minutes, 15 March 1966.
[136] Runcie to Ramsey, 30 Aug 1966, CCA GB3/6.

1966: "It was felt that we intend to have a closer association with the University for various causes, and it would be valuable to have in our number someone who was in the inner councils of the University and could advise us on matters such as residence qualifications for Degree and Diploma courses."[137] Maud declined the offer and Henry Chadwick, Regius Professor of Divinity and Canon of Christ Church, accepted on 26 November 1966.[138] This appointment proved important in strengthening the links between college and university.

Another proposal came out of a conference on recruitment at High Leigh organised by the newly-established ACCM. A suggestion was made that students should visit parishes to sell the idea of vocation in an effort to stem the decline of ordinands. It was decided that the College would participate in this project.[139] A correspondence with Dick Cartwright, vicar of St Mary Redcliffe in Bristol reveals that six men visited from 13 to 16 January 1967. A dialogue sermon was arranged for evensong and Runcie was to preach at the 9.30 eucharist. Runcie's introductory letter included pithy comments about the students and also on their parents. An outline of the visit includes the notes on the question under discussion: "Why are less men wanting to become parsons nowadays?" Students were to offer their thoughts on the slowness of the church to reform itself, and on the "reluctance of people to join creaky institution". Various headings were included for the way forward, which have a remarkably contemporary ring: "Breaking new ground; intellectual restatement; mission more than maintenance; looking for men of faith, men of vision, men of prayer; with sincerity, sociability and adaptability".[140]

A letter from Wilfrid Browning, who was director of training for the Oxford diocese, reported that no fewer than twenty-two parishes in the diocese were looking for a visit including Sandhurst; Adderbury and Easthampstead (in Bracknell).[141] As well as Bristol, visits were made to Sandhurst, Harpenden and Walthamstow at the beginning of January 1967. Other students were allowed to undertake "vacation projects" – for instance, attending the SCM consultation on the city; taking part in a youth leadership course; going to Lee Abbey or a Unity Retreat Conference at Lincoln. Two years later from 11-14 January 1969 the College made a similar visit to Newcastle Central Deanery. Twenty-seven men were distributed among twelve parishes. Runcie preached and celebrated at All Saints', Gosforth where he had served his curacy.[142]

However, such efforts did little to prevent the supply of ordinands from continuing to dry up, and the church commissioned the hard-hitting report,

---

[137] Runcie to Styler, 7 September 1966, CCA GB3/7.

[138] Chadwick to Runcie, 26 November 1966, CCA GB3/9.

[139] Governing Body Minutes, 6 September 66. See also letter from ACCM to Runcie, 25 July 1966, CCA P8/54.

[140] Correspondence at CCA P8/58-64.

[141] Browning to Runcie, 18 October 1966, CCA P8/65.

[142] Correspondence at CCA P8/96.

Theological Colleges for Tomorrow, which was published in 1968.[143] The Commission was chaired by Sir Bernard de Bunsen (Principal of Chester College of Education), Kenneth Howarth, Dean of Salisbury (and a former Principal of Wells Theological College), and Henry Chadwick (Regius Professor of Divinity at Oxford and a Governor of Cuddesdon). The Chief Secretary of ACCM, Canon Basil Moss, acted as secretary.

Runcie offered his thoughts on the proposals in his 1968 Lent Letter. While noting that talk was in the air about Theological Colleges for Tomorrow, he went on to state:

> This does not mean that we are arranging a farewell parade, holding a protest demonstration, or, which might be more likely, laying the foundation stone for our new buildings; but far-reaching changes will inevitably have to be made over the next two years before another Festival ... Hoskyns used to say that the Church was like a railway train always stopping at stations which blew up the moment you tried to get out.

In the proposed solution Cuddesdon was to be amalgamated with St Stephen's House in Oxford to create a larger and more viable institution. However, Runcie felt that it would be wrong to take this aspect of the proposals too seriously.

> It is only an example thrown out to give a particular edge to the basic argument on general principles. Indeed some of the proposals, such as the removal of Westcott House to Boars Hill, seem designed to underline the highly speculative character of this section![144]

Runcie, as chairman of the Principals and Staffs Conference, had given his views of the report to the *Church Times*: he noted the importance of entering into a closer relationship with a university, and also coming to an understanding of the constraints of the modern world: "To contract out of contemporary culture is to treat the Church as an asylum for the weak, or a kind of gigantic air raid shelter." He felt that the proposed college of 120 was too big and instead called for a "cluster of colleges" which, he felt, should co-operate in a common admissions policy, shared staff and common teaching programme:

> It sounds rather grand to talk about an ecumenical campus for pre-ordination training but something of this sort, by the surrender of one group of residential College buildings in Oxford, would be at once more radical and more practicable than some of the mergers proposed. If the Report can propel or alarm us into taking such a proposal seriously, it will be responsible for no small change.

---

[143] *Theological Colleges for Tomorrow*, London: CIO (for ACCM), 1968.
[144] Lent Letter 1968, CCA LL24.

At the same time Runcie felt that it was crucial not to lose the old principle of "withdrawal", which he considered was something not primarily geographical, but devotional. In any training programme there had to be "time to sit and read and think", which began "from a vast clearing of quietness around the offering up of worship". Similarly he felt that the need to be relevant could be a distraction from the real role of the priest which was about trying to "get into the gospel". He offered a rare moment of relatively unguarded passion:

> Much has been written and said about "disillusioned clergy", and it's no use dodging the issue or crying Peace where there is no peace. It is a highly complex problem, partly to do with the ecclesiastical paraphernalia, partly to do with the emotional insecurity of many young men, partly to do with the social problem of men stripped of status and without a secure niche in society, partly to do with theological upheaval and so on. It is a real problem and calls for much more affection and sympathetic interpersonal relations between the clergy; but I confess some disquiet at the direction of discussion about the role of the priest. It is so often insufficiently radical because it does not dig to the roots to discover what ministry is about, and runs away from so many of the hard questions about the gospel. I don't think the ministry comes alive by anxiously striving to "get into society". It comes alive by trying to get into the gospel. If a man has won through to a certain basic assurance in faith, if he has something to say with conviction and integrity, then he has what it takes to be a priest. All the other questions about the sphere in which that ministry should be exercised can then be dealt with. He will then be able to live with loose ends, with lack of clear status, all of which difficulties are to be found in Social Services as much as in the parochial ministry. Because I believe that questions about the ministry have to be settled by asking questions about the gospel, the first charge on our time here must be theology. It is my firm impression that the men for whom I have been responsible at Cuddesdon and elsewhere who are now most immersed and satisfied in various forms of ministry, parochial and non-parochial, are those who were most theologically alive in their time of training rather than those most devotionally orthodox, or nervously anxious to remain or become fully human – and that's not to say that I regard pious habits or human qualities as unimportant; but on their own they are quite insufficient foundation for the ministry of tomorrow.
>
> The theme has a wider relevance. In the old days when an ordinand went to visit a parish and asked what questions to ask, my advice would range round the daily routine, the existence of a parish policy, the age of the vicar's daughters – but now I always encourage them to discover quietly what is being done for the theological education of the congregation. So now you know! This letter is becoming *intense*.

Having forgotten his usual moderation, he finished with a lighter touch, by telling of "the curate who recently told his vicar after a year that he wanted to get out of the ministry. Questioned for reasons he replied: 'Well, the trouble with the laity in this parish is that they haven't read any of the books about the laity which I've read'."

In 1968 there was a long series of meetings and discussions in response to the de Bunsen Report, in which ACCM was becoming more closely involved. J. L. Reading was appointed as a "non-voting consultant" to the Governing Body, a role he already held at St Stephen's House. He wrote to Runcie anxious not to impose his will on the Governing Body: "As a matter of fact I have always strongly advised against any ACCM staff representative being allowed to vote if invited to attend meetings of the College Governing Body. It would put him in far too difficult a position."[145] On 25 March Runcie reported to the Governing Body on the follow-up meetings organised to discuss the proposals.[146] The formidable trio of the Bishop of Oxford, Henry Chadwick and the Principal represented Cuddesdon. Runcie also spoke about the informal discussions which had taken place with St Stephen's House. Although it was agreed that neither set of buildings should close (which in hindsight was an admission that the project was not considered feasible), there was talk of the possibility of a joint Governing Body, a joint admissions system, joint appointments and possibly a joint administration. He also spoke of the formation of a "cluster" of theological colleges in Oxford, which as well as the Anglican Colleges, would also include Blackfriars, Heythrop, and Regent's Park. On 1 October 1968[147] a further report was made to the Governing Body on the discussions with St Stephen's House: while neither institution could agree to amalgamation on one site, both thought "possibilities of co-operation in teaching and the operation of a joint admission scheme might be explored". The Oxford Cluster looked more promising and a Working Party, on which Runcie was the leading player, was set up. It recommended a considerable sharing of lectures, for example, on doctrine and worship, with some subjects, especially in the area of pastoral and clinical theology, being pooled between the colleges with lecturers moving round. Runcie reported on the conclusions of the Working Party: "we would not become one big institution, but would work together in such a way that disadvantages which might attach to our smaller size might be overcome and the best possible use made of local resources. This was thought to be some response to the principles which had been put out in the De Bunsen report."

By the beginning of 1968 Runcie was becoming increasingly anxious about the decline in ordinands from Cambridge, and he wrote to a number of deans to ask their views. In one reply the Dean of Downing, John Drury, spoke about his map of Cambridge with "mauve flags" for "loyalist strongholds". "Morale is good," he went on, "and admiration for our generalissimo's strategic acumen in establishing this position, unbounded. But there are uncertain areas to the right and left. Perhaps

---

[145] Reading to Runcie, 4 December 1968, CCA GB3/11.
[146] Governing Body Minutes, 25 March 1968.
[147] Governing Body Minutes, 1 October 1968.

a drop of propaganda leaflets on these areas would soften them up. I would like to call that phase 1. Phase 2 might use another centre of influence as Hardy is in charge of the chaplains' group. A visit by yourself in person to this might do much to consolidate and widen the scope of the campaign into the demilitarized zones. I have some men here who will be coming up for training at base in the next 2 years and will do all I can to see that they go to the right place."[148] Robert Hardy wrote back from Selwyn that Cuddesdon was felt by some to be too isolated from Oxford University, and was in competition with university courses elsewhere. Besides, he went on: "There is no denying the attraction of Salisbury and its new teaching methods, or the attractions of the industrial courses at Queen's and Lichfield."[149] Paul Lucas, Chaplain of Trinity Hall similarly felt that Cuddesdon was too isolated, and also that Cambridge had some theologians worth hearing.[150] The Dean of Pembroke blamed churchmanship: Cambridge was simply too Evangelical: "Anglo-Catholicism would appear to be in the doldrums. ... Remember how shrunken the chapel community is compared with the glorious fifties. I find evangelicals are the mainstay and the only people who seem to convert others at the moment."[151] Given the situation of the Church of England thirty years later, this might be regarded as a particularly prescient statement.

Through all these changes, life went on as usual in the college. There were many distinguished visiting lecturers and preachers. Michael Ramsey gave the Holy Week lectures in 1968 on God, Christ and the World,[152] and Knapp-Fisher returned for the 1968 College Festival. There were also the regular crises and minor problems. Particularly amusing is a letter received on 8 March 1968 by Runcie from a Mrs R. C. B. Griffiths of Westbury-on-Trym.[153] She had written after a letter had been published in the *Daily Sketch* which claimed to be from students at Cuddesdon College. The students' letter read as follows: "Although our experience may be somewhat limited, as young men studying for the church, we were amazed to observe that Tiffany Jones [a comic strip character] still wears a bra. Most of the girls we know, and certainly those who are photographers' models, do without. Shouldn't Tiffany, who is always 'with-it,' be without it?" The letter was signed "Students, Cuddesdon College, Oxford". Mrs Griffiths wrote in disgust: "I must say I feel uneasy at the prospect of perhaps having one of these young men as my vicar one day." Runcie replied in his inimitable style, admitting that two students had written from the College but that the *Daily Sketch* had

---

[148] John Drury to Runcie, 6 February 1968, CCA P8/88.

[149] Robert Hardy to Runcie, 7 February 1968, CCA P8/90.

[150] Paul Lucas to Runcie, 7 February 1968, CCA P8/ 92.

[151] Dean of Pembroke to Runcie, 11 February 1968, CCA P8/93.

[152] Ramsey to Runcie, 5 December 1966, CCA GB3/10. These lectures became the basis of his book, *God, Christ and the World: A Study in Contemporary Theology*, London: SCM, 1969.

[153] Mrs R. C. B. Griffiths to Runcie, 8 March 1968, CCA P8/102.

changed it to "Students from Cuddesdon College". He went on: "A protest has been made, but in these cases you know that nothing can be done ... Students are not what they were. Sometimes they can be very tiresome, but on the other hand they have qualities which my generation, and perhaps yours, did not have."[154] He evidently had a sneaking admiration for the perpetrators.

A snapshop of college life at this time is offered by the Report of the Bishops' Inspectors (Arthur Cyril Smith (Archdeacon of Lincoln), the Revd David C. St. V. Welander, Miss M. K. Powell) who visited the college from 12-15 May 1969. They concluded: "There is nothing remote from life in modern Cuddesdon training methods and techniques, despite being set in a village 7 miles from Oxford. Indeed, its unique setting in an attractive village and so near the University with its many experts in most fields of activity, is ideal for training the ordinand of today." The Inspectors also noted the beginnings of greater co-operation between the four Oxford colleges since the de Bunsen Report although they observed: "It is easier and more time-saving to move lecturers rather than students."[155]

In his Lent Letter for 1969[156] Runcie wrote again about the de Bunsen Report, which, he felt, had had "the effect so far chiefly in hastening the closure of one or two places and creating a seemingly endless round of meetings, working parties, and paper solutions". As chairman of the Principals' Conference he was particularly aware of the passions aroused in reshaping theological education, since theological colleges formed a fundamental aspect of the clergyman's identity. He felt that the idea of big colleges in universities took too little account of capital cost of reconstruction, as well as the shortage of graduate candidates, and the roots of colleges in communities. Despite the faults of the report, however, he felt that something had to happen, even if the independence of the colleges would make it impossible. Otherwise the iron law of the market would rule: "All Colleges can put up a defence but without a general agreement on policy, which at present seems impossible, the economic laws will shape the direction of providence."

Runcie went on to say that the existence of four Anglican colleges in Oxford was quite indefensible and that the Church's resources needed to be far more responsibly distributed. He noted that this was already beginning: joint programmes were being developed with Heythrop and Regent's Park. However he thought it could only work if Anglicans buried their petty differences: "This training is to be developed according to a consistent programme over the next three years, and it does make our churchmanship traditions ... look somewhat dated." He went on to defend Cuddesdon, but felt that its success should not make us blind to the need for change. In typical fashion he thought there was always the need to

---

[154] Runcie to Mrs Griffiths, 11 March 1968, CCA P8/103.

[155] Inspection Report, 1969, CCA GB3/12.

[156] Lent Letter 1969, CCA LL25.

guard against complacency. The following passage must have come as a strong challenge to his readers:

> Of course there are still qualities and standards for which this place is peculiarly marked. It is still jealous of its reputation for giving men the spiritual foundation for the ministry and the blend of definite system and quite informal staff-student relations is probably unusual even in theological colleges. ("In my day the College was a Republic" – Edward King, 1873). But having said all this I must admit that we have no monopoly in these things. So long as good candidates continue to present themselves and you all give us your support, we have a future in pre-ordination training. On the other had there is no desire in the present Principal's mind of keeping the place in existence simply for the sake of its past. Cuddesdon has done a great work for the Anglican Communion. It seems to me a duty to ensure that a history remains golden by recognizing when its story is complete.

He concluded by making a bold suggestion that perhaps the energies of the college could be redirected towards in-service training:

> I have sometimes nourished the thought that as we pioneered ordination training with the first purpose-built College, we might be right to switch to the urgent need for re-training older clergy in this century. ... After all, the Banks have Colleges for re-training and they are a fairly cautious part of the establishment! I am thinking aloud, but I hope not just filling up space. The College's present strength in a time of general perplexity might call not for complacency but perhaps a fresh lead and, who knows, a risk.

Discussions of the de Bunsen Report continued and on 14 March 1969 Runcie reported to the Governing Body the progress that had so far been made:[157] joint ecumenical training in pastoral theology had already started and was to be followed by joint teaching in social studies, worship, and preaching. In addition the Anglican colleges were to pool resources for the teaching of certain mainstream theological subjects during the coming year. A committee had been set up to explore the possibility of a Certificate in Pastoral Theology, and another was looking into a joint staff appointment and admissions system for the Anglican Colleges. It was recognised that some surrender of sovereignty by individual colleges would be needed to solve these problems. In the summer of 1969 Runcie reported to the AGM that a joint programme of training between the colleges was in the process of being planned, although it had not yet been worked out in detail what was to happen. Through all this change he reassured his audience about the future of the college: "Whatever the outcome of new plans for theological training, the Principal

---

[157] Governing Body Minutes, 14 March 1969.

would be very sad if Cuddesdon was not and did not continue to be something significant in training in the Church of England."[158]

By 2 October 1969 the proposals from the de Bunsen Report were looking more concrete:[159] there would be a reduction in number of colleges from 21 to 14 if this was accepted by the Church Assembly. Runcie thought that it would be difficult to see the Oxford Colleges suddenly merged into one – the Boars Hill site would be the only solution – but he did think that a reduction to two places, possibly one in Oxford and one in Cuddesdon, was the least that would have to be accomplished. Reporting on the joint teaching, he noted: "There was a general feeling at Cuddesdon that at least two thirds of the whole contribution in teaching and attendance was made by this college, and some of the programme would be better and more conveniently organised here." He also noted that the staffs of the colleges were meeting on a regular basis, and that the Oxford Certificate (which has since mutated into a Bachelor of Theology) was being established after a report "A Time to Plant". However, there was a good deal still to be explored in relation to the university, the non-Anglican colleges and ACCM. Perhaps most important in view of what was to happen a few years later, was the shared consultation between the staffs of Cuddesdon and Ripon Hall under the aegis of Martin Rogers and the Littlemore team.

Had Runcie stayed longer as principal it is difficult to say what might have happened to the shape of Oxford theological education. The strength of his personality might have put into effect something very different from what eventually emerged: a reduction to two colleges in Oxford would probably have been sensible, even if painful, and the move into in-service training might well have ensured Cuddesdon's survival in a very different form. Runcie, while he was always cautious and certainly no visionary, had the strength of personality to make things happen. In the months after Runcie's departure joint seminars were held on Tuesday afternoons in Oxford which generally provoked a good response. There had also been a wide ranging debate the previous November between staff and students on "Cuddesdon into the Seventies". One participant claimed: "The place itself, open to every wind of heaven, and founded on a hill, standing rock-like, looking as it were from the present upon the past and the future in one survey, seems to be a parable of the life of the English Church."[160] With Runcie's departure, however, the winds of change blew in a different direction, and while Cuddesdon and Ripon Hall eventually merged, the opportunity to form an Oxford Federation equivalent to that in Cambridge yet more closely associated with the university collapsed primarily because of party difference and a consequent lack of

---

[158] AGM Minutes, 24 July 1969, CCA AGM1/1.
[159] Governing Body Minutes, 2 October 1969.
[160] Lent Letter 1970, CCA LL26.

motivation. Personnel changes at the other colleges made joint planning far more precarious.

Even though as Bishop of St Albans he found himself on the follow-up committee to implement the Report (with Kenneth Woollcombe and D. R. Wigram), Runcie was too far removed directly to effect change in and around Oxford to ensure progress towards some form of federation. A letter sent to the Governors following a meeting on 18 November 1970 noted that the opportunity for greater collaboration had been missed:

> We regret that new tendencies at Wycliffe Hall are likely to make such comprehensive planning and even close co-operation more rather than less difficult. ... Our students make considerable use of Oxford and, in the context of any more comprehensive plan, would greatly welcome the provision, either in some part of the theological college buildings situated in Oxford or perhaps elsewhere, of a study centre where they could work during the day. This would be analogous to the use made of the Department of Education in Oxford by students from outlying colleges of education.[161]

Similarly, Dennis Nineham, Warden of Keble College and newly appointed as governor, wrote to Leslie Houlden at the end of November 1970, with the suggestion that the Governing Body should be more emphatic in our "disappointment that the Runcie Commissioners had not even had a bash at a single and creative ecumenical plan for ordination training centred on the Oxford Theological Faculty, and our hope that if any re-thinking was to be done, some of it might be along such lines".[162] Despite the many changes to theological training in the early 1970s and the reduction of places to 850, opportunities for a more coherent pattern of training centred on Oxford University, which was far better disposed towards the theological colleges and permanent private halls than Cambridge, were undoubtedly missed.

On 10 October Runcie received the letter from the Prime Minister, Harold Wilson, inviting him to take on the Bishopric of St Albans. He had earlier declined the offer of the Deanery of Guildford. He wrote a letter to his erstwhile curate, Ruston on 4 November 1969, where he spoke of his mixed feelings about leaving Cuddesdon:

> Now our roots are very deep. I feel that the work has built up so much over the last year or so that in some ways another man should write the next chapter, but on personal grounds Lindy is very happy here and she hates the thought of uprooting

---

[161] Letter to members of the Governing Body, 7 December 1970 (CCA G3/33).
[162] Nineham to Houlden, 27 November 70 (CCA G3/32).

after having made this house so lovely and got the children so well settled at school.[163]

On 25 October Henry Chadwick, who three days earlier had written to resign from the Governors following his elevation to the Deanery of Christ Church,[164] offered his congratulations:

> It is marvellous for St Albans, sad indeed for Cuddesdon. We are going to miss you both very much. In fact I have always looked forward to visiting you at Cuddesdon on occasions of special delight when Lindy would really bring us all down to earth and you would delight with some absurdity that had happened. Now you will be further off. I am glad you will be in the only position from which the C of E can effectively be altered and *moved*, viz. from the top.[165]

Chadwick withdrew his resignation and began thinking about a possible successor. "Do you think Alec Graham should be considered? He was offered (and then declined) a similar post. But I think he would be strongly attracted by Cuddesdon. I don't put forward his name as 'My Candidate' but as a fine man whose name ought to be before us." Names of other candidates soon began to emerge.[166] Appointing his second Principal, Carpenter wrote to the Governors about the results of the informal enquiries he had made:

> The name which has emerged with the greatest promise of being the ultimate choice is that of Leslie Houlden, of Trinity College, Oxford. To give his qualifications briefly: he is a theologian of recognised standing; he would form a direct link with Oxford generally and the theological faculty in particular; he is used to dealing with young men and giving spiritual counsel; he is competent on the side of business and administration.[167]

Carpenter reported that Runcie had already approached him and "he would seriously consider the offer of the post, if it were to come". Runcie wrote a farewell Lent Letter early in 1970 where he introduced his successor: "It will be valuable to have someone who is already a party to the debate about the shape of theological training and preparation for ordination in Oxford – the pace of co-operation

---

[163] Runcie to Ruston, 4 November 1969 (Oxfordshire Record Office, DD Par Cuddesdon b. 6 (h)).

[164] Henry Chadwick to Runcie, 22 October 1969, CCA GB3/16.

[165] Henry Chadwick to Runcie, 25 October 1969, CCA GB3/17. Chadwick resigned and was replaced by Dennis Nineham. John Barnett, Principal of Culham, also came on as a member (Ramsey to Runcie, 27 November 1969, CCA GB3/ 20).

[166] Houlden to Runcie, 6 November 69, CCA GB3/18.

[167] Carpenter to Governors, 17 November 1969, CCA GB3/19.

between different Colleges and denominations has quickened considerably in the past year."[168]

Assessment

Runcie gave his last address at Compline on 5 December 1969.[169] It was classic Runcie and displays something of his devotion to the Incarnation, specially the doctrine of self-emptying or kenosis, so central to the Anglo-Catholic tradition: "Christmas – a former principal liked Ash Wednesday. I like Christmas." He went on to point to the scandal of the incarnation, even suggesting (perhaps against himself) that "Moderation is not a Christian virtue – God's love is not moderate. ... Real spirituality means being content to accept life as it is because you forget anything is due to you." Perhaps reflecting on his own preferment, he suggested that it was all too easy to long for recognition, but this would be a "denial of the love of the God who emptied himself". He continued: "Does every man have the right to be a parish priest? Wilfrid Knox yearned for this, but he believed his friends when they told him he would be bad." As he embarked on his episcopal ministry, Runcie concluded: "We must be prepared for failure."

It was this kind of questioning, coupled with an immense self-deprecation that made Runcie such a great Principal, and it was this too that gave him the strength to lead the Church of England through the turmoils of the 1980s. His insecurity and his uncertainty helped make the faith credible in a world which often seemed to have little space for questions. All this was derived from a deep concern for the Gospel and the reality of prayer. As he wrote in his final Lent Letter:

> Since our theology here is not just a case of how much study we do, but is rather a preparation to govern our way of life and our way of ministry, it follows that the real question here is whether or not we care. Whether we care about the Faith. Whether we care about the Gospel. Whether we care about God. ... If we put off serious theological engagement and rest content at a tentative, rudimentary, jejune stage of belief, no wonder prayer is inauthentic or lifeless. Conversely, when anyone radical or orthodox, intellectual or practical, seriously thinks or reads as a believing man fascinated by the wonder of what God is, prayer is a possibility without the need of formal teaching.[170]

[168] Lent Letter 1970, CCA LL26.
[169] Robert Runcie, notes for Compline address, 5 December 1969, CCA P8/106,.
[170] Lent Letter 1970, CCA LL26.

Chapter 7

An Uneasy Alliance:
From the Merger to the Present Day

Robert Jeffery

Introduction

> The Revd Dr Richard Sturch animadverted that 160 books were missing from the
> Library; so ends the last meeting of the Senior Common Room and Chapter of
> Ripon Hall at 2.35 p.m. Sic transit Gloria mundi.[1]

Thus the Ripon Hall Common Room minutes for the summer term 1975 come to
an end. It was hard for the students at both Colleges to exercise a great deal of
influence over the merger of the two Colleges. The students were, after all, the
people in transit. It was the Governing Bodies and the wider Church who had to
bear the responsibility for such matters. At the same time they were greatly
affected by it and they were mainly very unhappy about what was going on. Indeed
Anthony Dyson worked hard to ensure that the students were not just the victims of
the negotiations. Expressing the great uncertainty and the need for change in 1970
he wrote in the College Annual Report as follows:

> The lesson is learnt that a theological College can only make its way today as a
> team enterprise. I have to acknowledge gratefully the help and support which is
> given to me personally by the staff and students, often with great generosity of
> time and energy. In particular it has been a year marked by an increasing part
> taken by the student body in the processes, which shape the pattern of life and

[1] This Chapter has been drawn from minutes of the Governing Bodies of both colleges,
as well as the Lent letters and Newsletters of the College. I am also grateful for
conversations and correspondence with Bishop David Wilcox, Bishop John Garton, Canon
Alan Dunstan, Canon John Clarke and various former students of both Colleges. I am
grateful to Mr John Davies, the College Archivist for his help.

training. In formal terms this has been manifested by the growth of the Staff-Student committee and the Worship Committee. But, in more informal ways, there has developed a conviction that the destiny of a theological college lies as much with the vigorous participation, enthusiasm, criticism and self-determination of the students as well as the labours of the staff. But the main challenge is not simply to initiate such structures but to see together that they are allowed to grow rather than fossilize.

The Wider Background

In order to put this whole process in context we have to go back at least as far as 1964. This was a key year in the life of the Church of England in many ways, but according to Callum Brown in his book *The Death of Christian Britain*[2] this was the period when the post war religious revival ended and when Church life started to decline. A major matter of debate was *The Paul Report*[3] which came about as a result of a debate in the Church Assembly in 1960 when Colonel Madge moved a resolution that "The Central Advisory Council for the Ministry should examine the whole matter of the payment and deployment of the clergy in very changing circumstances".Such a review was well overdue. At that time there were no proper pension provisions: much of the clergy's income still came from glebe which they had to collect themselves; there was no retirement age and a great inequality in levels of clerical stipends. Moreover, the deployment of the clergy reflected an age before the industrial revolution, and the rural dioceses tended to have more clergy per capita that the urban ones. The average stipend of the clergy was around £700 p.a. The chairman of the Advisory Council which commissioned the report was Kenneth Riches who had been Principal of Cuddesdon from 1945-1952. His subsequent experience as Archdeacon of Oxford and Bishop of Dorchester, and his growing experience as Bishop of Lincoln (to which see he was translated in 1956) would have made him very aware of the problems.

Leslie Paul produced an overview of the state of the deployment of manpower in the ministry of the Church of England. It was an influential document – but not perhaps in the way that Leslie Paul had expected. He began by noting the decline of the church. Only a tenth of those baptized actually attended church. Only one in four of those confirmed made their Easter communion. Both urban and rural dioceses were showing a decline. While he noted an increase in the numbers being ordained – which actually exceeded the number retiring in 1961 – he saw no guarantee that this would continue. Much more serious was the great imbalance in the deployment of the clergy between urban and rural parishes. This problem was

[2] C. G. Brown, *The Death of Christian Britain*, London: Routledge, 2001.

[3] Leslie Paul, *The Deployment and Payment of the Clergy*, London: CIO for Central Advisory Council for the Ministry, 1964.

taken up some years later in what was known as the Sheffield Allocation (named after a Report chaired by the Bishop of Sheffield, Gordon Fallows, and former Principal of Ripon Hall), which led to a gradual redistribution of clergy from the rural to the urban dioceses, working on a norm of 1:2000 for rural benefices and 1:6000 for urban ones,

Leslie Paul foresaw a trend towards shorter incumbencies and a movement from the north to the south of England among the clergy. He noted the social changes, family life and other stresses on the clergy and the very inadequate state of clergy stipends and pensions. He ended up making 62 recommendations. Looked at from the perspective of today, a surprising number of these recommendations have been adopted in one form or another. The development of what he called Major Parishes foreshadowed Team and Group ministries. Compulsory retirement at 70 with the possibility of retirement at 65 was adopted ten years after the report. He recommended the abolition of the clergy freehold for all, including bishops and archdeacons. He saw the need for a Staff College, which was mirrored by developments at St George's House, Windsor. However, he was over-optimistic in his statistics in relation to the numbers of ordinands and did not make recommendations about Theological Colleges.

So began what has seemed to be an endless reflection on the nature and training for the ordained Anglican ministry, which dominated much of central Church thinking for the rest of the century. The bibliography on the subject is considerable. The story of the emergence of Ripon College Cuddesdon is but a microcosm of the national scene. The sudden decline from 1964 onwards (noted in *The Death of Christian Britain*) moved very fast and the need to investigate the role of theological Colleges became inevitable.

At Cuddesdon, Robert Runcie was well in the driving seat as "Princeps". His Lent Letters to former students, all beginning "My Dear Sir", reflected on these matters and his own reaction to them. Never a rich College, Cuddesdon had attracted able students but the running costs were not easy to meet. Knapp-Fisher, when Principal, had suggested that Cuddesdon might follow the example of Kelham so that the students should do all the domestic work. It would be both spiritually enlightening and help to balance the books! Runcie attracted new money from various contacts and from old students and gradually the financial situation eased slightly. The 1964 Nottingham Faith and Order Conference, which had encouraged the establishment of Queen's College, Birmingham as a centre for ecumenical theological training, led Runcie to wonder whether that was the right way for Cuddesdon to go as well. Later he thought that the College might be increasingly involved in the ongoing training and retraining of clergy.[4]

Beneath the daily life of the College, such questions would not go away. They came to a head with the publication of the de Bunsen Report in 1968, entitled

[4] See above, chap. 6.

Theological Colleges for Tomorrow.[5] It was commissioned in January 1967, the committee working rapidly because of a sense of urgency in the task. They were aware of a rapidly changing church and knew that there were questions about how the independent theological colleges fitted in to the overall pattern of education and a more centralised church. They were agreed that the colleges must provide adequate education in theology, a community formation, the development of prayer, spiritual discipline and self-knowledge, and an adequate foundation of practical and professional training. The problem, which the committee faced, was that:

> In 1937 there were 24 theological colleges in the Church of England which could accommodate 1,125 ordinands. Today there are 25 residential theological colleges in England training 1,060 ordinands, but with accommodation for 1,169.

The committee pointed out that the independence of the colleges had been gradually eroded ever since the introduction of the General Ordination Exam (GOE) in 1922. Similarly the financial commitment of Central Church funds to theological education had increased rapidly and Local Authorities were beginning to refuse financial support for theological education. In fact three quarters of the costs were by then being paid by Central Church funds. It had been revealed in 1956 that a college needed at least 50 students to be financially viable. But in 1967 only seven of the 25 colleges had a viable number of students. There was a 10% drop in the number of graduates to just 35% of all ordinands. There was an increase in the number of married ordinands to 6%. At the same time, the average age of the clergy was getting higher.

At this point the de Bunsen Report moved to different concerns from those of the Paul Report. It tackled not just matters involved with the deployment of clergy to larger parishes and centres of population, but also discussed the need to provide the right quality of leadership for the church, both intellectually and equipped with proper leadership skills. Similarly, there would be a more diverse pattern of ministry (with specialist ministries like youth work and industrial mission) and growing patterns of ecumenical co-operation. They looked at the theological divergences of the colleges and their geographical setting. The report noted that many Colleges (not least in Oxford) related to Universities and others related to Colleges of Higher Education. It then considered the implications of links with theological faculties. The report decided that the ideal size for a general-purpose theological college was between 120 and 140, which they saw as educationally desirable and economically viable.

On this basis, they thought that the two colleges for older men at Rochester and Worcester should close and that the pattern of part-time training pioneered since 1960 by the Southwark Ordination Course would be desirable for married

---

[5] *Theological Colleges for Tomorrow*, CIO (for ACCM), 1968.

men with families. So they proposed an overall strategy to develop two different models of larger college: Firstly, there would be colleges which would offer degree courses and the General Ordination Exam. Secondly, there would be colleges for people who would benefit from the sort of education which was being developed in Colleges of Higher Education. They thought that there should be fourteen colleges offering a total of 900 places. In Oxford they suggested two new colleges formed through mergers of Cuddesdon and St Stephen's House and also Ripon Hall and Westcott House. In Cambridge they proposed a new college formed from Wycliffe Hall and Ridley Hall. In addition, there was a need for a new College in the North West of England. This would emerge from a merger of St Aidan's College, Birkenhead, Bishop's Hostel Lincoln and Hartley Victoria Methodist College. It was also recommended that the colleges at Cheshunt and Chichester should close. There were also some further recommendations which concerned the relationship of ACCM and the colleges.

The after-effect of the Report was one of real shock with several colleges seeking to defend their future and members of the House of Bishops rushing to the defence of their own "*alma maters*". The Governing Body at Cuddesdon considered a merger with St Stephen's House. An alternative proposal to merge St Stephen's House (then in Norham Gardens) with Wycliffe Hall even got as far as the planning stage. It proposed building a new College with two chapels, one at each end for very different styles of worship!

As was noted above in Chapter Six, the nettle was not well grasped, and the de Bunsen was followed in 1970 by the appointment of a committee of "Three Wise Men" who would visit every college and make firm recommendations to the House of Bishops. The number of candidates offering themselves for ordination was still declining. The Three Wise Men were very much from the Cuddesdon stable. They were the new Bishop of St Albans (Robert Runcie), Canon Kenneth Woollcombe (Principal of Coates Hall, Edinburgh and about to become Bishop of Oxford and Chairman of the Cuddesdon Governors) and D. R. Wigram. They recommended that the number of places for ordinands in training should be 850. This would be achieved by the closure and merger of Colleges but the colleges were left to sort this out themselves. From then on the future shape of theological education was never off the agenda. As the national scene shifted, so the Colleges adjusted and sought new paths. There were mergers of two Colleges in Bristol and of Salisbury and Wells. Rochester, Worcester, Birkenhead, Lichfield, Kelham, and Cheshunt closed in a very short period thereafter. There seemed to be a lack of strategic planning: Canon Armstrong, who ran the Worcester Course, pointed out that the church was closing down the cheapest patterns of training in the case of Worcester and Rochester.

The Merger of Cuddesdon and Ripon Hall

With this background we can now turn to the story of Cuddesdon and Ripon Hall over the last 30 years. As soon as the de Bunsen report was published both Governing bodies began to consider the future. Cuddesdon had a small and elite Governing Body with five members and chaired by the Bishop of Oxford. Ripon Hall had a Governing Body of twenty-seven members plus the Principal as Secretary and Lord Fisher of Lambeth, who died in 1972, as Visitor. There was no doubt that something had to be done. It looked as if the obvious merger would be between St Stephen's House and Cuddesdon. Both were in Oxford and both were catholic in orientation. Cuddesdon was full with 62 students and the forecast did not look bad. There were informal discussions with St Stephen's House, but it was considered that a cluster of the Oxford Theological Colleges working together might be a better option. In 1970 the Principals of Cuddesdon, Mansfield College and Wycliffe Hall all left, thus leaving the discussion in the hands of a new generation of Principals. Cuddesdon's distance from Oxford remained a problem. But by 1971 (after Leslie Houlden, who had been Chaplain of Trinity College, Oxford, had become Principal) Cuddesdon was facing an acute financial crisis. A lot of work needed to be done on the buildings, the kitchens had to be upgraded and the number of students was beginning to go down. New fire regulations required considerable alterations to the buildings. In running institutions there is a fine balance between number of residents, which will make the place financially viable, and the number of teaching and domestic staff.

Dr Anthony Dyson was a former student of Ripon Hall and after a two-year curacy in Putney returned as Chaplain in 1963. He became Principal of Ripon Hall after Gordon Fallows was appointed Bishop of Pontefract in 1968. It was in many ways a surprising appointment. Anthony was only 34, but he was a very outstanding person and a profound thinker, especially in relation to theological education. His first intuition was to seek to respond to the need for a new College in the North-west. He opened up negotiations with the Northern Baptist College in Manchester whose Principal, Dr Michael Taylor, who later became Director of Christian Aid, was one of the country's leading liberal theologians. It would have been a good theological match. The development at Ripon Hall of close co-operation with the Urban Ministry Project was another interest they had in common. The UMP was based in St Helier, Morden, Surrey, where Donald Reeves was Vicar, and served as a base for ordinands to experience urban life. Part of the experience included students "taking the plunge" and being made to live on the streets of London for three days with hardly any money. However, the Ripon Hall Governors were very reluctant to leave Oxford, especially when, at this point, there was little sign of any further drop in ordinands. Consequently it seemed sensible to open discussions with Cuddesdon, and in 1971 Ripon Hall and Cuddesdon agreed that if the numbers declined further they would begin serious negotiations over a merger.

The numbers did indeed decline. In his Lent Letter for 1974 Leslie Houlden wrote:

> By October 1973 the figure was down by 17% on the previous year. In the colleges as a whole, out of 882 places only 728 were filled. For next October there will be a further drop and the indications are that this will continue.[6]

He then went on to explain the difficulties of financing training. Local Authorities were refusing to fund places for ordinands as they had in the past, and Central Church Funds would not be able pick up the difference. A loss of four or five places over the previous two years had led to a deficit in the College of £30,000 each year. Furthermore, there was a great deal of work to be done on the buildings. The two Governing Bodies had therefore decided to proceed to a merger, with both Bodies appointing four people to form a working group. Houlden commented:

> It may seem to some, especially those who have seen little of the work of either institution, that they stand for such different outlooks. Of course this was once the case. But it is clear to those of us now teaching in the two colleges that, particularly during the last ten years, the educational policies pursued and the types of ordinands attracted by them have become more and more indistinguishable. In pastoral training, our methods are virtually identical. The academic teaching in the two cases has similar aims and aspirations. The liturgical practice has moved much closer together than would at one time been thought possible. And even in that indefinable area best labelled "ethos" it is hard to detect deep or significant differences.

Serious negotiations between the two colleges began in 1973. Not surprisingly, it was an unsettling time for all concerned. One member of the working group, the veteran Archdeacon of Oxford, Carl Witton-Davies declared that he was totally opposed to a merger of Cuddesdon, where he was a Governor, with Ripon Hall. The matters of major tension were the site for the College and the appointment of the Principal. It was agreed that the new College would start off at Cuddesdon, but that a new site would soon be sought. In relation to the Principal, it had originally been agreed that both would leave, and that the Archbishop of Canterbury should be approached to appoint a new Principal. In the end this was rejected and the following plan was agreed:

> That the appointing of the new principal of the new college would be in the hands of its governing body:

[6] CCA LL27, 1974.

That the Principal of Cuddesdon would be the acting Principal of the new college.

That he would resign in 1975, if by then the Governing Body of the new College was able to make a new appointment, and that in any case he would resign not later than October 1976.[7]

The Bishop of Oxford, Kenneth Woollcombe, played a considerable part in bringing the two Colleges together. A formal agreement by the two Governing Bodies to unite was agreed in September 1973 which was endorsed by the House of Bishops. Ripon Hall's commitment to a theology involving the interaction of Church and society was to be implemented by the College establishing the Institute for Church and Society, which would operate on a wider basis than the Colleges. The libraries would be merged to provide one of the best theological libraries in the country. Dr Dyson was appointed as a Canon of St George's, Windsor. It was thought his major theological expertise would be made available for those attending clergy and other courses at Windsor. He would also be Chairman of the Governors for the first three years. Peter Baelz, Regius Professor of Moral and Pastoral Theology in Oxford, who was the only person on the Governing Body of both colleges, became the Vice-Chairman. After three years Baelz became Chairman. Each college appointed four Foundation Governors who, under the Charter, could remain until they wished to resign whereas new governors and those under other categories (like those appointed by the Bishop of Oxford and by former members) had to be re-appointed every three years. The staff of the new College would be as follows:

Principal: Canon Leslie Houlden (Cuddesdon)
Vice Principal: Revd Alan Dunstan (Ripon Hall)
Revd Gareth Lloyd Jones (Old Testament, Ripon Hall)
Revd John Packer (Pastoral Studies, Ripon Hall)
Revd John Fuller (Ethics, Cuddesdon)
Revd Dr J. Geoffrey Cuming (Liturgy, Cuddesdon)

The Royal Charter provided for some considerable checks and balances between the two Colleges in relation to the Governing Body, with some members elected at the former members' AGM each year. The Privy Council issued the Charter in 1978. Anthony Dyson summed up the arrangement by claiming that the new college:

... brings together two colleges whose pattern of life, work and worship has been growing ever closer over the last decade. The liberal tradition of Ripon Hall will go forward in an institution, which will welcome students of all backgrounds and

[7] CCA GB1/1, 2 May 1974.

traditions. Many of the recent educational and training developments at the Hall will also be continued in the new college. We shall also learn much from Cuddesdon's concern with spirituality, and with that theological seriousness which has been a part of the Ripon Hall tradition from the earliest days.

The New College

So the new College began, although it cannot be said that it was an easy birth. Just after the arrival of the Ripon Hall students at Cuddesdon, the "For Sale" notice from the Boars Hill site, which was soon acquired by The Open University, appeared at Cuddesdon, but with these words added to it: "and in need of modernisation". This reflected the mood of the Ripon Hall students who were sad to leave Boars Hill, and felt that the Cuddesdon students had a superior attitude. The Cuddesdon students found it equally difficult. The uneasy relationship of the first two years of the merger produced many tensions. The two staffs did not easily mould together. There were resentments among the students either at having to move or about changes in the worship pattern, which they did not welcome. On reflection, the pressures brought on the Principal and staff were excessive. At the same time, however, there was a real determination on all sides to make it work.

At this point it is necessary to bring into play another rather strange factor in the situation. In the Cuddesdon Governing Body minutes as far back as 1969 there were references to "a distinguished person"[8] who wished to purchase the Old Vicarage at Cuddesdon from the College as his retirement home. It soon emerged that this was Dr Michael Ramsey, the Archbishop of Canterbury.[9] Thus at exactly the same time as there were delicate negotiations going on between the colleges, there were also some rather complex negotiations going on through the Archbishop's lawyer. Thus Michael Ramsey arrived just before the merger took place. And so began the very sad story of his peripatetic retirement, which is movingly described in Owen Chadwick's biography. Many people had doubted whether the rather remote situation at Cuddesdon was ideal for the Ramseys. He was away a lot and he and Lady Ramsey had to rely on others for transport. The house was altered to suit their requirements and the Governing Body very wisely, as it turned out, built in a clause to enable them to buy it back if the Ramseys left. They lived there for three years. The College was not as he remembered it and while some students greatly valued his pastoral advice and support, some others used his home as a sort of "Cave of Adullam", where they could complain about the College and what was going on within it. Moreover, as Chadwick pointed out, Ramsey was not sympathetic to the approach to New Testament studies which was exemplified by Leslie Houlden. The merger, which took place after Ramsey had

[8] CCA GB1/1, 14 March 1969.
[9] CCA GB1/1, 1 October 68.

been there for over a year, was even more disconcerting. Chadwick summed it up as follows:

> The old tradition of Ripon was of English modernism, which the undergraduate Ramsey learned to think of as superficial even when it was clever; though in young Ramsey's day the attitudes of Ripon Hall were very much more negative that they were in 1975, by which time it had become central in Anglicanism. Naturally in this union of Colleges the one tradition affected the other. The old traditions of worship continued. The trouble turned out to be, not the marriage of the different ways of thought or ways of worship, but the more intangible friction in the union of a group of persons living in their old buildings and another group of persons with different habits who moved into that building as a corporate entity. This was a normal human awkwardness. But it made life in the college rather uncomfortable in certain non-physical ways for a year or two; and the year or two happened to be while Ramsey resided.[10]

The pressure of the merger on students and staff at this time was not easy. It must have been particularly difficult for Leslie Houlden, who, as the Principal of the new College, was faced with this process of integration of Ripon Hall students into the buildings of the former college where he had already been Principal for four years. Mixed in with this was the question of homosexuality. This was always likely to be an issue in a single-sex institution and there has undoubtedly been a minority of homosexuals among the students through the College's history.[11] How this was to be handled was a matter which every Principal had to decide for himself. But in an institution where one is dealing with adults, who are meant to be making moral decisions for themselves, most principals felt that it was probably best dealt with individually and pastorally, unless it was a matter which was disturbing to other people or likely to create a scandal. As Chadwick puts it:

> Whether it was the atmosphere of the age, or whether it was the liberal tradition of open mindedness about a more conventional morality, or whether it was a very few people who happened to be there, the moral right or wrong of homosexual relations in ordinands and priests started to be argued with emotion and in this atmosphere several students came to consult Ramsey. He found he did not like being involved as an outsider in this predicament.[12]

It was undoubtedly even more difficult for the staff and the Governing Body. This

---

[10] Owen Chadwick, *Michael Ramsey*, Oxford: Oxford University Press, 1990, pp. 382-6, here p. 384.

[11] The problem was certainly not restricted to Cuddesdon. Canon Alan Wilkinson, Principal of Chichester Theological College at the time, was so anxious about the issue that he called for a Church Report which eventually emerged in the Board of Social Responsibility Report, *Homosexual Relationships: A Report* (GS 479), London: CIO, 1981.

[12] Owen Chadwick, *Michael Ramsey*, p. 385.

reflected something of the strains under which the staff were working. The unhappy story of Michael Ramsey at Cuddesdon stands in stark contrast to that of Professor Christopher Evans who retired as Professor of New Testament at King's College, London in 1977 to live in the village, and who has been a strong resource and support to the College ever since.

In 1976 Leslie Houlden decided to accept a post teaching New Testament at King's College London. Alan Dunstan, who had been acting Principal at Ripon Hall for its last year, found himself as Acting Principal again when Leslie Houlden left. He moved in 1978 to be a Residentiary Canon of Gloucester Cathedral. Thus gradually the staff and students changed and the college settled down. The numbers in the College began to stabilise, but there was a notable increase in the number of married students, which put considerable pressure on the accommodation. Various things were done to address this by renting or purchasing houses in the village. The work of the Oxford Institute for Church and Society went ahead with the appointment of the Revd Dr Christopher Lewis (now Dean of Christ Church, Oxford) as director in 1976. He collaborated with the Revd Robin Bennett, who also worked for Radio Oxford. The Institute published a series of papers of social issues, which were widely valued, and also arranged conferences and consultations.

The Process of Integration

After Leslie Houlden's departure, the post of Principal was widely advertised. It provoked a great deal of interest and an outstanding short-list was drawn up. After a two-day interview process (which has been the model used ever since for appointments and involves a presentation and meetings with staff and students as well as the interview panel), the Governors appointed Canon David Wilcox to the post. He was Warden of the East Midlands Ministry Training Course and a Canon of Derby Cathedral. He had trained and taught at Lincoln Theological College, and thus his origins lay in neither of the former colleges. He had also worked in the Church of South India from 1964-70 and was a member of the General Synod. This meant that he brought a breadth of knowledge of theological education to the post.

But there were still unsolved issues arising from the merger. The most crucial was the siting of the College. It had been agreed that Cuddesdon would be the initial site, but that a new site would soon be sought. The need for those taking theological degrees in Oxford was met initially by renting St Margaret's Vicarage in North Oxford for the use of those taking the Oxford University Honour School of Theology. Subsequently it was agreed to develop a split site with one member of staff and several students living in three houses in East Oxford.

In 1979 a new opportunity presented itself. The Society of St John the Evangelist (The Cowley Fathers), whose numbers were rapidly declining, decided to vacate their historic site in Marston Street, East Oxford, and move their mother house to St Edward's House in Westminster. They made an approach to Ripon College Cuddesdon to see whether they might be interested in the site. A major feasibility study then ensued with very detailed plans, but finally the Governors decided to turn down the offer. The number of married students was increasing and the need for a large amount of married accommodation would have been very difficult to fit into the Marston Street site. In the end the buildings were taken over by St Stephen's House, who had a much more saleable property to dispose of in Norham Gardens, and had fewer married students.

At the same time Ripon College Cuddesdon launched an appeal for the accommodation to be upgraded. The appeal never really fully took off, although the money raised was well used. Under David Wilcox the worldwide contacts increased and with the appointment of the philosopher of religion, Dr Janet Soskice, the College employed its first woman member of staff. The ecumenical nature of the staff began to develop. Both Janet Soskice and Paul Joyce (Old Testament) were Roman Catholics. This pattern has continued into the present, with a Russian Orthodox priest and a URC minister on the staff. The policy has been to employ the best staff, regardless of denomination.

The other major development at this time was the training of women at the college for the full-time stipendiary ministry, first as deaconesses and then as deacons: the first four women were ordained in 1982. There had for a long time been an exchange with the Church Divinity School of the Pacific at Berkeley, California and David Wilcox was asked if the college would accept for a year a woman training for the priesthood in the USA. The Episcopal Church had first ordained women as priests in 1972. This faced the Governing Body with a major decision. Not all the students were in favour of women's ordination but the Governing Body with the foresight typical of its Ripon Hall predecessor, decided that it was the right action to take. So the first woman in training for priesthood spent a year at Cuddesdon in 1979. Thereafter the number of women in training slowly increased, although it must be admitted that the first women students did not always have an easy time. The Governing Body was aware of this and tried to address it through appointing a part-time and a then a full-time woman Chaplain. Also Miss Katherine Ross, a governor for many years, deliberately put herself out to look after the women students. The Royal Charter, which came into effect in 1978, provided for two student Governors and it soon became the pattern to have one male and one female student Governor every year. So the College gradually became well established as a place that attached particular importance to the training of women.

The number of students' wives was also going up, so that the presence of women in and around the college was increasingly common. This matter also affected the training. The ordinands' wives varied in the way they expected to respond to their husbands' ordination. Some wanted to share fully in their husband's ministry, while others wanted to pursue their own lives and careers.

Special programmes were arranged for the wives including "Open Door Retreats". These became so popular that many of the men went on them as well. In 1980 the first married couple were both ordained to ministry. A new openness and flexibility was developing in the College with the result that when it became possible for women to be ordained to the priesthood the number of women studying at Cuddesdon became the largest of any theological college. When it became possible for women to be ordained priests in 1994, in the first round of ordinations, there were no fewer than 51 women who had trained at Cuddesdon. This was undoubtedly a factor in keeping the College full in subsequent years.

In the year before he left, David Wilcox devoted most of his article in the Annual Newsletter to an account of how the College was evolving. He began by comparing the College to a tree with trunk, roots and three branches. The tree trunk is the common life of the community. The College was, he claimed, "a warm, relaxed and welcoming community", which had been described by the last Bishops' Inspectors Report as "an adult College, combining tradition with liberality". The three main branches were:

1) the personal apprehension, through critical study, of the Gospel and the Christian tradition.
2) the pastoral studies programme with a growing knowledge of ourselves.
3) the daily pattern of corporate worship and private prayer.

For the tree to grow, he went on, it depends on the environment in which it is set. His further reflections on the nature of the College began by quoting a statement of aims made in 1906 by the founders of Ripon Clergy College:

The ideals which the founders desire to develop at Ripon College are:
(i) Love of truth, not a certain set of views received by tradition and labelled "The Truth", but of reality, the truth of things as it appears in the sight of God, so far as that truth can be ascertained by truthful methods.
(ii) Patient scholarship that thinks no pains too great to ascertain the exact meaning of any word or phrase in the Bible, or in the early Christian writers.
(iii) The use of historical methods – seeking to read the Bible not in the light of succeeding centuries (whether the 4th or the 16th) but in the light of their own day asking: "What did St Paul say to the men of his own day, and what would they have understood him to mean?" not "What can he be made to say to support my own views?"
(iv) The fearless welcoming of light from every quarter. The man who knows God does not fear light; seeking God in all, he will welcome every addition to our knowledge of the world around and the world within, assured that it can only throw light upon God and his truth
(v) The patient zeal to apply the truths thus ascertained to the pressing problems of individual and social life. The germ of all these can be implanted and fostered at the College.

Wilcox then went on to expand on this passage by pointing to its relevance to the modern College:

> though one might wish to quibble and qualify here and there, those five ideals seem to be to be remarkable in their relevance to our own tasks today. I simply want to add that we do seek to set ourselves high standards in academic matters as well as in other area, and that each person entering training may expect to be stretched to the utmost of his or her ability.[13]

He argued for more reflection on the nature of pastoral studies and pointed out the central role of worship, spirituality and spiritual direction. He was anxious to see that this entire programme was fully integrated. He then went on to reflect on the changing role of women in the Church, and also discussed other forms of training for the ministry. Finally, he pointed out (with some prescience) that while 40% of the students at the college were married, this could be a much higher figure if there were more married accommodation.

The Response to *Faith in the City*

In 1984 the Chairman of the Governors, Eric Heaton, Dean of Christ Church, resigned as chairman. He had succeeded Peter Baelz when Baelz had followed him as Dean of Durham. It was decided that, given the continued uncertainty surrounding theological education, it was important to have a member of the House of Bishops as Chairman of the Governors. Consequently, Michael Adie, Bishop of Guildford (and not a Cuddesdon or Ripon Hall man) was invited to take on the post, which he did with great vigour and discernment, even if one of the first things he did was to appoint David Wilcox to be his Suffragan Bishop of Dorking! Wilcox achieved a great deal during his period as Principal: he built up an able staff and outward-looking approach, as well as much integration between the different aspects of College life. There was by now little sense of "them and us" between the traditions of Cuddesdon and Ripon Hall, and the increasing number of women were being well cared for in the community. There were also three lay people on the teaching staff.

This was also the time of the publication of *Faith in the City*,[14] an investigation into urban life strongly backed by Archbishop Robert Runcie and setting a new agenda for the Church of England. There is little doubt that the thinking of the Report was reflected in the appointment in 1986 of John Garton as Principal. He was a former army officer, who had taught theology at Lincoln Theological

---

[13] Ripon College Cuddesdon Newsletter, 1985, pp. 1-7.

[14] Church of England Commission on Urban Priority Areas, *Faith in the City: A Call for Action by Church and Nation*, London: Church House Publishing, 1985.

College and been an inner-city Team Rector in Coventry. He came with a great commitment to urban mission as well as a real concern for inter-faith matters.

Early on in his time as Principal he felt that the question of the siting of the College needed to be resolved once and for all. The combination of Michael Adie and John Garton brought new blood on to the Governing Body with property and financial expertise. It was not long before they had established a radical plan for the future. There was a desperate need for more married and flexible accommodation. Thus it was decided to do what no college had done before, and launch a major appeal for £1 million to build new accommodation on the site. Architects drew up an imaginative design, which blended in well with the old buildings, and John Garton drew together a highly influential group of people, mainly from Oxfordshire, to run the appeal. In three years they raised the £1 million, which was a remarkable achievement. A by-product was the development of a large group of "Friends of Ripon College Cuddesdon" who, having been involved and seen the quality of the building and the training, have continued to give even more support to the College. Thus at a stroke the problem of accommodation was solved, together with raising a considerable amount of capital (mainly vested in buildings), which gives the college a very secure economic basis for the future. The Duchess of Kent opened the new building, named the Runcie Building, in 1990.

The commitment to urban mission had been an important part of the contribution of Ripon Hall to the College, mainly through the Oxford Institute for Church and Society. This now took a new form. The Institute ceased as a separate entity, but in its place a strong link with the Manor Team Ministry in Sheffield was established. John Packer, a former member of staff at Ripon Hall and of Ripon College Cuddesdon in the early years after the merger, was the Team Rector. A house was set up where some first and second year students spent a number of terms. The teaching in Sheffield was set against the background of the sort of poverty which *Faith in the City* had seen as requiring urgent attention. Bishop Kenneth Skelton, the retired Bishop of Lichfield, also contributed to the teaching for a number of years. When Packer left, he was succeeded by Richard Atkinson, a former student of Ripon College Cuddesdon.

When Alastair Redfern resigned as Vice Principal he was replaced by the Revd Dr Alan Billings, a Vicar in Sheffield, who was also deputy leader of the Labour City Council of Sheffield. In this way the urban commitments became more focused. Those unable to go to Sheffield were able to experience Council Housing ministry in the nearby village of Berinsfield, where the Team Vicar became an honorary staff member at Cuddesdon. This was a development of the programme which had begun under Runcie. Pastoral placements, and pastoral studies weeks also incorporated rural ministry. Inter-faith understanding has become an increasingly important aspect of the College programme. Students spend a short time living among people of other faiths, and leading scholars, among them the great Islamic expert, Bishop Kenneth Cragg regularly lecture at Cuddesdon. Students are thereby being equipped for the Church of today.

In 1987 the Report, *Education for the Church's Ministry* (known as ACCM 22), set and established a firm basis for the curriculum.[15] The College used this to reshape the curriculum, which was always very demanding, and to ensure a greater degree of integration between the different courses. Some students had for many years spent a year at the Venerable English College in Rome or the WCC School of Ecumenics in Bossey (Switzerland) or at the Church Divinity School of the Pacific at Berkeley in California. A more recent exchange programme for staff and students has been developed with The College of the Transfiguration in Grahamstown, which provides residential training for the Church of the Province of Southern Africa.

John Garton stayed at Cuddesdon for 10 years, leaving in 1996 to become Bishop of Plymouth. During his time the number of women in training increased significantly, especially after the passing of the legislation for the ordination of women to the priesthood, which was steered through the General Synod by Michael Adie in 1992. The pastoral care of women students had always been a matter of concern and the College has always tried to ensure that there has been a woman priest on the staff. In 1993 Michael Adie retired as Chairman of the Governors and was replaced by Bishop Tom Butler (then of Leicester and subsequently of Southwark). All in all, John Garton's ten years at Cuddesdon were marked by considerable well-managed change, and he left the College in a strong state. He had also managed to establish closer co-operation with the other Anglican Theological Colleges, and the other ecumenical Colleges through the Oxford Partnership for Theological Education and Training (OPTET). His successor, John Clarke also came from an inner city parish in Battersea although much of his earlier ministry had been in the Scottish Episcopal Church.

Training for Ministry in the Wider Church

Ever since the de Bunsen report there has been in the Church of England a steady flow of reports and reflections on the nature of ministry and its implications for training. A report advising a process of regionalisation for providers of theological education was issued for debate under the chairmanship of David Brown, Bishop of Guildford in 1981. The Paul Report was followed up by the Tiller Report, *A Strategy for the Church's Ministry*, in 1983.[16] This proposed a radical re-appraisal of the parochial system. A significant report on team and group ministries came out

---

[15] *Education for the Church's Ministry*, London: ACCM Occasional Paper 22, London, 1987.

[16] John Tiller, *A Strategy for the Church's Ministry*, London: CIO, 1983.

in 1985.[17] Taken together these raised questions about the sort of training which was needed in theological colleges. There had already been a steady development of regional non-residential courses. At the beginning of the 1990s there were two further highly-contested Reports: the first was by a committee chaired by Robert Hardy, Bishop of Lincoln entitled, *A Way Ahead*,[18] which made some very radical proposals including the closure of Mirfield and Oak Hill. After much lobbying these were not accepted by the House of Bishops which in turn set up a small follow-up group under the chairmanship of John Oliver, Bishop of Hereford, which reported in 1993 in *The Next Steps*.[19] This led to the closure of Chichester Theological College in 1994 and of Salisbury and Wells, and Lincoln in 1995. It also resulted in a degree of rationalisation of the regional courses which included the amalgamation of the Oxford Ministry Course (pioneered by Canon Wilfred Browning) with the St Albans Ministerial Training Course to form the St Albans and Oxford Ministry Course which provided part-time training for a large number of people across two large dioceses.

An initial increase in the number of ordinands in the mid-1990s, caused in part by the ordination of women, was not sustained through the decade with the result that in 2001 the General Synod set up a further investigation into theological training under the Chairmanship of John Hind, Bishop of Chichester and a former Principal of Chichester Theological College. This report[20] is now under active consideration and the role of Ripon College Cuddesdon in the future is under review as a result. It looks as if the College will retain a significant role as a centre for theological training, although this may be in a more diverse form than in the past and may well involve the creation of close partnerships with the Regional Course and the Diocese of Oxford.

The College has been inspected regularly by the House of Bishops in liaison with the General Synod Body for Ministry (it has changed its title several times from ACCM to ABM to the Ministry Division). In general these have been positive experiences with an affirmation of College life and work. The 1986 Inspection helpfully came at the same time as the arrival of John Garton and clarified some of the issues facing the College. The Inspection of 1990 was more controversial, having been used by some dissatisfied students to express their own personal

---

[17] *Team and Group Ministries: A Report by the Ministry Co-ordinating Group* (GS 660), London: CBF, 1985..

[18] Steering Group for Theological Courses and the Advisory Group on Full-time Theological Training, *Theological Training: A Way Ahead. A Report to the House of Bishops of the Church of England on Theological Colleges and Courses*, London: Church House Publishing, 1992.

[19] *Theological Colleges – The Next Steps. Report of the Assessment Group in Theological Colleges*, London: Church House Publishing, 1993.

[20] *The Structure and Funding of Ordination Training*, London: Church House Publishing, 2002.

anxieties to the Inspectors. It was this inspection that pinpointed the issue of the Principal also being Vicar of Cuddesdon. The 1997 Inspection came just after the arrival of John Clarke and again helped to point a way ahead. In 1997 there were 76 students in the College consisting of 49 men and 27 women (34 of whom were married). This is a very different pattern from that at the time of the merger. At every point the life of the College has reflected trends in the national Church, and it has always been sympathetic in its response to what was going on. However, the question remains as to what sort of Church the College is training people for. There is undoubtedly a need for a solid core of full-time professional clergy who will be in the ministry for 40 or more years, and who will provide the backbone of the church's ministry. Yet there are serious grounds, partly financial, for thinking that this is slowly being eroded; the future pattern of ministry may well be radically different. Through all the changes, the College has firmly resisted a drop in standards. It has continued to affirm the importance of serious engagement with academic theology in a residential community underpinned by spirituality. It sees the cultivation of an open and enquiring mind as essential for doing theology and being the Church in today's world.

The Parish of Cuddesdon

One of the unique aspects of Cuddesdon has been the close link between the College and the local community through the fact that since the foundation of Cuddesdon College in 1854 the Principal has also been incumbent of the benefice. This was something greatly valued by Robert Runcie and he saw its end with real sadness. It enabled the students to see that the Principal and other members of staff were firmly rooted in the life of the parish. At the same time two things need to be borne in mind. Cuddesdon was established at the time of the growth of the parochial system with every parish having its own incumbent. This reached its height at the end of the nineteenth century. However, in the last 30 years the number of clergy in full time ministry has been halved while the population has increased. Thus what was possible then is not possible now. In relation to available manpower the single cure was also unrealistic. But more importantly, the nature and work of a theological college principal has become increasingly demanding. The centralisation of theological training, the requirement to sustain academic standards, the ever-changing nature of theological education and the need for closer collaboration with other colleges, have all made the dual role more difficult to sustain. Thus John Garton became the last person to fulfil this role.

In resolving the matter with the Diocese of Oxford much was done to use the situation to the benefit of the College. Initially all but one of the four stipendiary clergy in the new Wheatley Team Ministry had been trained at Cuddesdon or Ripon College Cuddesdon and understood something of the situation. The appointment of John Fuller (a former staff member of Cuddesdon and of Ripon College Cuddesdon after the merger) as the first Team Rector enabled a smooth handover. The parish forms part of a cluster with Garsington, where the Team Vicar lives, and Horspath. More recently one member of the College staff has acted as a Non Stipendiary Minister in the parish. There is also a formal agreement for the College to continue to use the Parish Church for daily worship, and also a commitment by the College to continue to assist in community life with events, like the annual Cuddesdon Church Fete. The College is such a major presence in the Village that its interaction with the community is inevitably strong and is itself a unique factor in theological college life. The other theological colleges in Oxford are more University orientated and are in more institutional settings, having recently become Permanent Private Halls. Even if the Principal is no longer vicar, something of the flavour of the past still remains.

Community Life and Living

Probably the greatest changes which have taken place in the College have been in relation to the nature of the student community itself. A rather severe bachelor establishment under Knapp-Fisher and Runcie (when wives were allowed to come in and take baths only while the students were in Chapel) has been transformed into a community of students, many of whom arrive not only married, but also with children. A large number of children has been born in the College. The year 2001-2 saw almost as many children in the College as there were ordinands, and unlikely issues, including skateboarding, became major points of conflict in the community. The change had begun under Leslie Houlden, who wanted to produce a College that was not at all like the one he attended under Knapp-Fisher.

Several other problems emerged out of this changed community. One was the need to provide and care for the children who arrived in College with their parents. Their ages varied between 0 to 18, and some were children of members of staff. Another problem was the need to ensure that the single students did not feel isolated or neglected in such an environment. All this needed careful handling and much consultation: life did not always run smoothly. The odd riotous student or event or the difficult pastoral situation, such as when it seemed necessary to remove a student from the College, caused much anxiety and friction. While the married students felt themselves much more pressurised in relation to work than the single students, the single students often felt isolated. In many ways their increasingly normal human relationships were the common experience of the life of the College, and it is probably true that more was done to help students through their problems than would happen in many other situations. Each Inspection Report has raised issues which reflect some aspect of this area of community life. As in the rest of life, there is no simple answer to questions of relationships, but it all becomes a learning process. At the same time, the staff are very aware of these matters and only too willing to do all they can to resolve any tensions.

In the Cuddesdon days, the Revd Martin Rogers and later Beaumont Stevenson, successive chaplains of the Littlemore and Warneford Hospitals, ran group dynamics sessions. Stevenson began with the words: "I want to know why you want to be dressed up as Mother and called Father!" Later Mrs Wendy Robinson spent many hours teaching an understanding of pastoral care. Students also experienced this in their placement parishes. There has been a steady development of pastoral placements with the opportunity to deal in depth with questions of bereavement, dealing with AIDS patients, grappling with issues of sexuality, and the drug culture. Pastoral skills and support now play a major part in the training programme.

To some extent what comes to a Governing Body meeting is determined by the Principal and the staff, but the presence of the Student Governors slowly made the Governing Body meetings more open. At the same time, some students expected the Governors to be more involved in the College than was really possible. Every so often a dependency attitude would emerge, leaving the Governors and Principal to ensure that students took responsibility for their own decisions rather than projecting them on to others. The Governors see it as their business, alongside the regular Inspections and the requirements of the validation process, to keep the priorities of the College to the fore and to review and re-affirm them on a regular basis. Thus in appointing Governors there has been a need to balance contributions from those with clear expertise in theological education (including Anthony Dyson, Rowan Williams, John Barton and Trevor Williams) with those with an awareness of the wider church seen in the nominees of the Bishop of Oxford and General Synod representative, as well as those with financial acumen (in people like Martin Mays Smith and Alan Foster). There have also been a number who have provided continuity with the past.

The Governors have remained committed to the need for residential training, about which John Garton wrote in the College Newsletter for 1994. He began by analysing the different sorts of students at Cuddesdon and noted that it was often the mature students who most valued the residential element:

> They have seen it as vitally important not only because it provides time for study and practical experience, but also because of the way it can help with personal and spiritual formation. Far from being an ivory tower, a residential community can be a very challenging way of both doing theology and of discovering the truth about oneself, becoming aware of one's own strengths and weaknesses as well as learning to discern the talents and limitations of others.[21]

[21] Ripon College Cuddesdon Newsletter, 1994.

Conclusion

In this way the life of a changing community becomes part of the learning process for working and ministering in a changing Church. It is for others to draw out the implications of the story of Cuddesdon, and to see where the College is going but as someone who has encountered the college and has lived with it for the past thirty-one years (as a Governor but not as a former student of either establishment), I would like to affirm the very positive contribution it has made to the life of the church, and also the quality of those who have passed through its hands. This can be seen in the very significant roles in the Church many former members now hold. Indeed, it is hard to envisage the Church of England without the contribution which has come from Ripon College Cuddesdon. Ever responding to outside pressure, reacting to others, but keeping a strong sense of priorities, the College has a noble and notable history. Indeed, Anthony Dyson expressed the view that the new College might well become a form of "Staff College" for the Church of England. Throughout the history of the College there has been no desire to preserve its existence at any cost. Rather, its concern has been to be truthful, honest and faithful to the Gospel. As Robert Runcie expressed it in one of his Lent Letters:

> I do not think that the ministry comes alive by anxiously trying to "get into society". It comes alive by getting into the Gospel.[22]

This means being open to the Spirit, flexible about church structures and ever seeking the truth in love. This the College has always tried to do.

[22] CCA LL24, 1968.

Appendix 1

"The Training of a Priest": Sermon Preached at the Cuddesdon College Festival 1958

Michael Ramsey, Archbishop of York[1]

Mark 9:2: *He bringeth them up into a high mountain apart by themselves, and he was transfigured before them.*

Our festival today sends each one of us back to the days we first spent here at Cuddesdon, and evokes from each of us a gratitude, searching and specific. How do we begin to describe what Cuddesdon meant to us? It was here that we came to know and to love, each in our own time, one who taught and guided and inspired us. It was here that the ideal of what it means to be a priest came vividly home to us. It was here that we faced the truth about ourselves before the Cross of Christ, and with the very painful shattering of our pride discovered that we have no sufficiency of ourselves to think anything of ourselves. And, with memories solemn and searching, there mingle memories light and ludicrous, since, for all the seriousness of the purpose which brought us here, we were here as human beings with our own absurdities and our sense of the absurd. Learning to laugh at ourselves, we did not lack other things to laugh about. And how should we, if the Christian life is indeed the knowledge of Him who is the author and giver of laughter as well as tears?

It cannot be fanciful to see in what Cuddesdon meant to us a little re-enactment of the story of the Transfiguration. We were, in a way that was novel and alarming, "apart by ourselves". We were withdrawn. We were faced with what

---

[1] This sermon was printed in *The York Quarterly*, August, 1958. The version reproduced here is as delivered at the College Festival on 3 July 1958 and is slightly longer than the published version. A recording is at CCA Z9/4.

Newman calls the only "two luminously clear realities: the soul and its creator". We were apart, too, as those climbing a mountain. The discipline was not easy for all of us. Learning to pray is difficult. Learning theology is difficult. But we were apart, and climbing, because we believed that our Lord was so leading us. And He was leading us in order that He might give to us, here on this sacred hill, a glimpse of His glory. Moses and Elijah – our study of the Scriptures – helped us by their witness; but our study of the Scriptures was done to the end that our Lord might show Himself to us: Jesus glorious before His Passion. In contrition, in love, in gratitude we were glad that we had come, we were glad to be where we were, and we often said so: "It is good for us to be here." And then the cloud, the cloud: the conviction of the presence of God, the cloud that enveloped all, became very real to us: "*Deus fascinans, Deus tremendus.*" And then from the cloud there comes the voice, "Hear ye him". It was brought home to us that our God is to be adored not only but to be heard and obeyed in his righteous command, for never in the Christian dispensation is there the authentic cloud of the divine presence without the righteous voice of divine command: "Hear ye him." "Hear and obey." "Whatsoever he saith unto you, do it." We heard that voice. And we came down from the mountain.

In the years that have passed since we were here, the weirdest changes have been happening in the conditions under which our ministry is discharged – and this is true whatever our date may be, whether it was forty years ago, or thirty, or twenty or even ten years or five. In my day – a generation now just a little elderly, though not yet senile – I doubt if any of us would have guessed that there would be a Second World War within just over a decade, or that Communist Russia was destined to become so dark a menace to the world, or, to take another matter, that vast movements of population in this country were going to alter the shape of our pastoral work. Nor could we have guessed the extent to which industrial development was going to bring about the technological kind of outlook as the mental ethos of so many of the people: nor that the welfare state would ever really come to be, and when it came, would produce the mentality of comfort in the way that it has done. And who would have guessed that the epoch of social security within the state would also be the epoch of "near-catastrophe" in the world as a whole through the creation of weapons to annihilate the world itself? The saying of Charles Gore, "There ain't no new thought: there ain't nothing new", seems now less obviously convincing than it did when first we heard him say it.

Faced by these vast changes, we find that the pattern of our ministry has in many ways had to change. In some of those changes, for all that it that has distressed us, God has been wonderfully with us. Our congregations, never large in relation to the total population around us, are often more convinced in their allegiance, more instructed, more responsible, and above all more like the *ecclesia of God* realising itself week by week as one bread, one body, in the eucharistic offering. Our laity are discovering that they must be the evangelists, penetrating the community of their neighbours with their own conviction of the Christian faith. But all the while, over against us, a mental outlook is created in the people of the country by T.V., by radio, by newspapers, by novels and the rest – a mental background in which life and death, birth and marriage, home and work are discussed and argued about with the assumption that God and religion have no place whatever on the map. It is to penetrate this world of assumptions so far removed from the Christian faith that is our so very baffling task. Coming down from the mountain, we face indeed a faithless and perverse generation, with its dumb spirits dashing it down so that it foameth and grindeth its teeth.

So new and strange are the times, that within the Church of God those are found saying that "something new" is needed for us and the way we do things. "Something new." New pastoral techniques, new modes of evangel, and of course totally new ways of training our priests; and that has been put in very picturesque language, that we must not try to fight a modern war with horse transport and with bows and arrows. What of the plea for something new.

"Something new" indeed there must be. I mention three needs in the part of the church which seem to me to be very great.

(1) Within both the parishes and the industrial communities of the land we need groups of laity trained as "cells" of the ecclesia, such as yet embody the ecclesia in themselves, meeting, studying, praying, seeking together the will of God for themselves in the setting of their daily occupations, and drawing their neighbours where they can into their fellowship. This is happening. It needs to be happening more, not just as a sort of "supernumerary extra", but as part of the normal ecclesiology of our time.

(2) We need far more grappling with the influence of radio and television and all those things which mould the mental outlook of the people. The Church as a whole must learn far more of the use of these techniques, and in the parishes the priest and the congregation must know more of what their neighbours are watching and discussing, and thinking and reading about, and must be more ready to meet it and expose it.

(3) In the realm of theology itself, we need to break away from the notion, which still clings, that theology and the humanities are together the one mental discipline for a Christian, and that science is necessarily another world. We need theologians, if God will give them to us, who will think and write of God and man in the midst of those very mental disciplines which a scientific age is creating. "Something new." Yes, these are instances of "something new"; there are no doubt many others; and badly we need it.

Yet when the apostles were grappling with the worst manifestation of evil they had yet confronted, something that was baffling them completely, the dumb spirits dashing the poor boy to the ground, foaming and grinding his teeth – and there they longing for new techniques, for the techniques whereby devils had once been subject to them on their former missions now seemed of no avail, "Why could not we cast him out?" Our Lord, coming down from the mountain said only, "Bring him to me", and the only technique He mentions in rebuking the apostles is the "science of the saints": "This kind goeth not out save by prayer and fasting." Amid methods old and methods new, alike amid bows and arrows and the weapons of modern war, the art and the science of Christ and the apostles remain to learn and to practise, never to be taken as granted, never to be taken as assumed, always to be learnt and painfully learnt again, "Bring him to me", "This kind goeth not out save by prayer".

And this means *withdrawal*. And whatever new things we learn and do – and I do not doubt that the needs of them are many – let none of them blind us to the recurring need of withdrawal to the Mount. That withdrawal must needs have its place in the training of our priests. "Jesus chose twelve, that they might be with him." "Come ye apart into a desert place and rest awhile: have leisure awhile." "He brought them to a high mountain apart by themselves." I do not see this withdrawal exaggerated in the life of our Church, or in the counsels of our Church in its search for divine wisdom under the guidance of the Spirit of God. Rather does it seem all too widely forgotten and imperilled that today, for our own many failures in this, for our own forgetfulness of what Cuddesdon taught us, we ask forgiveness, and we ask for our own renewal in the climbing of the holy mount.

"He brought them up to a high mountain, apart by themselves, and he was transfigured before them." It did not mean that He had left behind Him the conflicts of the Galilean ministry which had gone before, or the conflicts of the Via Crucis which were to follow. That perhaps was St Peter's error, longing to linger on the mountain scene of glory and thinking that it was perhaps possible to leave all that was irksome down below. Rather was it that, when our Lord went up to be transfigured, He carried with Him every conflict, every burden, both of the days behind or the days ahead, up there to be transfigured with Him. And when *we* go apart to be with Jesus in His glory, it is so that our frustrations, our limitations and our cares may be carried into that supernatural context which makes all the difference to them. They are not forgotten: they are not abolished: they can still be painful. But they become transfigured in the presence of Jesus, our crucified and glorious Lord. And when we have carried our frustrations up to our Lord in His glory, we find in the days which follow that He so generously brings His glory right down into the midst of our frustrations. "My peace I give unto you." "These things have I said unto you that my joy may be in you, and that your joy may be full." "Be of good cheer, I have overcome the world."

"It is good for us to be here." With grateful hearts we shall be taking leave again of the place which means more to us than words can ever tell. But wherever we may be, we are allowed always to go apart by ourselves and to "climb" where we may see the glory of Jesus. And if we are even but trying to do this, He is able generously all the while to be changing us into the same image from glory to glory.

"A Strange Land":
Sermon Preached at the Cuddesdon
College Festival 1966

Owen Chadwick[1]

Psalm 137:4: *How shall we sing the Lord's song in a strange land?*

The traveller, returning to this place, has a feeling that he comes home. The heart lifts in gratitude at what once was. The memory discards the moments of pettiness and retains the moments of beauty. Many years ago you knelt in this church at the presence of God in the sacrament of the altar, and you knew that you glimpsed the vision of truth. You were at home. No strange land.

But now as you walk the churchyard and perambulate the bishop's garden, you experience a twinge of melancholy. They were high ideals that then possessed you. They possessed you the more readily because putting them into practice lay in the future. You were not then troubling yourselves about coming down into the dust. The aspiration had nobility. But it was noble like the idealism of a boy who does not know how ideals become corrupt as they seek to express themselves in society. We were idealists partly because we were immature, partly because we were ignorant. But whether immature or ignorant, still we were idealists. And now? Your twinge of melancholy may pass into a stab of penitence.

For it is a strange land in which God's people live. I must retain my ideals among people who do not share them. I must demand moral principle where voices question the axioms on which my principle rests. I must retain simplicity where the economic structure demolishes an old-fashioned virtue like thrift. I must sing though some tell me that it is the song of a dreamer. I must pursue a Christian

---

[1] This sermon was printed at the request of those who attended the 1966 festival at which a new lecture room of the College to be called The Graham Room was opened.

policy though I know that any or every practicable policy means compromise with non-Christian men. I am no longer so immature. I am no longer quite so ignorant; and I know that I am a stranger in the land.

History has this utility; the student knows that however bad things seem at the moment, there were times when they were worse. If you have a sense of the past, you are not likely to be so elevated by the momentary victory of today, nor so downcast at the momentary defeat of tomorrow. The Catholic Church is a tree with deep roots, which hold fast whether the upper branches shine in the sunlight or bend in a gale. The mind goes back to the evening when from this hill the eastern sky was livid with the light of London burning, and here young men longed to help, and felt helpless, and were half-relieved that they were out of the fire, and then ashamed that they felt relieved. The mind goes further back to the days when austere Edward Willis, Vice-Principal and second founder of our office-book, unwitting caused the second onslaught upon the College; how quaint old Golightly, decaying at last in his mind, issued his penultimate pamphlet among so many pamphlets, *A Solemn Warning against Cuddesdon College*;[2] and how Bishop Mackarness needed to protect us at the diocesan conference, not against the comedy of Golightly, but against more formidable assailants. The mind goes further back to him who in his simple person reflected the best in the high Anglican tradition of pastoral care, John Keble; who advised our founders, and composed us a hymn (though we dare not use its words unaltered), and wrote letters so precious to Liddon that Liddon took special care that they be preserved. Religion, taught Keble, if it be true religion, is never popular. If it is popular, it is not true religion. God and the world are sundered far. Face it that the Christians are a protest against the society in which they live. Face it that their kingdom is not of this world – Jerusalem my happy home, when shall I come to thee? Ye are strangers and pilgrims, you can hear St Peter's word (I Peter 2:11). You have no long time to stay. The hooves of the galloping horses can already be heard as distant thunder. The sacrament of this altar, which to us is peace, and rest, and comfort, was founded in a sacrifice of pain and loneliness. Will the man wholly at home in the world ever be wholly at home in God? What doth it profit a man if he shall gain the whole world, and lose his own soul?

There is the first division of this text: How shall we sing the Lord's song in a strange land? If we would sing to the Lord's tune, the land ought to be strange.

The second division of the text is the Lord's *song*. A song, a hymn. How shall I sing? How shall I reason the Lord's philosophy? How shall I practise the Lord's Commandments? How shall I organise the Lord's company? Go before television and pretend that religion is only an argument. Go into Church Assembly and pretend that we only need efficient administration. Go into the Women's Institute and pretend that religion is only social reform. Despise not an argument, despise

[2] See above, Chapter Three.

not efficiency, despise not social reform, three necessaries of Christian endeavour. But when we were young men, and Cuddesdon forced us for a few terms to neglect social reform, and be more silent in argument than usual, and know nothing of ecclesiastical efficiency, then it was as plain to us as it has ever been, that the multi-coloured work of the Church is taken up into worship; that we end not merely in philosophy, not merely in the Church Commissioners, not (I dare not say "not merely") in the commandments, but in the Lord's song;

> O fons puritatis, Jesu Domine,
> Me immundum munda tuo sanguine
> Cujus una stilla ...

Cleanse us, unclean, with thy most cleansing blood – it was a hymn which they had, unforgettably, at a eucharist when the nave altar was first here. I know a member of the College who has never since been able to sing *Adoro te devote* without a vivid image of Cuddesdon church.

The third division of the text: *How* shall we sing the Lord's song? Of course in penitence and in faith. This psalmist was only melancholy. He thought that Palestine was the Lord's land, and that Babylon far from home was not. So he was aggressive, over-defensive. It was an excess. He built a Chinese wall; a wall of the Law to keep out the world. He clung to his orthodoxy not because it was truth but because it was orthodoxy. It is a spirit which can afflict Christians; strangers in the world, build high the bastions against the world. Fortify the sacred trenches with barbed wire. Be so passionate in your love for Jerusalem that you end by blessing those who bash in the heads of its enemies' children. Russian persecution bred a touch of this in Eastern Orthodoxy; African persecution bred a touch of it in Tertullian; Garibaldi bred it, calamitously for all Christendom, in the Italian Ultramontanes of the last century. Liddon had a flavour of this spirit in his youthful early days at Cuddesdon; as though this place was a fortress, a barricade against the passing life of man. Liddon was one of the greatest of Victorian Christians. Yet, more than Liddon, Edward King knew that this world was God's world, that his purpose for the world is to be trusted, that change, even a change that looks menacing, may be brought within the scope of providence.

We had a touch of the fortress-mentality in my generation. The future historian of the College may look back upon the end of the thirties to see a touch of excess. That excess was not ignoble. In the days of Munich, and Prague, and the rape of Poland, and friends being killed, and our hands seeming idle, it would have been ignoble if there had not been a touch of excess. What, when friends and companions are settling the fate of humanity, nothing but say prayers, and study the old Fathers dusty on the shelves, and work for a future church when there might be no future church to work for? Sometimes we silence our inward questionings by excess of zeal. We were not always wise. Our Principal was teaching us the serene Christian philosophy of Gore and Temple. But the books which we liked to read were not serene. They were the fiercest of theologies; *credo quia absurdum* terror-divinity. We preferred authors who dipped their pens in blood. We talked much of remnant theory. We thought much of "little flock" texts. We had more of Liddon than of King in our make-up.

None of this was due to our Principal. He was like a rock. When we could switch on our radio and listen grimly to the baying of *Sieg Heil* from a hundred thousand throats at a Nuremberg rally, it was not easy to see that God rules over the earth; that He is still King, be the people never so impatient. But Eric Graham knew with his whole being that the world is still God's.

He was a man of many natural gifts. He had a fine mind; not sufficiently sceptical in its questionings to make a first-rank philosopher, far too charitable in its judgements to make an historian, but a mind of system, clarity, coherence. He had the happiest of homes. He had a dry delicate penetrating sense of humour. He had a deep sense of the tradition and authority of the Catholic Church and yet he was deeply Biblical, Scriptural in his religious outlook. He gave devotional addresses which not seldom we failed to understand. He never pressed us. No emotionalism, no excess of fervour, no hurry, no suggestion that we must be saints by tomorrow. As a director of souls he was immensely gentle; so gentle that stern old Jansenist critics might even have charged him with too little severity in his direction. In words there was no pressure whatever. Yet there was a pressure upon us. This pressure came from his rule of life. He disciplined his personal conduct to an extraordinary degree.

He knew of the little flock texts. He knew of the theology of the sanctuary, none better. But he also knew of God's providence for the world. Never for one moment did he encourage us to read authors with gall in their ink. Never for a moment did he waver in his faith in the divine governance of the world.

It was King who elicited Graham's reverence. He once declared Edward King to be "the fairest flower of the Oxford Movement". On our ordinations he gave us each a copy of King's Pastoral Lectures. Some of the acts of Edward King would have been impossible to him. When Joseph Wolff, the strange pastor and traveller, came to stay in the guest room at Cuddesdon, he rang the bell early in the morning for a servant. The chaplain appeared. Wolff did not know that it was the chaplain. He demanded to be shaved. Edward King went away, returned with razor and bowl of lather, and shaved his distinguished guest. Such an act would have been difficult for Eric Graham partly because the chaplain of a college may sometimes do what its head may not, and partly because, though a hospitable pretence, it was a pretence, There was nothing but truth in the man. He knew that he must teach us – and very good at it he was. He knew that he must visit in the parish – and we thought that his shyness prevented him being good at it – whether this was so or not is under God's eye alone. Whatever he did, it faced the altar. We could not help facing the altar; not only because there was an altar to face, not only because we were surrounded by natural beauty, not only because the community had a way of life and a tradition (though that was of the highest importance), but because we met here the servants of God. The harmony was unmistakable. It was the Lord's song.

You are strangers and pilgrims in the land. The land ought to be, in some way, strange. But let us get the reason right. Because we live amidst easy clamour, and brash publicity, and argument more for the sake of noise than for the sake of truth, we rightly retreat and find our sanctuary in the stillness before the altar of God; somewhat as in this church, during the weeks of Dunkirk, men found in Cuddesdon church a seal of eternal peace as they knelt near the sacrament reserved at the east end of the chancel. A most blessed sanctuary. But a sanctuary to reach outwards. Not a hiding-place from the shrapnel of the world. Let us not hedge our sanctuary against a world that we presume to be hostile. Let us not begin to be Pharisees; defending our purity with the obsolete muskets of vanished campaigns; buttressed by a holiness which at last is not the holiness of faith but of Leviticus. Let us get the reason right. You are strangers not because this earth is given over to the powers of darkness. The earth is the Lord's, still the Lord's. You are not fully at home here because your eyes are fixed upon a city whose foundations are eternal and not of earth. Perhaps my people reject my gospel; they are God's created beings still; of kindness and courage and sometimes thirst for truth; a people to whom we must go, whether they will hear or forbear. The world is not demonic but sacramental. "Turn the stone and thou shalt find me, cleave the wood and there am I."

How shall we sing the Lord's song in a strange land? Why not? The Psalmist hung up his harp upon the willows by the water's edge and would not sing. He knew Palestine was holy, and that was all he did know. The land, though strange, is not the land of Baal, nor of Moloch, nor of Dagon, nor of Thor, nor of Wotan, nor of mammon, nor of Stalin. It is still the land of the Lord, the Creator, the Almighty, Maker of heaven and earth, and of all things visible and invisible.

Here then are three divisions of this text: how shall we sing?

the first, the land ought to be strange; for what shall it profit a man if he gain the whole world and lose his own soul;

the second, it is a song; for religion ends in the worship of the whole man;

the third, it is a strange land because we look for another country; not because it is a land of savages and devils.

When, a few years ago or many years ago, you knelt before God in the sacrament of this altar, it was not possible to doubt his reality and his power. We came to this College questioning, hesitant, sceptical; and the questioning of my generation was multiplied tenfold by the onset of war. But here in the quietness of worship we found a reality unmistakable. We have all moved far from this retreat. We are still hesitant, still questioning; and now we know that truth is less tidy, and that words are more impotent even than we then thought them. We have soiled ourselves in a heap of the world's soot. But we do not forget what we once have seen. Despite all that has happened to us since those Cuddesdon days, it is still impossible to doubt God's reality and God's power; the Lord is King though the people be impatient; he sitteth between the cherubim, be the earth never so unquiet. *God of God, Light of Light, Very God of Very God, begotten not made, being of one substance with the Father*, the great Nicene words are as powerful now as those years ago. The truths by which we then learnt to live are truths still; and when we are faithful to ourselves we know them still to be living truths.

How then shall we sing the Lord's song in the modern world? How shall we not?

Index